A THOUSAND YEARS
AND A DAY

A
THOUSAND YEARS
AND A DAY

Our Time in the Old Testament

CLAUS WESTERMANN
Professor in the University of Heidelberg

Translated by Stanley Rudman

FORTRESS PRESS
PHILADELPHIA

CONTENTS

INTRODUCTION

THE Old Testament has begun to speak afresh to our generation. We are in the process of rediscovering it. In the
nineteenth century, and at the beginning of the twentieth,
the question was becoming increasingly insistent: had not the time
come to remove the Old Testament from the Christian Church,
from its preaching, its teaching and its Bible? In my own country,
Germany, external pressure aimed at compelling the Church to
abandon its 'Jewish' book was needed in order to face the
Christian Church seriously with the question, what this book still
really meant for it. The question stirred many to re-examine and
listen again to the book which was the Bible of Jesus Christ. This
questioning and investigation yielded much fruit now apparent in
the life of the Church today, in the study of theology and further
afield.

Yet the question posed by the outsider—whether the Church
could ignore this book or whether it was still necessary for its life—
was not the ultimate reason for this reappraisal. The Old Testament
began to speak afresh to our time during the years when so much
was changing. It spoke to us because we were in a similar position.

This book spans a thousand years. A thousand years have contributed to it; before the book which we possess today could grow
out of the first records, ancient lyrics, historical narratives and the
stories of God's call, a long period of time was needed. It is a long
journey which leads to the destination reached in the New Testament. What is reported in the New Testament can be compressed
into the events of a day, the day on which, according to John's
gospel, the Son of Man was 'exalted'; the crucifixion as well as the
resurrection is included in 'exaltation' or 'glorification'. The one
day to which the accounts of the four Gospels proceed as their

destination is also the goal of the Old Testament. A thousand years of history were the indispensible prelude for the coming of this day. This one day cannot, in fact, be understood apart from the long journey which led up to it. The thousand years would have had no conclusion, no goal, but for this day.

A great deal happened on this long journey. Every stage of a nation's journey, from the call of one man, Abraham, and the growth of a kingdom right up to its collapse and the growth of a new community of hope, is recorded in the Old Testament. But the journey of this people is not the whole story; the people of God is a nation among nations, a part of humanity, and sharing with humanity in the whole of human nature. The journey that is described for us leads through every dimension of human existence. There is nothing human which is not touched upon somewhere in the Old Testament. The sweep of this book is such that it covers the stars in their orbits and the smallest creature on earth, the pyramids of the Egyptian empire and the beginnings of Roman rule; it deals with the great epochs of human history as exemplified in the history of one nation, and it extends from prehistoric periods, reflected in its myths, to the earliest beginnings of civilization, from the life of the nomad and the roving hunter to the development of the highest civilization. It describes what it means to be a man in all its inexhaustible richness: childbirth and old age, children at play and young people in love, friendship and marriage and work in all their aspects. There is no human activity which does not find a place somewhere in this book—including the first traces of science. All forms of communal life, all basic forms of social and political life, have their place in the journey through the thousand years of the Old Testament.

But all this—and only a part of the story has been told so far— is firmly rooted in God's activity in men's lives, in man's relationship with God: for God has created man in his own image. Everything that concerns the life of man and his existence in the world is dealt with in the light of God's presence.

It is precisely for this reason that this book can picture man so soberly, without any idealism, and just as he really is—with his faults and his potentialities for evil, and with all the enigma of his disobedience and his wanton sin.

Belonging also to this journey of a thousand years, therefore, is the answer of man, his response to the mighty acts of God—his conversation with God, expressed in lament and cries of joy, in supplication and praise, in singing and weeping. One such expression which grew out of this story of God's dealing with man, and which still has power to speak to us today as it did then, is Psalm 90. It is the word of a man who was as human as any man described in any history book, and it is the word of rejoicing that our human existence, such as it is, along with *everything* in it, contains Another on whom we can depend—Another who does not change throughout the centuries.

> *Lord, thou hast been our dwelling place*
>   *in all generations.*
> *Before the mountains were brought forth or*
>   *ever thou hadst formed the earth and the world,*
>   *from everlasting to everlasting thou art God.*
> *For a thousand years in thy sight are but as*
>   *yesterday when it is past, or as a watch in*
>   *the night.*

I · THE PRIMAEVAL HISTORY

The Primaeval History

THE Bible deals with the whole wide world—including the stars, the trees of the field and the sand on the seashore. It deals with men from the earliest days to the present, and right up to the end of the world. The central theme is the story of the *one* chosen people leading up to the coming of the *one* Saviour. But this one Saviour came for the whole world, and his message is directed towards the salvation of the whole of mankind. The first chapters of the Bible, like the last, speak of the world's furthest bounds, of the beginning and end of history, and of the origin and destiny of mankind.

The first eleven chapters of Genesis, the so called 'primaeval' history, are concerned with the origin of the whole world, and the whole of humanity. These first chapters of the Bible were never intended to do what is, in fact, impossible for them—namely, give a historical or scientific description of the origin of the world and the human race. They are the product of a confession—that God is the Creator of the world and the Lord of its history.

It was quite clear to those who first heard these early chapters of the Old Testament that they were being given a description of the very beginning of God's activity, which was centred for them in the act of deliverance at the beginning of their history and in the guidance and protection of the nation right up to their own day; an activity which was the foundation of their history and existence. They had met this God and his activity in the solid facts of their own history; they had no choice but to recognize that their God and Saviour and Lord was the one from whom *everything* originated, and that he was their Creator and the Creator of the world.

They praised him as Creator; in their songs of praise they expressed their joy at being alive and their joy in the greatness and beauty of the world. In the creation psalms, of which there are many in the Psalter but which are also to be found in the book of Job and elsewhere, we meet the actual heartfelt words used by these people of their Creator. We should really read these creation psalms and make them a part of us prior to reading Genesis, if we wish to understand the creation story at the beginning of the Bible properly. Praise of God, the Creator, does not presuppose the creation story, but quite the reverse: praise of God is the source and presupposition of the creation story. The present narrative is, in fact, a developed and expanded confession of faith in God as Creator.

This helps to clarify a further point which is important for our understanding of the first chapters of the Bible. When God is praised as Creator in the psalms of the book of Job or Deutero-Isaiah this is not done mechanically or formally, always in the same words, but with an unlimited richness of forms, vocabulary and metaphors. Praise of God, the Creator, like his Being, has many voices and forms; it cannot be squeezed into a single type of expression. In this, basically, lies the reason why the creation of the world and mankind is described in more than one way at the beginning of the Bible and why two accounts of creation stand next to each other. Their importance lies in their distinctiveness, and they were never meant to be harmonized by our logic—if, indeed, that were possible.

1 · *The Writing of the Five Books*

T H E two creation stories at the beginning of Genesis—1.1-2.4a and 2.4b-3.24 (or to 2.25)—come from widely different periods of history; Gen. 2-3 probably arose in the ninth century BC and Gen. 1 in the sixth or fifth century BC. The first books of the Bible— the Pentateuch—are not the work of a single author, nor even the later editing of a single man. (The Bible never says that Moses wrote the five books named after him; that is a later conjecture.)

They are the result of oral tradition, which lived on in the customs of the people and above all in their worship.

We said above that Israel's confession of faith in God as its Saviour from deadly peril lay at the root of the whole transmission of the Pentateuch. This confession had the character of a proclamation—even if extremely brief—of the saving activity of God. An additional clause concerning the entry into the promised land was attached independently to the confession that God had brought Israel out of Egypt. Such a confession, with its proclamation of the mighty acts of God, already contained within itself the seed for further development in a fuller account. The earliest form of this expansion consisted in an orderly enumeration of the most important events of God's saving activity among his people. This brief historical creed' (as von Rad calls it) was recited when the people were assembled for worship, in the manner of Joshua's affirmation when the people were gathered together at Shechem (Josh. 24). A good example of its place in the sacrificial offering of the individual Israelite is Deut. 26.

Behind each sentence of this confession of faith, in fact, stood a whole history or whole number of histories. They were related among the people and they had their special focal point among certain tribes, in certain families, at holy places and on festival days. In this way they were passed on for decades and sometimes centuries, from generation to generation, from parents to their children, and certainly, also, through men and women who were particularly expert and talented in telling these stories. As long as the tribes had a separate existence the stories also lived among the tribes, for they were important to the life of the tribe and its members, and belonged to its environment and circle of interests. This was where the patriarchal history, in particular, originated.

In the process of Israel becoming a nation through the saving work of God and his guidance all these oral traditions were crystallized in the confession of faith. Thus, a historical work depicting the whole of Israel's history as the history of God's dealing with his people grew up round this kernel. The earliest part of the work goes back to the time of David and Solomon, somewhere in the ninth or perhaps even tenth century BC. It is called the *Jahwistic* source because throughout it God is called 'Jahwe'. About a century later comes the *Elohistic* source (God is called 'Elohim'), which many scholars take to be only a supplement to the Jahwistic source, although, in fact, it could be a quite independent account.

The so called *Priestly* source—so called because it originated from priestly circles and displays a marked interest in the cult, the priesthood and priestly tradition—arose much later, just before or just after the end of the exile (6th or 5th century BC). These three sources or *strata* of tradition are joined together in the Pentateuch, in such a way that the Priestly source forms the framework and the older traditions are inserted in it. The combination of traditions from many centuries was so well done that a history genuinely new, genuinely complete, came into being. Yet at the same time the older traditions were guarded with such fidelity that scholars 2,500 years later have succeeded in unravelling the strands of which the work previously consisted. This has made it possible to sketch in broad outline the history of Israel from the earliest time.

This work of Pentateuchal criticism, the so called 'source—criticism', has, it is true, led to many unnecessary and dangerous abuses, but on the whole it has made a very useful contribution to our understanding of the Old Testament and, therefore, of the whole Bible. It brings real enrichment and clarification to our understanding of the Old Testament that we now hear several voices bringing their report, and several witnesses bearing their testimony to the mighty acts of God in the first books of the Bible. Today we discern more clearly than before a distinctive period, a distinctive vocabulary and a distinctive theology in each of the different parts which compose the whole. This makes the character of each individual history more clear and precise. At the same time, because the early historical narratives have been set in relief chronologically, it is possible to co-ordinate Biblical events with the history of the surrounding world more reliably. Beside their confessional and credal character, the various *strata* of the earlier narratives of the Bible have the additional value of a historical document.

Recording the history of the basic events of salvation by means of several allied witnesses, instead of by means of a single writing, is paralleled in the New Testament. There is a difference: in the New Testament, the four gospels are separate accounts; in the Old Testament, the corresponding accounts are joined together to form a single account. In both Testaments, the variety of testimony is appropriate to the events recorded, which portray the activity of God in our world. This is an activity which, precisely because the many-sided accounts come from different men and from different times, withstands all our efforts to classify what happened wholly according to our contemporary concepts and modes of thought.

2 · *Two Accounts of Creation*

T H E differences between the two creation narratives in Gen. 1.2 must strike every unbiased reader. The older narrative only alludes to the creation of the world in a subordinate sentence at the beginning, before proceeding straightaway to the creation of man. Its style is simple and picturesque, in the manner of a folk tale, and is sometimes directly reminiscent of the language of the fairytale. The later account speaks of the creation of the world comprehensively and systematically, interpreting and arranging the facts, in a heavy imposing style, which sometimes sounds like a cosmic litany, with its recurrent, stylized expressions.

All that is said in these first chapters of the Bible stems from reverent obeisance before God's majesty and from amazed and wondering affirmation of the divine possibilities which surround everything. At the back of the account of creation in the first chapter stands the question, 'Where did everything come from?' Behind the account in the second chapter stands the question, 'Where did I, such as I am, come from?' And both answer: 'It is our helper and our Lord who brought us and everything else into being'.

In addition to this, however, both witnesses have their own distinctive message. At the bottom of the account of the creation of the world in seven days there is already a recognition of periods in the creation of the world. It is, for example, recognized that the origin of plant life is prior to that of animal life, and that of fishes and birds to that of land animals. The number and specification of the periods of creation is comparatively unimportant; it is the account of creation in deliberately consecutive periods that is important. Behind this account is an unmistakable acquaintance with scientific thought. Animate matter is seen to be divided into *genera*, in the same way that creation is seen to take place in periods. The story does not tell of the creation of particular plants or animals, but of the creation of the different species of plant and animal life. The basic knowledge of the structure of plant and animal life in species is prior to the Priestly account of creation, in fact.

Connected with this is a third observation: the first works of God in creation consist in making a division. God divides the light from the darkness, the waters above the firmament from the waters beneath it, the dry land from the sea. This description of God's activity in creation is again based on knowledge of an elementary scientific principle: a complex whole can only be understood when divided and defined. Even if it has still a long way to go, the first trace of one of the basic concepts of scientific work in the nineteenth and twentieth centuries, namely the concept of analysis, reveals itself here. It is the same basic knowledge which is revealed when God's creation is depicted in terms of division. All this may sound very surprising and very strange. And we should remember that this is only *one* aspect of the Priestly account of creation. But this one aspect should not be denied or ignored: in describing the creation of the world by God this account has taken over the scientific knowledge which had already been gained at the time of writing. Here, at any rate, there is *no* opposition between faith in divine creation and the first groping beginnings of science.

This can be illustrated from yet another angle. There were creation narratives among Israel's neighbours also, and many features of the Bablyonian account are echoed in the Old Testament. The Babylonian account of the creation of the world has a definite mythical character; it is part of a divine drama. In the Book of Genesis, the only parallel to this myth is in Gen. 1.2, particularly in the name *Tehōm* ('the deep'). This is actually the name of a mythical monster, in Babylonian 'Tiamat'. In addition, there are a number of passages in the Psalms in which the mythical element is occasionally more obvious because of the poetic use of language. For example, on one occasion God is reminded of his work in creation by these words: 'Thou didst crush Rahab like a carcass' (Ps. 89.10). This is only one of many indications that Israel was acquainted with the mythical explanation and description of creation and that in speaking of creation even Israel itself occasionally had recourse to the language of myth. The actual creation myth, however, in which a plurality of divine beings is presupposed, is passed over in the Old Testament. For the creation story in Gen. 1, there is only God. He alone, sovereign and unrestricted by any other forces, is responsible for the origin of the world. The world is not the arena for a battle of mythical forces, but simply the world, simply the universe, simply nature. The 'demythologizing' of the world, undertaken by the Old Testament belief in the *one* God as creator of heaven and earth, was the necessary presupposition of a scientific understanding and investigation of the world.

This, then, is the one main feature which characterizes the creation stories of Gen. 1. Systematic, descriptive and classificatory discussion of the world is included in the discussion about God, which, as we have already said, has almost the character of a litany. A powerful, imposing style is used in honouring God as Creator. This chapter is a tremendous hymn of praise to God the Creator. The majesty of the Creator is seen above all in the fact that he creates through his 'word'—his power of command and jurisdiction reaches beyond the sphere of persons to the borders of all creation. 'For he spoke and it came to be: he commanded and it stood forth' (Ps. 33.9). And whenever it is said at the end of the day, 'And God saw that it was good', this recurrent expression is voicing exactly the same recognition that sounds loudly and jubilantly throughout the Psalms, in which man is summoned to praise God along with the whole of creation (esp. Ps. 148).

3 · Creation and Science

I F a description of creation which undoubtedly betrays traces of a scientific approach has been inserted into what is really a hymn of praise in Gen. 1, this is of far reaching significance for us. Praise of the Creator, if properly understood, need not exclude scientific investigation of the growth of the world; but it can fully support it. A scientific passion for investigating the origin of the world can, if properly appreciated, still be joined with praise of God, the Creator. The Church's repudiation of the beginnings of cosmological exploration at the time of the Renaissance and its rigid adhesion to the cosmology found in the Bible can perhaps be understood in terms of the situation of the Church at that time, but it is by no means the only way supported by the Bible. If the Priestly writing could include contemporary insight into the growth of the world in its praise of God, the Creator, then in principle the way is opened for linking the scientific insights of later periods also with the recognition of God as Creator—even if they stand in opposition to the cosmology of the Priestly writing. Science developed further in opposition to belief in God as Creator, but this was a historical rather than a necessary development. Today there are growing signs that the Church is revising its deliberately suspicious attitude to the scientific investigation of origins. At the same time scientific work is beginning to recognize its limits and to find its way, in various fields, to a new affirmation of the creation-faith of the Bible.

While the first account of creation reaches its goal in the creation of man, the second begins with this. The important sentence in the first is 'God created man in his own image'. This means God created man to be in a personal relationship with himself. Man is God's likeness insofar as he may listen to God and talk to him, humble himself before God and praise him. The other side of this message is this : human existence can only find fulfilment in personal relationship with God. A man who no longer has a personal relationship with God is no longer a man. Fully developed and mature personality cannot be found without God. A man for whom God no longer exists and for whom God has become irrelevant must, whether he wants to or not, look for a substitute Another. If he can no longer cry to God, he must cry to something or someone else; if he no longer trusts in God, he must place his trust somewhere else. For God had created man to be in a personal relationship with himself; man can never completely destroy this relationship.

What is expressed in the first account of creation in this one fundamental sentence is expressed in the second account by means of an incident in which God and man meet. That man owes his existence to God is depicted in the first account by the idea of the 'likeness of God', in the second account by means of an incident which brings man face to face with God and thus reveals the truth of human existence. The picture of the creation of man in Gen. 2.7 is considerably more primitive than that of the Priestly writing; it is the voice of a tradition which stretches much further back into the history of mankind. God breathes the breath of life into the man who has been fashioned from the dust of the earth; in other words, the life of man—as long as man remains—is still the gift of God. His breath, and therefore his body, soul and spirit, is existence given by God. This God-given existence is marked by three fundamental conditions in connection with its creation : it receives food and at the same time work (Gen. 2.15); it receives a commandment of God (2.16-7); and it receives community and by this continuity (2.18-24).

God's command that man should cultivate and guard the garden in which he has been set *precedes* man's disobedience. Moreover, work as such is by no means included in the curse subsequently pronounced on the ground. On the contrary, work is integrated with the existence of man by the command of God. An existence without work is neither a real nor a full existence. Even in the twentieth century, in spite of the tremendous ramification of what is possible and what is necessary in the work of men, we can understand all work, in view of this double command at the beginning, as ordained by God. All work that is expected of a man ought to have some part somehow in the cultivation and care of the soil entrusted to man. Where work which a man has to do cannot possibly be understood in the light of this command, it ought not to be expected of a man.

4 · To Cultivate and to Guard

M A N was forbidden to eat of one of the trees in the garden. This command is not to be understood as a limitation; man has quite enough with the fruits of the other trees. Rather, the intention of the command is to connect man with God in his daily life in a special way. This command symbolizes God's claim on man's obedience. While man respects this barrier, he respects God. The command is framed with men's highest potentialities in mind and takes them seriously; it believes man is capable of making God happy by his obedience.

Man betrays this hope; he is not obedient; he disobeys the command. But this only happens when community, the third condition of being a man, has been added. Both the first and second accounts of creation agree on this point: man was created by God to live in community; it is not good that he should be alone. In both accounts marriage is seen to be the basic form of human community. The Biblical confession of faith in God as Creator includes the full, clear affirmation of the fact that man and woman belong to each other. And that is true throughout the Bible. The Bible never allows celibacy to be rated higher than the estate of marriage in man's life before God. If a man is once commanded not to marry—as, for example, in the case of Jeremiah—this is the result of a unique command in a unique situation. Much harm has been done by the Church having, over a long period, stamped the union of man and woman in itself as 'sin', or at any rate as somehow blemished. The future of community life will depend a great deal on whether these clear and unambiguous words of the Bible about marriage as the basic form of all human community are taken seriously again.

The creation narrative of the Jahwist does not see sex as the

crisis, the danger point, of community life; the crisis is the appearance in the community of temptation, and the growth of sin. The
picture of temptation and guilt in Gen. 3 is one of the world's
masterpieces of narrative art. Behind the narrative stands the question of why man is destined to die. Why does man, the creation of
God, go to his death? Why is life a deathward existence? The
narrative connects this deathward trend with the disobedience and
the guilt connected with it. The woman was enticed to break the
command, man followed her. The temptation to disobedience is left
standing in all its enigma. The voice of temptation proceeds from
one of God's creatures—no attempt is made to explain the source
of evil; on the contrary, it is asserted that the source of evil is inexplicable. The fact that men still live after disobeying the command, although death had been threatened as their punishment,
also remains without explanation. It is the inexplicable and,
apparently, inconsistent mercy of God which allows men time before their death. It is a mercy which forgives. Men try at first to
hide themselves from God; when they are caught they try to push
the guilt from themselves on to others. But this only shows how
the guilty pair are thrown back completely on forgiveness. They
tried at first to hide their nakedness themselves; in the end God
clothes them both in order that they may continue to live with each
other and with him without being ashamed (v.21). This conclusion
to the story of man's creation shows with a simplicity that is full of
deep meaning that man needs God's forgiveness to be able to live.
But the man who has broken God's law can now live only in
separation from God's abiding presence. The garden in which he
was with God is for ever closed to him (vv.23-4). He lives now in a
world where he has to face the realities of death and guilt.

Such is man! The truth of human existence is portrayed in this
narrative with inimitable artistry. It does not seek to picture either
a historic or prehistoric occurrence, but to expound the confession
of faith: 'I believe that God created me'. It is vital, however, that
it is developed as the description of something which *happened*.
We shall never understand this story if we only use it as a source
for concepts, into which human existence before God, guilt and

deathward existence can be fitted. If the Church has derived its teaching about original sin, the fall of man and the origin of evil from this story, this need not be understood as anything more than an *essay* at interpreting the story. The concept of original sin is especially dangerous and open to misunderstanding; we have to be very careful with it. The attempt to derive concepts from this story is of doubtful value for another reason, too; the Bible itself, both Old Testament and New Testament, almost never refers expressly to this story of man's disobedience. The importance which this story has in the teaching of the Church is out of all proportion to the Bible's own reserve. This reserve is clearly intended to indicate that this story of how man first became guilty should be left as it is. It ought always to be read afresh and every generation will probably understand it differently. It will be wise, therefore, not to understand it on the basis of hard and fast presuppositions, but to allow it to speak directly *as history* to every new generation in order that they too might hear for themselves what man is like.

5 · From Cain to Babel

T H E account of creation and the expulsion from the Garden of Eden is immediately followed by the story of the two brothers, Cain and Abel, which is clearly intended to develop what has been depicted in Gen. 3. It is meant to show what men can do when separated from God. It is another story of temptation. It is a further instance of man's inability to withstand temptation. It has already been demonstrated in the previous story that the disturbance in the relationship between man and God must lead directly to a disturbance in the community life of man. The story of Cain and Abel shows how this disturbance caused by separation from God can lead to the extermination of human life by a man, in short, to murder. Careful consideration should be given to the motive for the murder. God accepts the sacrifice of Abel, but not that of Cain. The reason for this distinction is not explained and is not meant to be. It just is so. Cain, therefore, has to assume that God is more

favourably disposed to Abel than to himself, or even that God is
favourably disposed to Abel but not to himself. For Cain it is a matter of God's favour. Behind the murder, then, is a motive which is
pure, worthy and upright. It is the way in which Cain seeks to win
God's favour again—namely through the removal of his brother—
that is wrong, quite wrong. He is told that it is wrong. Cain knows
what he is doing; but he does it all the same. The murder is committed. Here, at the beginning of the Bible, it is being stated with
genuine, deep knowledge that man is such and that human nature
has the power to commit murder. It is not that men can be divided
into murderers and non-murderers, robbers and non-robbers, but
that we are all involved in this situation at some point or other. It
is only the final consequence of the fact that we are no longer enclosed together with God. We are outside, where hate as well as love
is found. It is important that this first murder is the deed of a man
against his brother. Real burning hate only arises when two people
are close together. All hatred is, at bottom, hatred of one's brother.

The punishment of Cain is expulsion from the land. He must
now wander about restlessly. The only reason why Cain does not
have to pay for the murder is based on the story's position at the
very beginning of history. The story is meant to show that from
the beginning man has the power to murder and that there cannot
be any atonement—even by the punishment of death—for it. The
murderer remains within the history of mankind which now
begins; at all times and in all places from now on he will have to
be reckoned with. The opposition of Cain and Abel is a characteristic of the world in its present state.

The story of Cain and Abel has yet further significance in relation to what follows. The Jahwistic narrator wants to show in the
first chapters of Genesis how humanity created by God, beginning
with the first disobedience of Adam, has become involved in a
downward trend which can no longer be arrested by man himself.
The story of Cain and Abel is an acceleration of this trend; mankind, separated from God, contains the germ of destruction within
itself. This trend is continued in the following chapters.

In the first verses of Gen. 6 an ancient myth raises its head in the Bible—a fragment on the 'Sons of God', who had union with the daughters of men, a union from which giants were born. 'These were the mighty men that were of old, the men of renown.' The narrator wants to point to a further danger-point of humanity by his use of this fragment of a myth: the obliteration of the distinction between God and man, the growth of a species in which Superman challenges his creatureliness. One consequence of going beyond the bounds of creatureliness is the flood, a castastrophe for all mankind; only one family, that of Noah, is rescued. In previous generations the account of the flood has been treated as fantasy like the rise of the Titans or giants. Today people are very much more cautious. As far as the giants go, archaeologists today reckon with the possibility that the stories and tales of giants which circulate among many nations are based on accurate recollection. It is true that nothing definite is known about this yet, but we have to reckon with the possibility that a pre-historic period of human history is, in fact, being dealt with here.

Reports, saga or legends of a colossal flood which wiped out humanity are to be found in many parts of the globe. Here, too, investigation accepts the view that historical facts lie behind these stories. The excavations of Sir Leonard Woolley in Ur of the Chaldees have proved most impressively that a mighty flood must once have destroyed all life in the valleys of the Euphrates-Tigris area in the dim and distant past. It is not important whether the history of the flood in the Bible goes back to this catastrophe in the Euphrates plain or to another catastrophe. We have no reason to doubt that an actual event stands behind the story. It is not, however, for historical reasons that the story is recorded by the author, but in order to affirm that, in view of man's increasing depravity, the earth's continued existence was only possible through God's continued protection.

The final story in the line which descends from the account of creation tells of the building of the Tower of Babel (Gen. 11.1-9). It is based on a folk tale which contains legendary features; it was intended to explain what was remarkable to the still nomadic Israelites about the city of Babylon: the half-ruined, turreted temple (the Ziggurat whose remains have been brought to light by means of excavations and whose form is quite easy to imagine as a result of attempted reconstructions), the confusion of language in a metropolis and the strange name of the city. This final story about mankind and its way of life in the early period, immediately prior to the call of Abraham, points to a very extreme course of action which is open to man—revolt against God. Perhaps a correspondence between Gen. 6.1-4 and 11.1-9 is intended. In the former passage the revolt against God was described as a mythical event, in the latter as a technical operation. In Gen. 6 there were superhuman beings which destroyed the boundary between the Creator and the creation; in Gen. 11 it is the work of men. The tower whose pinnacles reach to heaven is meant to surmount the boundary between high heaven and earth. No matter how primitive the story sounds to us today in the context in which it is set, it shows the first trace of *hubris* which finds expression in the works of man.

In suggesting that the two motives of the master-builders are 'to make ourselves a name in order that we might not be scattered abroad over the whole earth' the story touches on what are two decisive motives for the great technical works of early times. The first is fame. The building is a monument to the builder; the mightier it is, the greater the reputation of the one who erected it. In addition to this personal motive there is a more political one. In all great empires, from Sumerian times to the present day, the rulers have endeavoured to give their empire a focus, which, by reason of its imposing size, should act as a power house which rules the whole from the centre and thereby holds it together. It has often happened in the history of humanity that the buildings which are meant to perpetuate the name of the builder and hold together the kingdom of a powerful ruler have grown to an unnatural size. They have often become the expression of an individual or group's exaltation above the ordinary man; this is fatal. In Israel one of the expressions always repeated in praising God was that he destroys those who have exalted themselves too high. The story of the Tower of Babel makes the same point. God comes down and destroys the building erected from a mania for fame and power because it has grown too high. And now, very appropriately their punishment is the confusion of tongues, 'that they may not understand one another's speech'; and those who built the tower are scattered over the face of the earth. There is a suggestion here of the profound perception that the very arrogance of a work of engineering can lead to destruction and meaninglessness. Perhaps there is already here a presentiment that the greatest technical achievements of man, as, for example, the invention of the machine, have led also to the greatest divisions between men.

This story, coming as it does, directly before the fresh phase of God's dealing with men in the call of Abraham, with which the journey of salvation begins, points forward to the New Testament. In the story of Pentecost the confusion of tongues was brought to an end as a sign, with the result that men of very different languages heard, each in their own language, the Apostles telling of the mighty acts of God. In radical opposition to the attempt of men to immortalize themselves in a building, the top of which reached right to heaven, the Man, to whom the history beginning with Abraham leads, humbled himself to death on the Cross. This act has laid the foundations of a new understanding to span the abyss of meaninglessness. Its language was intelligible to all who took it seriously.

II · THE PATRIARCHAL HISTORY

1 · Abraham and the Promise of the Blessing

T H E R E is a peculiar similarity between the events recorded at the beginning of the Old and the New Testaments. Both are to begin with simply concerned with the birth of a child. In both, it is a child who has been promised and who is destined to fulfil a greater promise.

In the primaeval history which precedes the patriarchal histories, the narrator has created out of much older history a connected account which traces the line of the Fall in a world created by God. A Fall which is not really consistent with creation by God but which is the insuperable, threatening truth, from the disobedience of the first man and the subsequent fratricide and the revolt of humanity to the building of the tower which was meant to reach to heaven. God's decision to preserve this earth—quite inexplicably —has been set over against the possibility of the complete annihilation of creation. That is the background for the story of the call of Abraham. With the call to Abraham something new is set in motion. A call of God goes out to one man; and God continues to go with him on his journey. It is the beginning of the history of the chosen people, a special history in the vast totality of world history. Beginning with this call to Abraham God proceeds to deal with the world in a different way. World history and 'salvation history' are separated, and the message of the Bible deals only with this salvation history from now on. Yet it still deals—though not obviously—with the whole, with the world, with humanity and with creation. God is still the Creator and Lord of what happens throughout the world, but in his dealings with the whole he works out his purpose through the call of *one* man, and *one* chosen people and *one* mediator, in whom his work for the whole reaches its goal.

At this point, in the transition from primaeval history (Gen. 1-11) to patriarchal history (Gen. 12-50), two things happen which are vital for us today. First, it is clear that the Bible thinks in terms of *periods*. Every period of time is not the same as every other for the Bible. It recognizes periods in human history. Later it will become even clearer that no book of antiquity reveals such a deep understanding of history as the Bible. In saying at this point that God has dealt differently with men in different periods and in seeing that the relationship of the points 'God—world—mankind—nation—individual' was not always the same, but formed quite new patterns as the periods changed, the Bible has accepted the basic fact of historical change or historical development and expounded it in what it says about God. The Bible affirms that history means growth.

Secondly, God's dealing with the whole world is, from the call of Abraham onwards, a *progressive* work, which is not always immediately recognizable as a concern for the whole world, for all nations and for the whole of humanity. It is at this point in the Bible that by far the deepest secret of human existence is seen to be divinely ordained: the immeasurable, invisible and unprovable secret of how the one is a member of the whole, the smallest a member of the greatest: the secret of the representation of the whole by a part of this whole.

A call goes out to Abraham to leave his homeland, his father's house and his whole environment and set out for a land which is soon to be pointed out to him. The call is confirmed with a promise. He is to give birth to a great nation. But the promise goes even further than this: all the families of the earth will be blessed in him. With these opening words (Gen. 12.1-3) the main theme of the patriarchal histories is announced. It is not to be understood without the prospect—even if it is unfulfilled—of the fulfilment of the promise. The seed of Abraham became a great nation; it received the land promised to Abraham, and there became in the process an empire with which both small and powerful neighbours had to reckon. In its growth into an empire Israel saw its true origin not only in the physical fatherhood of its tribal founder but in the

call (which was at the same time a promise) which came to Abraham
and in which this future was announced to him by God. The
account of the promise made to Abraham was the result of a confession of faith, the confession of a people who knew their existence
was rooted in a word of promise from God. They finally became
a nation through God's saving activity in rescuing the Israelites
in Egypt from bondage and bringing them into a homeland of their
own. But even before this beginning as a nation they knew that
their early history which described the journey of a family rather
than a nation was brought into existence through the promise and
call which came to their father Abraham from the same God who
saved them.

The Bible begins with the fact that God spoke and it was done.
The second period, which deals with God's journey with this one
man and with this one people, begins with the word spoken by God
to this one man. And when this second period is brought to an end
there is a new beginning: the Word became flesh. It is God's word
that binds world history together as a whole, according to the
testimony of the Bible. The promise to Abraham forms a link
stretching from the moment in which he received it to the moment
in which the promise was fulfilled. 'Word' in this context is never
simply 'What is said'; it always results in action. From the word
comes history. Here at the beginning of Abraham's story a link
of event and promise, which will span vastly different periods of
history, is made. This link stretches much further into the future
than the life of this one man. When will all the families of the
earth be blessed in Abraham?

For Abraham himself, the man to whom this promise was made,
the future, which is full of such far reaching promises, is compressed in what, by contrast, seems at first a very slight and insignificant event: namely, that he should receive a child. The
promise which spanned the world was compressed for him into the
expectation of a child. Abraham had broken his connections with
his family to answer God's call. In the world of those days he could
only have a future if he had a child. If he were to die childless,
his life would sink into the oblivion of one forgotten; it would be

as if he had never lived and the promises would sink with him into oblivion.

Sarah, his wife, however, bore him no son. The promise that he should become the father of a great nation became more comprehensible to him when he was promised a son (Gen. 17.15-22; 18.9-16). But he had to travel a long way before the actual birth of the child, which is not recorded till 21.1-7. Abraham followed the call to leave his native country for an unknown land which God would soon show him. Then, however, the obstacles began. Famine hit the land, Abraham retreated and made his way with his wife to Egypt. The offensive story, so hard to understand, of how Abraham surrendered his wife to another man is told here (Gen. 12.10-20). Behind it stands an older story which was once independent; it has parallels in Gen. 20 and 26. The theme of this earlier story was the danger of the Great Mother. It was related how the tribal mother once fell into serious danger but made a brilliant escape. In the history of Abraham the story is set in a new context and thus receives a new meaning. It is the first incident recorded about Abraham after he had received the promise; only notes on Abraham's journey come between. How will he receive the promise into his life? How will it work out in his life? The story answers: in this first test Abraham did not trust God sufficiently. He failed. Abraham passes off Sarah his wife for his sister, in order that he may not be killed if an Egyptian desires to have her. He knows that they are lawless in Egypt. They are at everyone's mercy there. He sees only two possibilities: destruction or the surrender—temporarily at any rate—of his wife. He saw no third possibility. He did not realize that God who had promised him great things could save him and Sarah, the father and mother of the promised one, in a way he had not foreseen. Everything took place as Abraham had foreseen it. The beauty of his wife causes a great stir, news of the beautiful foreigner comes to the ears of Pharaoh; and how easily at this point could Pharaoh have had Abraham done away with in order to possess Sarah! Abraham's plan seems to stand the test brilliantly. As brother of the beautiful woman he even receives presents. Then something happens on which

Abraham had not reckoned. God, the all-powerful, intervenes. Abraham receives his wife back again; he is allowed to leave the land with both her and the gifts—but as one who has been made to feel ashamed at the smallness of his faith and who has had to be taught by the mighty lord of Egypt that his own Lord was the more powerful.

This first story of Abraham, in which the 'father of faith' brought no honour to this name, tells of a test which is really quite modern. What Abraham discovered during his journey to Egypt when he made his proposal to Sarah is well known to us today; a feeling of complete helplessness in the face of a colossal power which can dash us in pieces without anyone taking any notice, a power so mighty that it could dispense with justice. What can a man sacrifice to escape from the brutal, deadly attack of such a power? What can one individual do against these machines of power which have at their disposal every means of exerting pressure? Have moral considerations any meaning in this case? We know these questions only too well as a result of the experience of the last hundred years. And we should not delude ourselves on this point: there are many, very many people today whose life has been threatened by such a colossal power and who have made the decision which Abraham made. Our story makes two comments. Abraham was ashamed, he had not reckoned with God's possibilities. This is very important in view of the concentration of power which has become possible in our time. There is no power on earth and never will be which God cannot—even while it is increasing—upset, restrain or check despite all human expectations. The alternative, which Abraham thought confronted him, never exists in such an absolute form that a man must say: 'Either I surrender what God has entrusted to me or I must die'. God always has another possibility even when none of us sees it.

Secondly, although Abraham was made to feel ashamed at his lack of faith, God, nevertheless, continued his dealings with him. The strength of this story lies simply in the fact that not a single word of judgement was spoken. Without actually saying so the story implies that this is what we men are like. We do not always stand up to great power. We are not always strong in faith. Abraham was like that too. But God took him further on his journey. The journey's destination is not, in any case, a perfect man. The promise meets another obstacle; Sarah bears no children. This time it is Sarah who seeks a way out—a solution which in the world of those days was both possible and common. She gives Abraham her maid as a concubine (Gen. 16-21), in order that she may give Abraham a child. This way, too, in which men thought they could help God's promise along, was rejected by God. Abraham was to receive a child from Sarah. This is exactly the same as in the case of the previous obstacle—God proceeds to a third possibility which men had overlooked. Abraham was not only to receive a child— that was equally possible with man's solution. Sarah, Abraham's wife, was to share in the fulfilment. This was only possible by means of a miracle.

This is the context of the news brought by God's messengers; they announced the birth of Ishmael to Hagar as well as the birth of Isaac to Sarah. These messengers are referred to frequently in the story of Abraham: the angel of the Lord meets Hagar when she is fleeing from Sarah (16); the 'three men' visit Abraham at the entrance to his tent and announce to him the birth of a son (18); two angels warn Lot and save him from the destruction of Sodom (19); the angel of God saves Hagar and her child from dying of thirst (21), restrains Abraham from sacrificing his son (22), and protects Abraham's servant on his way to the city of Nahor (24). These frequent references to the messengers of God or angels in the stories of Abraham are not accidental; for these stories remind us very much of an earlier period long before the present when the difference between God and man, and between God's world and man's world, was not yet felt to be so absolute. It is true that God is a long way from man but he can send his messengers and these messengers come in the form of a man and they can be met on the roads of this world. In every narrative which speaks of God's messengers God himself can enter in place of the messenger, and *vice versa*. The messenger, rather than acting as an independent being distinct from God, represents the deeds or words of God which affect the earth. There is another group of stories at the beginning of the Old Testament which speaks equally frequently of angels: the stories in Judges. There is, in fact, a peculiar correspondence to be discovered between the two sets of angels. The meaning of the angel in the story of Abraham revolves round the birth of a child; in the history of the Judges, the angel usually announces the liberation of the nation from its enemies. In the former case, it is to the greatest plight of woman—childlessness—the angel brings good news. In the latter case, it is to the greatest plight of man—oppression. A strong continuity which spans the whole Bible begins to show itself: the two lines of good news, which have their source here in the first beginnings of the people of God, will one day open out into the good news of the birth of a child, whom God has destined to be the Saviour of the world.

The severest trial Abraham has to face comes after the child was born. God tested him by commanding him to sacrifice Isaac his son. Behind the narrative stands a historical occurrence of great importance, not only for the people of Israel but for many nations: the replacement of human sacrifice by that of animals. In the land of Abraham's wanderings human sacrifice had been practised. This has been proved since by an abundance of discoveries in that region, especially in the shape of building-sacrifices. When a house was built a child was buried in the foundations; clearly, from all the evidence, a practice continued over a long period. Later the prophets protested passionately against the sacrifice of children, which obviously found its way into Israel from Canaanite practice. There is no doubt that children were sacrificed in Canaan. In Israel it was forbidden from the beginning, not because God could not demand it, but rather because he himself had said that he did not want this sacrifice. The laws of Israel tell of the abolition of the sacrifice of the first born; but behind them is a story which stated once for all that God does not want this sacrifice. The story of the sacrifice of Isaac, as transmitted to us, is only a late distant echo of that story of the abolition of this custom. It no longer conducts a polemic against child sacrifice, but simply describes it as an already very distant background. The point it seeks to make is rather different.

It reports that God puts Abraham to the test, and at the end it says: 'Now I know that thou fearest God'. But this is only the framework of the story; the one who has to bear the suffering does not know why it is happening to him. For him it is an event which can be summed up in the sentence 'God provides himself an offering' (Gen. 22.8, 14). For him, the story begins with the command: 'Sacrifice thy son!' It ends with the command: 'Do not sacrifice him!' He can only interpret the first command as meaning that God is thereby disregarding his promise. Accordingly, if he follows him, he is obeying a God whom he can no longer understand. Now, in this hour, he says 'Yes' to God's third possibility, which is way beyond the alternatives he had the power to foresee. Abraham holds fast to God against all human possibilities and against God's earlier word. If he says to his son 'God will provide himself an offering', then he is balancing what God can do against what God has said. This conversation between father and son on the way to the mountain where the offering is to be made is without comparison: *And Abraham took the wood of the burnt offering, and laid it on Isaac his son; and he took in his hand the fire and the knife. So they went both of them together. And Isaac said to his father Abraham, 'My father!' And he said, 'Here am I, my son.' He said, 'Behold, the fire and the wood; but where is the lamb for a burnt offering?' Abraham said, 'God will provide himself the lamb for a burnt offering, my son.' So they went both of them together* (Gen. 22.6-8).

Let us ask ourselves what is the meaning of this story in the Bible as a whole. We can distinguish broadly speaking three clearly defined periods of sacrifice in the Bible: the prehistoric period of *human* sacrifice; the period of *animal* sacrifice from the patriarchs to the end of the monarchy—coming to life once more after the exile and continuing up to the destruction of the temple in the year 70 AD; and, finally, *the replacement of animal sacrifice*, which was constantly offered over a wide area, by means of another sort of sacrifice which had a unique character. This was implied and prefigured in the representative suffering of the servant of God at the end of the prophetic line (in the servant-songs of Deutero-

Isaiah) which in turn points forward to the suffering and death of Christ, a sacrifice 'once, for all', as explained in the Epistle to the Hebrews.

None of the types of sacrifice as such and none of the interpretations as such are the right or the wrong ones. Each has its own time. Each signifies a period of humanity. The assumption underlying the whole history of sacrifice is that God can claim the highest and costliest from us; he can claim the unblemished perfect sacrifice. Over the whole earth, for many thousands of years it has been an intrinsic part of human existence to offer sacrifice to the gods or God. The Christian belief in the sacrifice of the one for the many can only be properly understood against this background of thousands of years of sacrificial offerings.

Today it is possible to speak of a fourth period of sacrifice. The place of God or gods has been taken by that of human organizations, which claim their sacrifices. The time during which men have thought that they were not obliged to offer any sacrifice to any God or in which they have ceased to know anyone to whom they could gladly offer their sacrifice is infinitesimal compared with the thousands of years of human history in which sacrifice has been an integral part of life. But already in this short time it has been demonstrated in some places that the demands for sacrifice made by human organizations can be more terrible than any sacrifice ever made to deities. The human sacrifice demanded by the totalitarian state is the distorted counterpart of human sacrifice in remote antiquity, the sacrifice which Abraham no longer needed to bring.

The rest of what is reported about Abraham says little more than we have seen already. A remarkable figure! Almost every feature of greatness—as we understand this word—is missing. How is it credible that such an account of the father of the nation— which does not even try to represent him as an outstanding man— could arise? The general impression is that of a man who is always having to give up something. He had to give up his father's house, he had to give up his titles, he had to give up his attempts to enjoy security in life, he had to give up his own son. It is true he receives everything back again—and abundantly too; but that does not alter the impression that Abraham is a man who was always having to give up something. If we want to say anything in Western terminology about his life's work, his achievement, his contribution to anything, his effort and exertion, his activity and creativity, then we should simply have to stand there with empty hands. Abraham is *the man who had to give way*. We should not forget, therefore, that this picture of Abraham was given to a nation which was at the height of its political importance. A nation that knew and very much appreciated purposeful activity, great achievement and genuine leadership, and that looked to its future with high hopes. This was the nation to which the authors of the patriarchal history presented such a father!

It proves one thing at least. What a powerful figure God must have been to this people! That Abraham is pictured as the one who must give way is an indirect testimony to the majestic reality of the God who does his work in *such* a life and founds the history of his people on it.

In the middle of the story we are told that Abraham's chief characteristic was this: he trusted in the Lord. Consequently later ages have called him the father of faith. There is a direct inversion of the truth if he is seen as a 'hero of faith'. A correct understanding depends on noticing what is important about this figure: he heard a call and followed it. In following this call he gained a future, the future which had been promised him.

Understood in this way, this figure of Abraham has something important to say to modern times. We live at a time in which the individual is more than ever under the threat of being swallowed up in the crowd and of no longer being able to discover a life that is really his own and worthy of man. This story says to people today: extrication from the crowd does not depend on something special or exceptional; this is not the way to become an independent individual. It depends on a man ordering and planning his life in response to a call which binds him as an individual with eternity. His life can then really be the life of one who must give way. But in affirming the call, he has attained to the unique dignity of man, the individuality of one called by his own name by God.

2 · *Jacob and the Struggle for the Blessing*

T H E second group of patriarchal stories has for its theme the
quarrel of two brothers, one of the great themes of world history
to the present day. The two brothers are rivals; literally, 'two who
live by the same river' (and draw water from it). Two brothers who
grow up in the same house, in the same environment, by the same
spring and with the same inheritance, are by nature rivals. The
basic source of all conflicts, ever since the world began, can
be located in the fact that we have to live together. The Bible has
seen and described the basic importance of this conflict for community life in the two pairs of brothers Cain and Abel, Jacob and
Esau. By describing hostility between brothers *twice* within a brief
space at the very beginning of its story, in the primaeval and patriarchal history, the Bible has from the outset pointed to this rivalry
and competition of men as existing both among the people of the
world and among the people of God. There is not only rivalry among
men which can result in murder or war between brothers, but there
is also rivalry in the province of those called by God, in the province
of the promise. As the facts of church history show, and as the
New Testament says, this rivalry between brothers is included in
the brotherhood of Christ's Church right from the band of the
disciples and the earliest Christian community; the possibility of
rivalry is by no means excluded. Brotherhood in absolute harmony
and without a single quarrel would be an idealistic falsification
of what it really means to be a brother. Absolute harmony between
brothers is not normal.

The question is not whether there may be rivalry in a 'true
brotherhood', but how it is dealt with. It can be dealt with in such
a way that the rival is removed. This possibility will always exist
to the end of the world; it is one of the possibilities of human intercourse, which the *whole* of humanity, not only the murderer, has
to put up with. This is affirmed by the story of Cain and Abel just
as much as by Jesus's interpretation of the command 'Thou shalt

not murder'. Rivalry can, however, also be dealt with in such a way that the two rivals remain neighbours in some way or other. For such a relationship to issue in complete agreement or complete goodwill is very exceptional. As a rule one of the rivals or competitors will become the first and the other the second; one will have the advantage over the other, or one will become superior to the other. The scenes and forms of strife between brothers are capable of infinite variation; but this rivalry is in itself an abiding fact of corporate existence throughout all ages. The modern Jacob and Esau still confront each other just as in the group of stories in Genesis; only the forms of this confrontation have changed. A decisive difference is the shift of emphasis from the political to the economic which we are experiencing. Instead of 'rivals' we have 'competitors'. Economic competition is simply a new form of the old sibling rivalry. Recently economic competition has assumed yet another form through the fact that in the race to investigate new sources of energy a special branch of scientific work is coming to the front of the economic war, an event which again brings with it unsuspected consequences.

For everyone who stands anywhere in the struggle for existence today rivalry in some sense of the word is unavoidable. That is true for every member of the Christian Church also, for there are brothers who hate each other here too, whether we like it or not. All rivalry, competition and opposition have their origin in the family, where two brothers grow up together in the same circle. In the Jacob-Esau stories (Gen. 24-36) the brothers' quarrel revolves around a single issue: the blessing. In the quarrel over the birthright it is the father's blessing which is the issue; in the climax of the third part, the story of Jacob's return it is again the blessing which is the issue; and again in the intervening section which relates Jacob's stay with Laban it is the blessing which is the issue—even if in a quite different way.

The idea of blessing in the world of the patriarchs occupies the place which the idea of success has in modern times. 'Success' which even today is still a concept which defies closer definition. Striving for success and working for success play an important rôle in our society; and yet it is conceded by everyone that there are those who succeed and those who remain unsuccessful in spite of much perseverance and exertion. One man succeeds, another does not; and no method for achieving success can alter this. In our word 'success' there are still echoes of the mystery which once found expression in the word 'blessing'. Blessing in the Bible is a force which man has no power to control but which takes possession of him. It is a force which is active not only among men but beyond, in every living creature, indeed in the whole of creation. Blessing is the power of growth. It is active in the threefold fertility of womb, flock and land. This threefold fruitfulness is very well portrayed in Deuteronomy (e.g. 7.13). It is quite clear that, each in its own way, the three groups of patriarchal narratives have to do with the blessing; the Abraham stories with the blessing of the child, the Jacob stories with the blessing of the flock, and the Joseph stories with the blessing of the corn. The patriarchal history begins with the promise of the blessing (Gen. 12.1-3) and it ends with the blessing upon all the sons of Jacob (Gen. 49); in between we have the story of the struggle for the blessing, the story of the rivalry between the two brothers. It is assumed that only one of the sons can be blessed by the father and that the blessing of the father can only be transmitted through *one* line. There is only one who is blessed, that is, who is the heir. The conviction that only one can be blessed has imprinted itself in the right of primogeniture, which is the earliest privilege in human history. In order that the life force of the father may be concentrated as it is passed on to the coming generations, the possessions must remain in the hands of the same person; therefore only one can be the heir and that is the first born among most peoples. The right of primogeniture has had a fundamental significance for those periods of human history when the economy was dominated by agriculture (and cattle breeding). It is only the age of industrialization that has gradually brought this ancient, universal right of privilege among men to an end.

The story of Jacob and Esau describes how this right was set aside. The blessing is God's free gift and is not tied to any rule. How the stream of blessing shall move through history has not been fixed once for all. It is reserved for God to decide through whom he wishes it to continue. The conflict between Jacob and Esau is described in two acts—at the beginning (Gen. 25-8) and at the end (Gen. 32-3); in between we have Jacob's stay with Laban (Gen. 29-31), to whom he had fled from Esau. In the first and third parts it is a matter of obtaining the blessing, in the second part the consequences of this are described.

We should not approach this story with our modern criteria. It has been a great mistake to make models out of the figures of patriarchal history. Jacob is not by any means a model. He is not an example for either good or evil. Every such classification misses the meaning of the stories. It should be seen as the story of two rivals fighting for the blessing and what God makes of this struggle.

Isaac, Abraham's son, becomes the father of twins by his wife Rebekah. She had been childless for a long time and had made her grief known to God, and Isaac had pleaded to God for her. She was told that she would give birth to two sons and that the elder would serve the younger. The fact that Esau was the first born of twins, however, only made it clear that the question which of the two should inherit the blessing was still not decided. The conflict is prepared for in two stories which precede the act of blessing by the father. In the story of the pottage of lentils (Gen. 25.27-34) Jacob obtained Esau's rights of primogeniture by a trick. In fact the story once had quite a different meaning. Once upon a time it played off two classes against each other, the farmer against the hunter, as happens in the folk stories of many nations. The story makes fun of the fierce and foolish hunter who lives for the moment, while the farmer thinks of the future and cheats the greedy hunter. This story of the farmer and the hunter, which is certainly very old and well known, is set in quite a new context in the patriarchal history. As a separate folk-tale it reflected an event in the life of the community which signified a radical change for Israel as for many other nations: hunting as a livelihood was replaced by farming, the hunter lost his importance. This piece of history is transferred to Israel's patriarchs, and thus the change in men's way of life, which

is reflected in this story, the change-over from one stage of civilization to another, is inserted in the history of God's dealing with his
people. The elder will serve the younger. The stream of the blessing
proceeds through Jacob.

The story of Gen. 27 is a climax in this respect; the crisis comes
in the hour that the father feels his end approaching and desires
to pass on the blessing to the first-born. It must be frankly admitted
that Jacob here deceives his father with the help of his mother and
cheats his brother in order to obtain the blessing. His mother would
be thinking of the announcement that the elder should serve the
younger; but that alters nothing. That this act of Jacob's was regarded as a trick is shown by a later reference in the prophet Hosea
(12.4). This story, too, is based on a much older folktale. The clever
farmer outwits the stupid hunter again. This old story belongs to
a period in which, as in many of our fairy tales, the end justifies
the means, and one must think of groups at loggerheads in which
trickery and deception are acknowledged as the superiority of the
cleverer. We repeat : these stories are not to be judged by the
criterion of an 'ethic for individuals'. The reception of this old
story into Israel's patriarchal tradition is more than simply an act
of preservation, however. It is an affirmation of the fact that the
nation of Israel as embodied in its tribal founders does not stand
out by its quality among its neighbours. It is like its tribal founder,
Jacob. It is a people for whom sinning is not only a possibility but
an actual fact, an important component of its history. The journey
which God made with his people does not exclude deception.
Through this story at the beginning it is clear once for all that those
who are called by God are not better than others. Attention is here
drawn to the fact that in three places in the course of this nation's
history a single man is especially important for the whole : Jacob
the tribal father, Moses the leader, and David the king. A serious
lapse is recorded about each of these three. With merciless realism
failure, transgression and sin are included in the facts about God's
people. The great, the leaders, and chief men are not excepted.
There are no ideal figures here and no spotless models. Already
we are beginning to guess why Christ stands at this journey's end.

Jacob emerges from this story as the one with the blessing. But the story continues. His fortune is in no way assured because he now has the blessing. He has to flee from his brother Esau. It is true that Esau in this story is always the one who is taken in, the stupid one who is imposed on, but in spite of this he retains the sympathy of the reader. That he should fight for his rights after the death of his father and that he should want to kill his brother who has taken everything from him is understandable. Their mother intervenes a second time and persuades Jacob to flee right away from everything that had been promised him in his father's blessing, to a place where he is without rights, without succour and an object of pity. It becomes clear very quickly that trickery does not pay.

The one with the blessing becomes a refugee and subsequently a servant. He comes to his relative Laban, his mother's brother. It is here that his father's blessing takes effect—in quite a different way from what Jacob had expected. He becomes rich in cattle, rich in the blessing of children from his two wives for whom he had served and from their maids. It is here in a foreign land that the fathers of the future tribe of Israel were born. But one must look at the other side of the picture, too : Jacob, the tribal father, spends many of the best years of his life as a servant in a foreign land in exile from his father's house. He is sent to the rulers of a foreign land and handed over to them. In the hour for which he had waited during seven years of service he himself was badly cheated; instead of receiving the betrothed maid for whom he had worked all those years the elder sister was substituted and he had to serve another seven years—an implicit parallel to the younger and elder brother motif—and finally he had to flee from his father-in-law also, because he was not sure whether one day he would not lose everything again. He had come as a fugitive, he had to leave as a fugitive. All the wealth he had acquired meanwhile and even his life was jeopardized by the anger of his brother whom he goes to meet. The destiny of the nation to which he gave birth is clearly reflected in the story of the tribal father. A nation which knows itself blessed by God and yet has to serve in a foreign land; a nation richly endowed by God and yet without any certainty of possession; a nation which cannot escape from the circle bounded by blessing and guilt, protection and danger.

Two events at the beginning and end of Jacob's flight are the focal points of the story: two encounters with God, on which the whole history of Jacob hinges. The first is Jacob's dream when he is running away from Esau (28.10-22). Again we must distinguish between the older story, which was told long before it was inserted into the group of stories about Jacob and Esau, and the new meaning which it received through this insertion. Bethel was a Canaanite and perhaps—as has been maintained recently—a pre-Canaanite shrine, the earliest remains of which have been dated to the third millenium BC by excavators. A stone pillar stood there as a symbol for God. The Israelites took over the shrine, just as later so many pagan shrines became places of Christian pilgrimage or worship. Bethel became one of the chief shrines of Israel. It was in Bethel and Dan that Jeroboam erected his bull-images; it was in Bethel and against Bethel that A.nos preached. Whenever pilgrims came from the country to Bethel they were told the story of how the shrine originated. Then they heard how the nation's father, fleeing from his brother, had spent the night there; how God had appeared to him and he had had a wonderful vision in the night; and how in the morning he had erected the mighty stone—all by himself!—and made a threefold vow, which was proved by the holiness of the place up to that very day on which the pilgrims were listening to the story. In the middle of the story comes the sentence with which Jacob awoke. *Surely the Lord is in this place; and I did not know it. How awesome is this place! This is none other than the House of God* (= Bethel), *and this is the gate of heaven* (28.16 ff.). This sentence, together with the story in which it comes, demonstrates with unique power and clarity the discovery of the holiness of a place. Every holy place once originated in a manner similar to that described here: through an encounter with God. There is no place on earth which is holy 'in itself'. A place can only become holy through an encounter with God. And the place as such can never preserve holiness. Bethel had already been a holy place for a thousand years before the patriarchs of Israel entered the land. Nevertheless, Israel attributed its holiness to that one night when God appeared to the father of the nation here. And it is only in the context of the history of God's dealings with this people and of their response as worshippers here, that it is a holy place for them. Thus it was possible that this place was not holy in any way for Amos; for him it had been profaned through the idolatry and false worship which were current. If Israel did not remain true to the God who once spoke to their father Jacob at this place, then the holiness of the place also disappeared, its destruction could be proclaimed by the prophets, and—as happened under Josiah—it could be demolished and profaned. This is the first consideration which throws light on the real importance of this story for us. We are staggered by the fact that this thousand-year-old shrine of our story could in fact be completely destroyed and yet we, who live in the twentieth century, can still, in a radically changed world, hear the words which were uttered on that occasion in response to God's self-revelation—a revelation of the Holy—and understand them. The time of holy places has now passed, as far as we are concerned. We can no longer see in any place on earth the spot where the entrance to God's dwelling place is and where his messengers ascend and descend. But the revelation of the living God, which evokes fear and at the same time brings pardon, has retained its reality for us over thousands of years.

Jacob has only just practised his deception on his brother—which causes his immediate flight from the sphere of his father's blessing into the unknown—when God promises him: 'Behold, I am with you and will keep you wherever you go' (28.15). Such is the God of the Bible. He does not deal with us according to our sins. His works are incomparable and immeasurable by our judgement.

The second story, the struggle by the river Jabbok, likewise has roots which stretch a long way into the pre-history of the Old Testament to a time far, far beyond the experiences recorded here, when men had no distinct belief in a personal God or even a plurality of gods, but their world was full of spirits, strange beings of various sorts who visited men with friendly intent, granted men's wishes and helped them, or raised uncanny opposition, fell upon them and attacked them. It is in this early period of history that the story of the struggle by the Jabbok has its roots. And long before Jacob passed by the place with his family and his herds, apprehensively advancing to meet his brother, tales were told of the river-spirit at the ford of the Jabbok, who fell upon men who wanted to cross in the night and sought to kill them but who had to return to his lair as soon as day dawned. This very ancient, certainly pre-Israelitic narrative was changed so that it became a component part of Jacob's life story. If we read this story today and ask 'With whom then did Jacob really fight?', and if we are alarmed by the wildness of this mythical, legendary account, then we must realize first of all that, even at the time when the authors of the patriarchal history included it, it contained strange ideas which had already long disappeared. The grandeur and impressiveness of the composition of the patriarchal history, especially for us, lies in the way it risks incorporating very old, pre-Israelitic traditions in order to let the nation's patriarchs traverse in this way the violent periods of the past and in order to incorporate all these long 'outdated' traditions into the account of God's mighty works for his people. If the confession of faith in God as Creator were taken seriously then his ways must include all the regions of pre-history and its traditions.

Through its incorporation in the story of Jacob the attack of the river-spirit has become a fight with God himself. To be sure it is God in a strange, bizarre disguise who meets Jacob shortly before he reaches the destination of his long flight and falls upon him like a demon. Here for the first time in the Bible is a narrative which shows that God can become an enemy. It is exactly as God is represented in this story that Job speaks of him in his struggle with God and temptation: *He has torn me in his wrath and hated me; he has gnashed his teeth at me; he has siezed me by the neck and dashed me to pieces* (Job 16.9 and 12). God can become a man's enemy. This very old story, with its roots deep in animism, can express this better than an abstract account which can never be so vivid and real. The realization that God can, by a terrible change, become a demonic enemy of his people and his saints is intrinsic to the story which begins with the nation's father. Not only Job experienced this; the laments of the Psalms contain accusations against God: 'Thou hast become my enemy'. The prophets declare to Israel that God will strike his own people like a tearing, wild animal, and the songs of lamentation after the destruction of Jerusalem look back to this. *The Lord has destroyed without mercy all the habitations of Jacob; in his wrath he has broken down the strongholds of the daughter of Judah; he has brought down to the ground in dishonour the kingdom and its rulers* (Lam. 2.2). Jacob emerges wounded and victorious from his fight with God. He holds God fast and wrings a blessing from him: 'I will not let you go unless you bless me'. He receives a new name. 'You shall no more be called Jacob but Israel; for you have striven with God and men and have prevailed.' He receives the name not of victor, however, but of 'wrestler with God'. This name is the real characteristic of the story which began with the one named Israel. Here began a struggle with God which consisted of a long series of defeats and at the end of which the struggler was told 'you have conquered'. It was the beginning of a struggle which accepted that God could become hostile and in which men thought of God as the enemy. It began the history of struggle with temptation. There is a direct road from this victory of the wounded Israel across the great stages of Israel's history to the hour in which the Man on the Cross cried 'My God, why hast thou forsaken me?' and in which he too received a new name, the name which is above every name.

On the following day Jacob met his brother Esau. The meeting is described in detail. In the middle of it stands the scene of greeting. Esau greets Jacob as his brother, he embraces and kisses him. Jacob, on the other hand, greets Esau as a vassal greets his lord: he throws himself down before him and entreats his mercy with a costly gift. In order to understand this one must know what a greeting meant in those days. It was no formality but a social event of great importance. By throwing himself down before Esau Jacob recognized him as his lord; and that Jacob did this in the hour of meeting after long years of separation confirms what is undoubtedly

the truth of the matter. Only such an interpretation makes sense
of the Jacob-Esau story as a whole. The mother had been informed
before their birth that the elder would serve the younger. In fact
the younger had obtained the blessing of the first born by cunning
and deceit. But it had not brought him what he expected of it. He
had to flee and become a servant. The blessing, it is true, fell upon
him. But now, again, it really seems as if the opposite of what she
was told had come to pass: Jacob, the younger, but the possessor
of the blessing, does obeisance to Esau, the elder, the unblessed; he
humbles himself before Esau with his large family and gives him
of his possessions. The story of Jacob wants to get across to the
children to whom it will be told that they cannot possess God's
blessing simply on the ground that they are the blessed; God remains the master of his blessing and he can lead his blessed ones
along hard and difficult paths. It can happen that it is precisely
those that he has assured of his help and protection whom God
teaches to think of him as a terrible enemy—an experience which
Esau the unblessed never knew. Later, there will come a time in
which the sons with whom God blessed Jacob will come to him
with a bloodstained garment. In this hour he is the deceived one;
and years of suffering return. At the end of his life he stands before
Pharaoh and says: *The days of the years of my sojourning are a
hundred and thirty years; few and evil have been the days of the
years of my life* (Gen. 47.9). Such was the life of the one who received the blessing. And it was through his life that the stream of
blessing continued into the future, the future of the people of God
in whom the history of Jacob continued.

3 · Joseph and the Peace of the Family

T H E third group of patriarchal stories, in which Jacob's son
Joseph is the central character, deals with events affecting father
and sons, and one son in particular. In the Abraham group the
stories turned on the propagation of life by the parents, from father
to child, in other words on the vertical, genealogical line of man's

journey through history, which begins with the birth of a child. In the Jacob group the horizontal line entered also: the rivalry of brothers was the problem here. In the Joseph stories there is a further addition to these two basic motives: tension arises between the three parties—brother, brothers and father. While the two motives which the first two groups of stories deal with describe the chief components of the family, only this third group, the Joseph stories, in which the motives of succession and co-existence are brought together, really deals with the family as such.

One or two observations should be made at this point. It may be that the Old Testament has something important to say here about our present problems of the family. We stand today at a juncture where the basic forms of human life and community, which developed from the human race's settled mode of life, have entered upon a period of change. In the period now closing rural forms of life have determined the real distinctiveness of community life. These forms can no longer meet all the requirements of the changed mode of life of our changed world; this shows itself even in the family.

For this reason the Joseph story has its own special interest for us: it stands at the beginning of the period now ending. If we ask today what form family life ought to take in our changed world, we shall do well to look where the family as we know it took shape. Everything which we now take for granted, everything in fact which we no longer notice because it is too self-evident, is here still at an early stage of development. It is seen with surprise, with awe and with fear, and what is seen has become a story. The Joseph story is different from those of Abraham, and Jacob and Esau, in another respect also; it is told in a connected way. It is an entity in itself rather like a novel, whereas the Abraham group consists simply of more or less independent separate stories only very loosely connected, and the Jacob group, as far as this goes, stands somewhere between the other two. The Jacob story as a whole has a certain continuity through Jacob's flight and later return.

There is a third difference of the Joseph group from the other two which must be noticed. The stories of the Joseph group are

nearest to the lifetime of the narrator (i.e. the era of David and
Solomon). From the point of view of the narrator and his hearers
the Joseph stories are by far the most modern. That applies also to
a certain extent to our own point of view. What takes place between
God and man in the Joseph stories takes place, so to speak, in the
lifetime of the narrator: God rarely appears to a man (only once
does he appear to Jacob in a dream—Gen. 46.2-4). We are a long
way from such stories as Gen. 18 or 32. There are no conversations
between God and man (such as in Gen. 18 about the judgement of
Sodom). There are no physical visible manifestations of the God-
head. All traces of mythical thought are absent. One could almost
say the Joseph stories betray a certain worldliness. Almost everything which happens admits of what we call a naturalistic explanation; the whole narrative breathes a modern, enlightened air.

The theme of the Joseph story is peace in the family. 'Peace'
(*shālōm*), the usual greeting among Semitic speaking people, means
the well-being of the community. In order to understand the development of this theme in the story of Joseph and his brothers
we must try to attune ourselves to a different wavelength from
that of our contemporary world. In our world, family dramas are
not generally headline news. What is happening on the political
scene occupies the headlines for us; plus what we find every day
in the columns of the daily newspapers—events in the economic
world, in cultural life, and film and stage, on the streets and in
commerce. In the whole range of our experience, family dramas
rank only second or third in importance, or simply become part of
the background. They only become important among men who
have a name; kings, film stars, and the leading sportsmen. But if a
man who was once surrounded with the glare of publicity retires
from the limelight, the most stirring and gripping drama may take
place in his family life without it any longer exciting interest.

In the world of the Old Testament what happens in the family
is of prime importance. A man does not have a 'private life' in
addition to his standing in the public eye, but his private life describes his real life; it is the scene of what actually goes on, where
men's characters are formed, where they conquer and are defeated,

fail and prove true. It is in this light that we must try to understand these stories.

Peace in Jacob's family was disturbed by Jacob loving his son
Joseph 'more than all his other sons, because he was a son of his
old age'. Liking led to favouritism; and this engendered hatred
among Jacob's other sons and led to the plan to murder Joseph.
The eldest brother dissuaded them from carrying out this plan
and Joseph was sold into Egypt; this had to be concealed from the
father by a lie. As a result peace in Jacob's family comes near to
breaking point and healing seems no longer humanly possible. The
story describes how the community life of this group was, nevertheless, restored. The scene of the second part of the story is the
great world. At the court of Pharaoh—with a background of stirring events which are closely interwoven with the Egyptian empire
but which, despite their dimensions, remain in the background—
what had been broken long ago at a distant moment in the life
of a family was restored. In this way everything becomes part of a
well-ordered, silent hymn of praise to God, who blesses men with
peace (*shālōm*) in their community life and who alone is capable of
restoring peace when it has been broken. There is a hymn of praise
to the God who humbles and exalts, who leads men along unfamiliar paths and who in his actions is by no means always recognizable as a righteous God, who is able to bring together what has
been separated by a great distance, who directs the kings of the
earth like the hungry creatures of the field and who has a purpose
in all his ways which is for the peace of men. But what has just
been said about God is to be inferred from events rather than explicitly stated; there is no exaggeration, but simply a story telling
its own tale.

Interwoven with this is reflection on the events which make up
the life of a community, and above all of a family. The starting
point was the preference of the father for his youngest child. This
preference is not condemned but simply stated as a fact. It *is* a fact
that parents love a child born to them late in life differently from a
child whom they had before the prime of life. If we say that they
love it 'more', that probably gives the wrong idea: but that it is

a different love is simply a fact. The child born while they are still young will probably go a long way through life with them; the child of old-age enters their life as they approach death. In the child of old age the parents love the part of their life which remains when they go. This must have been experienced even more strongly in a world in which life was only understood in terms of the succession of generations, as a stream flowing from one generation to another.

It is only wrong where this quite natural preference leads to favouritism. In the gift of the 'coat of many colours', better translated a 'long robe with sleeves' (RSV), the father's liking becomes an open fact. The distinction sets the youngest on a level above his other brothers; he is thereby 'something better' and that is bound to have hurt the brothers.

Joseph's coat meant a great deal in a world in which clothes still had a definite social function. For thousands of years in settled communities clothing has been recognized as an indication of social standing. The democratization of clothing has brought about a great change in human society. The cry for equality which spread over Europe as a result of the French Revolution received perhaps its most concrete expression in the matter of clothing.

The garment motif extends through the whole Joseph story; one of the signs of great narrative artistry. The coat becomes the evidence used by the brothers to hide what they have done from their father. A garment results in his condemnation when he is accused by the wife of his Egyptian master. At the height of his career he is decked with the garment of the governor by Pharaoh himself. There is another reason too for his brothers venting their malice on him— Joseph's dreams. This dream motif is a later addition from an earlier source but it runs through the whole story. We cannot go more closely into the connection of the two strands of the narrative at this point; they run through the Joseph story from beginning to end and make us recognize that the story has its origin in oral tradition, in the course of which it received different recensions.

The garment motif reveals a predominant interest in the way men live together and in the events of community life, in which the basic form of community is always the family. The dream motif, however, clearly announces a political interest in addition. Joseph's dreams declare that he will be exalted high above his brothers and even above his parents too. His brothers ask angrily: 'Do you want to be king over us?' Behind this can be discerned the question which was troubling the people of Israel 'Is kingship permissible? May a man be exalted so high above his brothers?' The historical account of the beginnings of kingship in Israel still enables us to recognize that kingship in Israel only arose in times of severe crisis and under strong opposition. These are the problems which provide the background to Joseph's dreams.

The brothers had conceived a hatred for Joseph. Their hatred had a justifiable aim: the advancement of justice. But their method of recovering the equal rights of which they felt deprived, the undivided love of their father, was a failure. It is very significant that their anger was directed not against the person most responsible, their father, who favoured the youngest son, but against the one he favoured. This feature of the narrative also, even though it is barely visible, is based on keen observation of the way men live together. When one individual is singled out for special protection, instead of the father or leader or chief giving himself equally to all, a group of people who belong together is altered; this was seen, and the importance of it recognized. Today, too, it is a generally observed fact that those who have been slighted, if they are afraid of the one in authority, do not settle the matter with him but direct their hatred at the one who has been protected, and thus the rift in the community only becomes worse.

Similarly, their mutually agreed plot to murder Joseph can only be planned when they are well out of their father's reach. This plan makes it classically clear what is the chief motive behind premeditated murder: it is to get someone out of the way. At the same time the utter stupidity of such a decision is demonstrated: murder never clears the way for the murderer. The brothers desire to recover the undivided love of their father, and this desire is justifiable. But hate makes them blind. The first specific result of their deed is to block the way to their father's love. Their plan of murder is very much like that of Cain. The deprival of love and something like jealousy are at the back of both incidents. In both cases the anger, from which hatred subsequently grew, was justified to a certain extent. If we take these stories seriously, as God's word, then it is clear that the Church cannot withdraw into a bourgeois respectability away from those who are usually stamped as criminals and lawbreakers by the law abiding. The Joseph story at all events knows nothing of such a withdrawal. It has a burning interest in what are called 'criminal events'. Right from the beginning we are brought into contact not only with a plan to murder but the sale of a man, punishment and prison, the course of justice, suspicion of espionage, and false accusation; and all this is included in what happens between God and man. God does not simply wash his hands of men who have decided to kill their brother in cold blood. He continues his dealings with them.

The reason why the plot against Joseph was not carried into effect needs special comment. The reason lay in the position of the eldest brother. If, in the absence of the father, a situation arose in which an authorative action or decision was called for, then the eldest brother assumed the father's functions as a matter of course. (He is called Judah by the older source, Reuben by the later source.) This is the origin of our modern, vague and overworked concept of 'responsibility'. On the brothers' return the father will ask the eldest: 'Where is Joseph?' He must face the question and give an answer. Therefore the responsibility is his. Because he is responsible he intervenes after the formation of the plan to murder Joseph. He has to think further than the others; he has to make the answer. He does not have the same authority as the father; he is only one of his sons, one of the brothers. But the question that the father will put to him later and which he must withstand compels him to act 'responsibly' in this moment. It is true that he cannot prevent the deed—he is naturally on the side of the brothers—but he can prevent the worst.

It is a wonderful position, this position of the eldest brother. It applies right up to the present day. Here lies the secret of genuine authority. Genuine authority is only possible and can only be preserved where there is someone who knows that he must answer to another and higher authority. The possibility of genuine authority depends on the preservation of some trace of this derivation from the father's authority. Authority and responsibility belong together at the point where the one who is exercising authority knows that one who is empowered to do so will question him and that he must then make answer. A person who knows no-one to whom he must answer cannot, in fact, act responsibly. Nor can he have any genuine authority.

The eldest brother on this occasion could only prevent the worst. What happened—insofar as he agreed with his brothers—is still bad enough. Joseph is removed all the same; but without bloodshed; he is sold as a slave. This crime also has to be concealed from the father. The father is shown the fictitious evidence of an accident: 'a wild animal tore Joseph apart'. The brothers will remember this hour much later; they themselves will have the fictitious evidence of a theft which they are supposed to have committed held before their eyes. And they will be helpless in the face of this evidence, just as their father at this hour is the helpless prisoner of their false evidence.

The brothers succeeded in removing Joseph, the disturber of the peace, but they achieved nothing by it. In his helpless grief their father was even more intensely attached to his lost son than he had been before when Joseph was still at home. The rift between father and sons was not healed; it was only made worse.

The scene changes and now the story of Joseph really begins. It is a success story. What we call 'success' is called 'exaltation' in the Bible. That God exalts the insignificant from the dust is an important sentence in Israel's praise of God (e.g. Ps. 113). The story of Joseph's 'exaltation' is like a brilliant, rich variation on this theme. In early Israel such a rise in status—a rise right from slave to Governor—was a new and quite fantastic possibility. In a purely agricultural environment nothing like that ever happened. The scene of this rise in Egypt corresponds throughout with the historical facts: in Egypt at that time this sort of thing was possible, and Egyptian sources report several instances of something similar.

But the social aspect of the event is not the decisive one for the narrator. He wants to emphasize that Jacob's family history, the history of broken peace in the house of Jacob, continues in the person of the one who is removed by his brothers and sold as a slave. The story continues by saying that 'God was with him', as we are told. God restored harmony again to a group of people by being with the one who had been thrust out from this group.

How God was with him is described with little effort at edification but very soberly. By degrees Joseph worked himself into a high position with the man who had bought him as a slave. Then— without any fault at all on his part—he was knocked down again from this height to which he had painfully and slowly attained. This episode with the Egyptian's wife, which is told with wonderful artistry, is, unfortunately, usually interpreted quite wrongly. There is no suggestion that when confronted with this immoral woman Joseph withstood the temptation successfully because of his 'chastity'. The masterly portrayal of this scene is much more concerned to make the point that Joseph declined to break faith with his master. Because of all the goodness which his master had shown him a natural barrier, keeping him back from his master's wife, raised itself of its own accord. This scene gives a clear hint—that is still relevant today—that to isolate sexual matters, and to make hard and fast rules for sexual conduct without setting it in a larger context, is a questionable procedure which cannot be supported from the Bible.

At all events, if a man or a woman is faced with temptation similar to that of Joseph in this scene, a decision is made which quite certainly cannot and should not be limited to the so-called 'sexual', but must be brought into relation with his or her whole life. If he resists the temptation this is not to be imputed to his purity or chastity but to the power of a real integrating force in his life which was operative at that moment, as in Joseph's case. There is something else important for us to notice about this scene. What happens between man and woman is described quite openly: 'and she caught hold of him by his garment and said "Lie with me!" ' Every reader will perceive that just because the language is direct the description of the whole scene is clear and unambiguous. We could learn something from this.

That Joseph preserved the confidence his master had placed in him proves of no avail. He is thrown into prison. This is a decisive point in the whole story of Joseph. In refusing to deceive his master Joseph kept faith with God (Gen. 39.9). 'How could I commit so great a wrong and a sin against God?' he says. God had been with him up to this hour and now he has a chance to show that he is obedient. This God, however, immediately after his expression of trust brings him into prison! The narrator intends to say through this that God really is like this. He does not allow his deeds to be calculated by men, even by his own. He is not the dear God of pious history where everything always goes right. 'He is the righteous worker of miracles, who can exalt and humble at will.' It is possible that a decision made in obedience to God can bring a man directly into catastrophe. This is quite a realistic estimate. There is no question of an appeal.

But even in prison there is a possibility of improving one's position. In the words of our story 'God is with Joseph in prison also'. God can do his work in a prison. It is a sad fact that many people today only became aware of this when ministers of religion went to prison not as prison chaplains but as prisoners. Consequently people never noticed earlier the particularly beautiful and authentic touch in the development of the story of Joseph which we understand again now: the exaltation of Joseph from prison begins with the fact that he enquires how things are going with his fellow prisoners, whose master he had been! Anyone who has been in prison knows what that means.

In response to his enquiry the court officials who are in prison with him tell him their dreams, which they themselves could not interpret. The original dream motif is taken up again. Through his skill in interpreting the dreams Joseph comes before Pharaoh again and becomes his Governor. Behind this motif of dreams and their interpretation stands an early stage of Israel's experience of the revelation of God. In early times the dream was a common way for God to speak to man. On this occasion, however, there was a new, additional factor. God was speaking to men outside his own people, but they had not the key to understand such words. They must look for someone who can unlock the words of the dream for them. Here we find the first traces of the faith of Israel to which the words of God have been entrusted, not for themselves but for the world. As a member of the people of God Joseph can reveal to others what God has in mind for them.

But this motif contains yet another explanation: in the interpretation of Joseph the prophetic word—the word which points to the future and gives direction to the present—can be heard announcing itself from afar.

The dreams, the hidden words of God, which need interpretation, are supplemented by something quite different: the advice of the clever steward, the wisdom which grasps a situation and puts forward the correct solution. There are indications here of the early golden age of wisdom of Solomon's period (cf. 1 Kings 10) which corresponds exactly to the enlightened spirit of the Joseph stories. Wisdom in this early period is in the main practical cleverness, watchfulness and unerring aim in the human decisions of everyday life in all its ramifications, but never a specialized subject along with others, as philosophy later became.

Joseph's wisdom proves itself in the province of commerce. In this extract we re-live the hour when commerce began to emerge as a special province of life. In a nation of farmers it was seen for the first time that between production and comsumption, output and use a new independent factor had arisen—the mastery of the fluctuation between over-production and under-production by means of a planned economy. It should be noted here that there had been a planned economy on such a large scale in Egypt long before Joseph, and the Egyptians certainly did not learn it first from Joseph. What the story can teach us is not primarily how a planned economy originated but how a still quite young and agricultural nation reacted to the large scale commercial undertaking of the neighbouring empire. Reflected in the Joseph story we can perceive two reactions of the Israelite to this encounter. Firstly, the new possibilities which were opened up in the area of commerce were worked into the praise of God who preserves life. 'God thought it good to make and preserve many people' is the final comment on Joseph's work in Egypt. It is a simple, strong faith which here associates, quite as a matter of course, the enterprise of commerce—which at that time was only just making itself independent but today has grown to a tremendous extent—with God's goodness which preserves men from starving: a faith which knows itself called above all else to praise God. This does not prevent it from recognizing and affirming that the enterprise of men, their clever plans and prudent execution, as such are under the friendly protection of God. God's way of preserving many lives in this story is indirect; not through the intervention of a direct miracle but through the wisdom which he gives a man who then makes plans and puts them into action. This section of the Joseph story shows that the division of labour (cf. Gen. 2.15) is recognized and accepted by the Bible. The growing independence of commerce and the ventures of human industry into new fields are linked with faith in God and accepted with gratitude. If the constantly expanding work of men in the fields of commerce, technology, science, etc., has increasingly detached itself from faith in God and become a 'law unto itself', then this is perhaps due to the fact that there has been a declension on the part of the Church from the affirmative and grateful attitude which can be found throughout the Bible, and which our story illustrates. It is a good sign if today a different view seems to be setting in.

The conclusion of the Joseph story brings together the two series of events in their different settings in dramatic style and thus leads to the solution and healing of the rift in Jacob's family and to the restoration of harmony (shālōm). Here we shall find the statements on the life of the community which the author finds most important. Two scenes of simple narrative are set next to each other: Joseph's brothers are invited to a celebration banquet by the powerful foreign lord. There are high jinks, there is plenty to eat and drink, all the brothers' worries and anxieties seem to be at an end, everything in the garden is lovely—and the listener waits eagerly to hear that Joseph at last allows his brothers to recognize him. The best opportunity to do so seems to be at this feast. It does not happen. The narrator wants to convey that the rift could not be healed with this sort of reconciliation. It would not be a genuine solution; real forgiveness is not possible in such a manner. In sharp contrast to the festive banquet that evening stands the scene next morning. The caravan of the departing brothers, richly laden with corn, is stopped on the way, the golden beaker is found in Benjamin's sack (the false, fictitious evidence!) and thus all the brothers' plans are upset. Once again it is the oldest brother, the responsible one, who must put the situation right. He speaks the word which is decisive for the whole story: 'God has brought thy servant's guilt into the light of day'.

Real, healing forgiveness can only take place where it meets with an open confession of guilt. The brothers had found it necessary to conceal what they had done from their father. They succeeded. Life continued. Apparently ruin was averted. In a completely different place, long afterwards and in a completely different context Judah admits that God has uncovered what they have done. In doing so he acknowledges the continuity which God gives to life. In real life it is not usual for a fault to be confessed to straightaway so that it can then be forgiven. Real life is much more as the narrator shows it here. God continues his dealings undeterred with those who conceal what they have done. But one day the time comes when they see that concealment has not been a success. It happens in a situation in which the brothers are dealt a heavy blow through no fault of their own. The responsible one makes a stand and discovers how to say 'yes' openly to his guilt. Thus he, and his brothers with him, is able to receive forgiveness. Their peace can return. The narrative is saying in what happens here that human community life cannot exist without forgiveness. Equally clearly guilt and forgiveness cannot be forced into a set pattern, whether it be an intellectual system or a system based on acts of confession and penance. A fault is not always necessarily discovered, acknowledged and forgiven in the place where it happened. These events are never completely at man's disposal; they remain in the hands of God, whose dealings span long periods and great distances.

In addition to accepting his guilt the eldest brother is now ready to do something which is aimed at making amends for what he did wrong. He offers voluntarily to take the punishment on himself in place of the accused Benjamin, in order that their father may receive his beloved son back again and in order that the peace of the family may not be completely destroyed. It does not come to this because the reconciliation of Joseph with his brothers makes this sacrifice unnecessary. The readiness for this sacrifice clearly points beyond the Joseph stories. Here for the first time the thought is expressed that some day an individual may have to intervene and surrender his life in order to preserve the unity of the community. On this occasion it was not necessary but some day it could be. Emerging in the distance is the figure of the servant of God, of whom the unknown prophet of the exile says: 'Upon him was the chastisement that made us whole'.

III · THREE WORLDS

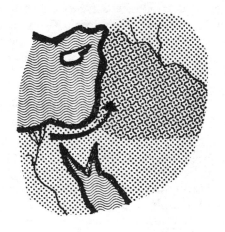

1 · The Rivers, Palestine and the Wilderness

BECAUSE Biblical history is concerned with events of this world, it is partly limited by its geography. The history of both Old and New Testaments acquires its drama through the close proximity and opposition of three regions: the great river valleys in the North and South; the small hill country of Palestine in between; and the great desert between the river valleys.

None of these three regions should be omitted from the drama of the history of God's people. They form the three boundaries of the area with which the history is connected. More than that they are themselves so deeply involved in what happens that without them nothing can be understood of the events which took place in the thousand years of history of God's people. God's giving and taking, God's saving and protecting, the people's obedience and rebellion, its return to God and reformation—none of this can be reported without one of the three regions playing some part not only as a place but as a symbol.

The great empires in the river valleys, of the North and South, represent for the Old Testament something like what is called 'the world' in the New Testament. As a result of its situation between the great river-empires the small land of Palestine was from the first destined to have less political importance; but, in addition, the ups and downs in those two neighbouring empires necessarily had an effect on the small country in between, and this meant both constant danger and constant attraction at the same time.

Already in the days of the patriarchs the prosperity of Egypt had exercised an attraction in times of famine; but had subsequently threatened to destroy Jacob's descendants by forced labour. The nation's history begins with the deliverance from Egypt, and the return from exile in Babylon represents God's last great act of deliverance. In the intervening period the young nation had the possibility of settling down in Canaan and developing into a flourishing kingdom, as long as the two great powers did not intervene. In fact the only time when Israel formed a strong state, internally secure and respected abroad, in the era of David and Solomon, was only possible because at that time for once in a thousand years both the empires of Egypt and Babylon were suffering from defeat. Already at the division of the northern and southern kingdoms on the death of Solomon, Egypt was involved in the background. And from now on the two kingdoms of Israel and Judah, weakened by division, were tossed and battered to and fro between the movements of the two great empires, until the northern kingdom succumbed to Assyria and the southern kingdom to Babylon. The exiles were transported to Babylon, while a remnant fled to Egypt, and Judah became a Babylonian province. With the end of national sovereignty the struggle for spiritual independence against the rulers of the great empires was continued in an opposition which spread right through the nation. The struggle waged by the various factions within Judaism was always concerned with the influence of the 'world', represented by the powers which had succeeded to the inheritance of the great Babylonian empire, first the Persians and then the Seleucids, until finally the small nation tried once again to free itself from foreign rulers in the wars of the Maccabees, but had to admit defeat. In the last act of Israel's history Roman rule took the place of neighbouring powers. The last wild resurgence of the Jewish nation against Roman domination in the year 70 AD led to the complete destruction of Jerusalem and the country. But in between another history had been begun, the history of the crucified King of the House of David.

The most important fact about the second region, *the land of Palestine*, has now been stated. It is 'the land in between', and it has never been able to free itself for any length of time from the superior strength of its great neighbours. That a history whose further developments extend to the present and which has exercised a formative influence on the West for two thousand years could arise in this small, poor, unfortunately situated country cannot be understood from the geographical, material and human conditions. What took place within this setting defies our normal criteria. One thing at any rate was very special in the relation of the people to their country. Israel always looked upon this land as given to it by God. They never forgot that they were once slaves in a foreign country and that God promised Israel this land, brought them into it and then made it their own. The land was and remained a trust, which could also be reclaimed. It was never a possession of which Israel could boast. Even so, it was for Israel 'a land flowing with milk and honey'. This was how Israel had once seen this land from the wilderness. The somewhat penurious land retained this lustre throughout the centuries: it was the gift of God's goodness, the gift of a homeland to his people.

The wilderness is the area between the great empires and the mountains of Palestine. All Israel's great journeys led through the wilderness. On the occasion of the two great deliverances at the beginning and end of Israel's history the way from servitude to freedom led through the wilderness. The way through the wilderness had to be accepted whenever the people took up the message of freedom. The wilderness was for Israel the true place of protection. And this is one of the most· surprising and most important facts in the nation's history: the years of wandering in the wilderness, the time which was hardest and severest and heaviest in losses, was later called by the prophets the only time when Israel was faithful to its Lord.

In the eyes of the farmers of Palestine the wilderness was a place of fear, deadly danger and horror. It was a specially frequent theme in prophetic announcements of judgement. 'I will make your land a wilderness.' The wilderness was always to be feared. But in spite of this Israel never forgot that the wilderness could be the place of refining, and that a man like a community could be changed in the wilderness. Remembrance of this extends into the New Testament. John the Baptist preaches repentance in the wilderness; Jesus is tempted in the wilderness. In the middle of the Old Testament it is particularly the message of Second Isaiah which proclaims the nation's return from exile in Babylon, through the wilderness. Right at the very beginning stands the call : 'In the wilderness prepare the way of the Lord !'

From the beginning the wilderness had symbolic significance for Israel—it is expressed most explicitly in Second Isaiah. The journey through the wilderness was and remained an important part of this nation's history. It had the wilderness behind it, but it also kept the wilderness ever before it. It could always be called out into the wilderness again.

2 · An Outline of the History of the People of God

E x o d u s and Deuteronomy tell the story of the chosen people's wanderings. These books are in fact the essence and foundation of the Old Testament. It has already been stated that the historical writing of Israel had its starting point in the confession of faith of those who had been saved by God, proclaiming what God had done for them. This confession of faith or hymn of praise (Ex. 15.21) was then expanded into a detailed narrative. This description of God's saving activity which began Israel's history is to be found in the first chapters of Exodus (Ex. 1-14). The whole Pentateuch is built up from this central fact. The account of the deliverance at the Sea of Reeds (Ex. 14) is followed by the account of Israel's journey through the wilderness and its preservation there, leading up to the arrival at Sinai (Ex. 16-8). It is preceded by the account of the distress to which the message of deliverance was addressed, connected with an account of the man who was the mediator of the deliverance, Moses (Ex. 1-13). The account of the journey through the wilderness after the departure from Sinai is continued in Num. 10-32. The story ends with the death of Moses, related in the last chapter of the fifth book of Moses (Deuteronomy).

This account is interrupted in two places; first by the book of Leviticus, and then by Deuteronomy. When the Israelites arrived at Sinai they received the Law there. This consists primarily of the Ten Commandments alone (Ex. 20). In Ex. 21-3 one of the first codifications of law, which originated in the period shortly after Israel's settlement in Canaan, is added. Ex. 25 to Num. 10—that is, the last chapters of Exodus, the whole of Leviticus and the first chapters of Numbers—represent a large collection of laws belonging to a much later period. In other words: as the five books of Moses (the Pentateuch) have been handed down to us, the first part of Exodus and the last part of Numbers merely form the narrative framework of a large collection of laws. (The narrative comprises approximately forty chapters, and the giving of the law sixty chapters in Ex.-Num.) It is understandable that in Jewish tradition the whole Pentateuch received the name 'the law' (*Tōrah*).

The second interruption is the fifth book of Moses, Deuteronomy. It is inserted at the point where the people of Israel have conquered the land east of the Jordan, but have not yet crossed the Jordan; it is prior therefore to the settlement in Canaan itself. The whole of Deuteronomy—up to the last chapter—is a speech delivered by Moses to the people at the moment prior to the crossing of the Jordan. In the middle of the speech (Deut. 12-26) there is another collection of laws reminding the nation of everything God has done for them and urgently exhorting them to obey and remain faithful to the *one* God who has brought them so far. In the opinion of many scholars Deuteronomy is the introduction to the second great historical work which follows the Pentateuch and which comprises the books Joshua—II Kings and describes the time from the immigration into Canaan up to the Babylonian exile. As a result of this introduction being attached to the Pentateuch as the fifth book of Moses (it is inserted before the account of Moses' death, which now stands at the end of Deuteronomy) these two historical works are joined firmly together.

If we now separate these two large interruptions for a moment, we have before us in the first part of Exodus (Ex. 1-20, 24, 32-4), and in the second part of Numbers (Num. 10-36 partly), the foundation facts of Israel's history—the deliverance from Egypt, the journey through the wilderness, and the advance to the Jordan where Moses died.

This account contains all the basic elements from which the

drama of Israel's history developed. Drama is given to the events by the relationship of the people of Israel with their God. In one respect the term 'history', as used here, is very different from what we call history in the twentieth century: God is a partner in the events of this history. It would not be possible to leave out this transcendent or irrational element from what happened and to represent the history without this. If one were to try, there would not be much left of this section of Israel's history: nothing but a few vague accounts whose context and historical value would be doubtful. A history of Israel which thinks in the concepts and categories of modern historical writing only begins in fact with the settlement in Canaan. And from this point on, Israel begins its first serious involvement with the history of the surrounding world, the Middle East. However, the historical account of the occupation of Canaan, which begins here, and of the growth of the kingdom up to the Babylonian exile, cannot really be understood without what went before. Not only this first section, consisting of the settlement in Canaan, but the whole history of Israel has been built up on the foundation of a confession of faith, a proclamation of God's activity, and it can only be understood from this point of view. The fact that this nation understood its origin as God's work, its land as his gift, its journey as his leading, its growth as his blessing and above all its catastrophes as his judgement cannot simply be abstracted from this history and what remains then be termed historical. There are too many places in which God's dealings are deeply rooted in the separate historical events, for which all non-transcendental explanations fail. That Christianity exists today as a historical fact, deriving from the people of God of the Old Testament, and that at the same time the Jewish people have not ceased to exist bears witness to the fact that what the Old Testament brings news of is something other than the history of one nation among others. This record, as long as there are men to hear it, guard it and expound it, will keep alive the question whether this history can be detached from God, whether it can be conceived apart from God and his activity.

It is against this background that the early history of the people

of Israel, the history of the nation's wanderings, should be read.
The construction of the book of Exodus sets out clearly the chief
factors in what happened at the beginning of the nation's history.
The account begins with the wretchedness of slavery in Egypt and
describes how they were rescued from this plight (Ex. 1-14). Following this, and belonging to it, is the account of their being guided
and protected on their journey (Ex. 16-8), for the Israelites were
not only promised that they would be brought out of the land
of Egypt but also that they would be guided into a new, fair land.
But this is only one aspect of what happened. It would not be complete if the reaction of those to whom these things happened were
omitted. This reaction is everywhere and at all times the same:
the rescued would like to thank their rescuer and to make him a
present of something. The response of the rescued seeks expression
both in word and deed. Directly upon the account of the rescue at
the Sea of Reeds (Ex. 14) follows the hymn of praise from
the rescued (Ex. 15), the kernel of which is Miriam's song (Ex.
15.21):

> Sing to the Lord, for he has triumphed gloriously;
> The horse and his rider he has thrown into the sea.

The other aspect, the response of the rescued in deed, consists
chiefly in simply following the guidance now of the one who had
helped them. This is described in Ex. 16-8. But this is not the end
of the matter. Those who had been helped in this way want to serve
their helper by doing more than following his commandments and
walking in his ways. In order that they might serve him, however,
he must reveal his will to them. The reason for the insertion of the
Sinai-event into the collection of laws (which was itself an addition)
is as follows: it is a necessary result of the deliverance that the
liberated respond to their liberator in action. As they do not know
how and by what means they can serve him, he must declare his
commandments to them at this juncture. Thus it is not accidental
that much later collections of law also found a place here.

Up to this point God's activity and the people's response have
been described consecutively. In Ex. 24 the two are brought to-

gether in the covenant which God makes with the people. From a transaction in which God is on the one side and the people on the other comes something lasting and permanent, an agreement which binds both parties. What began with the promise of God to those who cried to him in their need might have been terminated by the making of the covenant. The covenant could then have gone on for ever without anything really new happening: God continuing to reveal himself to his people as deliverer, leader and protector; the people serving him in following and obeying the commands which God made known to them.

But now something comes in between. The account of the covenant being made is followed immediately by the account of it being broken: the story of the Golden Calf (Ex. 32-3). (In between stands the beginning of the priestly collection of laws, Ex. 25-31, which is continued in Ex. 35-40.) The people do not hold fast to the promise to follow God who rescued them.

Perhaps many readers feel at this point that the course of events is familiar to them. It is, in fact, broadly speaking the same event which Gen. 2 and 3 describe. It becomes clear that Israel's understanding of the true nature of man sprang from its God-centred history. The story of Adam and Eve in the Garden of Eden is a reflection of the basic outlines of historical experience gained by this people from its relation to God. What has imprinted itself on the nation's history as valid, fundamental and important, has been extended to human existence generally. The salvation-event on which the nation's existence was grounded is analogous to the creation of man; in both cases preservation follows. As God gives his command to the nation, so he does to the man in the Garden of Eden. In both cases the command is broken and this breaking of the command is fundamentally inexplicable. Now, however, comes the decisive point; the history of God with his people continued in spite of this break, and in exactly the same way God continues his dealings with the man who has broken his command. In Ex. 34 this is described in such a way that the covenant of God with his people is renewed in spite of his anger and judgement. Here, then, if anywhere in the Bible is evidence of an unmistakably clear continuity : the drama of Israel's history is, in broad outline, the drama of the human race. God has his special history with the people of Israel, but this, too, is concerned with the whole, with humanity. This continuity points in a very definite direction : Israel is like man, and man is like Israel; both fail to obey. The history of man, like the history of Israel, is based on the fact that God continues dealing with them in spite of their disobedience; he does not treat them as they have deserved. After Adam and Eve broke the command and sought to hide themselves in their disobedience and to exonerate themselves, God gives them clothes in order that they might continue to live in each other's presence and in his. It is the same event that is described in Ex. 32-4 about the people of Israel, after they have disobeyed God. In this case, the forgiveness of God is shown in the renewal of the covenant. The Israelites will again break this renewed covenant, just as men proved disobedient, even after God had given them a new possibility of life. But the fact of the renewed covenant points to a future for those who fail to obey; it points to forgiveness which opens a new possibility of life. When prophecy was coming to an end, the prophet who finally proclaimed the approaching judgement of God on the remnant of the state of Israel speaks of the new covenant and the possibility of new life following God's catastrophic judgement (Jer. 31.31), and what he says here is fulfilled in the coming of Jesus Christ, in the 'new testament in his blood'. The word 'testament', which translates the Old Testament word for covenant (*berith*) on the basis of the Greek word *diathēkē*, is the strongest evidence of this connection. In the history that follows the period of the wanderings nothing really new happens to dispute this. The main lines of this history are firmly laid in the account of the book of Exodus.

There are three great periods which follow on the period of the wanderings. The first spans the time from the crossing of the Jordan to the rise of the kingdom. The pattern of events in this period (mainly the period of the Judges) is described retrospectively in the second chapter of Judges. We shall find there that it is the pattern supplied from the book of Exodus which determines this period also :

> *The people cry to God out of their oppression.*
> *God hears and sends them a helper.*
> *Through this mediator the people are set free.*
> *The people make their response in praise and obedience.*
> *The obedience does not last long; the people forsake God.*
> *God steps in as judge and brings new distress on the people.*

Naturally this is a later stylization and systematization of the history; it is never so schematic in actual fact. But it does—in a rather clumsy way—recognize retrospectively that, in the history of a community which knows that it stands in a relationship with God, everything that happens is to be set within a large framework that allows real history to be born out of experiences which follow one another meaninglessly and are endured blindly. The cycle outlined in the above pattern, however, would necessarily lead to complete meaninglessness, if those who consistently failed to obey could not expect that a new act of God could create new possibilities.

The second period is that of the monarchy. The place of the ever newly summoned deliverers (the Judges) in each fresh crisis is taken by the permanent political institution of the monarchy. The pattern of events remains the same by and large as in the period of the Judges. The reaction and response to God's saving and preserving activity on behalf of his people is divided differently now, however. It does not depend only on the people now, but equally on the king and his obedience. The king decides for the whole nation; consequently his disobedience has an effect on the whole. If the king turns from God his political decision proves a new factor which endangers the people of God. That is why the line of prophets stands by the side of the line of kings; the prophets step into the breach which threatened at this point. They cannot prevent the breakaway from God in the period of the monarchy leading to catastrophe, but through their preaching of judgement they succeed in preventing the people's faith in God's activity from being involved in the catastrophe.

The judgement on the disobedience of the nation and its king causes a complete political rupture, but at the moment when the judgment is executed the last of the prophets looks forward to a new covenant. The parallel to the events in the book of Exodus is especially clear at this point.

The last period, which begins with the Bablyonian exile and extends to the coming of Christ on the one hand and the final destruction of Jerusalem on the other, no longer has a definite recognizable pattern. Israel is a province; it no longer has a separate history of its own. It is a period of waiting. Israel waits for a new covenant, a new deliverance and a new and a different king, God's annointed. That the new deliverance, the new deliverer and the new covenant will be quite different from anything that happened in Israel previously is seen most clearly by Deutero-Isaiah, the prophet of the exile.

IV · THE PILGRIM PEOPLE

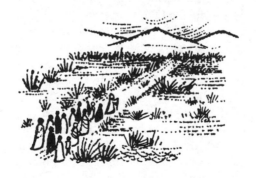

1 · Israel in Egypt

THE two great neighbouring kingdoms of Egypt and Assyro-Babylon had ceased to be nomadic before we hear of them. When Israel settled in Canaan both kingdoms already looked back on a thousand years of continuous civilization. The Sumerians, whose civilization had been brought to an end by the old Babylonian civilization, were already a settled people as far back as our earliest sources. The Egyptians in their river valley, which was enclosed on both sides by the desert, had known no migrations in a thousand years. Israel, however, preserved the traditions dating from the time when it was nomadic as the foundation of its history. In these traditions it kept alive important, deep-seated differences which separated it from its neighbours.

For this very reason the Old Testament has special importance as an historical document. Contained in the account of the history of this one small nation are two great periods of humanity. It portrays the transition of a nomadic into a settled nation, embodying the experiences of both periods. This is of special importance for the human race at the present stage of history. One of the results of ethnographical study in recent years has been to show that in very many places of the globe a way of life based on hunting and picking the wild fruits of the earth has preceded an agricultural way of life. The transition to a settled state had been accomplished in the transition from one to the other. Most civilized nations, even if they have experienced nomadic wanderings in historical times, have forgotten them and not preserved their experiences. Settled civilizations strip off only too soon the hard experiences of nomadic wandering.

For humanity as a whole settled life has undergone a change today. A great part of mankind is no longer settled in any real sense.

Today there are nomads again, nomads of the machine and nomads of the admass. No one knows yet how this new nomadism will develop and work out. In this situation what the Old Testament says of the experience of a nation that always retained something of the nomadic quality is especially important. The background of the book of Exodus is the pyramids of Egypt, the tidal wave at the Sea of Reeds and the smoking volcano in the wilderness. The most elementary and powerful natural events, and buildings which have lasted for thousands of years and are still standing—all this is appropriate scenery for the birth-pangs of Israel. The history begins with the fact that men call to God in their need. The primaeval history (Gen. 1-11) ends with the history of the building of the Tower of Babel. At the beginning of the nation's history stands another building. One of the Pharaohs—probably Rameses II (c. 1292-1225) who built the two store-house cities of Pithon and Rameses—had a group of Israelite workmen among the tens of thousands who were engaged on his buildings. They originally entered the land during a time of famine. It was no longer known why they were such a relatively closed group with such a strong group-feeling. They interested the Pharaoh only as labour. It is a situation which has never ceased, beginning at a certain stage of human history and continuing for at least six thousand years through all political and social changes right up to the present day; the labour value of the downtrodden is exploited by individuals or groups who are in power. Down the centuries the reason for this has always been the same: the edifices of great powers. Whether it is a matter of pyramids, great cities or political systems, is immaterial. It is always a matter of 'making a name for themselves' or of the summit of this building reaching to heaven. And the erection of such a building always necessitates the work of nameless masses, who in the course of such a building are nothing but labour which is 'taken on'. If this labour force remonstrates in anger against its slavery the same methods as are described in the first chapters of Exodus are always used: the pressure of work is increased and provisions cut down.

It is of the utmost importance for the understanding of the Bible as a whole, that the basis of the whole, God's act of deliverance, turns on a need which is largely a social need, the oppression of men by men. It is not only important for the nation of Israel which was brought into being by this deliverance. We shall see later that Israel never forgot this beginning and hundreds of years afterwards still based its social laws on the following reason : 'Remember, you were a slave in Egypt'. It is also important for Christianity to whose Bible the Old Testament belongs. The nation of Israel received its first heavy blow, which was never healed, through the fact that Solomon's successor preferred to increase the service of the Israelite farmers for the king rather than alleviate it. The result was the division of the kingdom. A decisive reason for the subsequent collapse of the two halves of the kingdom, one after the other, was the failure to observe the social teaching of the prophets. They finally forgot—and above all the kings forgot—what had been told them at the beginning when they were delivered from slavery in Egypt.

It may be that the heaviest blow Christianity has met in the course of its two thousand years of history to date is connected with the fact that it did not take seriously the oppression of workers at the beginning of the industrial era, and really failed to see it in the light of the Bible, so that others had to arise to resist this oppression. Possibly, too, however, the development of socialism and communism up to the present points to the insuperable problems for which the fundamentals and perspectives can only be found in the Bible. In the account of an oppression at the beginning of the book of Exodus it should be noted particularly that no attempt at anything like a revolution is made by the Israelites in spite of increasing hardship. Two very different factors lead to a change. One is the life force of this group. Three times it is said in this chapter : Israel increased. The Egyptians had to resort to doubtful measures to suppress this growth. Finally Pharaoh gives the command for all male children born to the Israelites to be killed. This same measure brought about the rise of the nation's deliverer. One thinks instinctively of the parallel in the New Testament, the murder of the children of Bethlehem. Both stories make the same point : where God wants a deliverer for his people, all the powerful measures of the mighty cannot prevent it. There is another connection also

between the stories in that every story of deliverance pre-supposes
the birth of a child. This was the theme in the Abraham group of
stories. Here it returns again, but not only as a family event as in
the Abraham stories: but as an event of historical significance.
The Egyptian empire with all its tremendous power is opposed by
something apparently so small as the irrepressible life-force of a
group of Israelite workmen, who threaten to become dangerous
to Pharaoh simply by their fertility. Here for once is an indication
of what the blessing given to the patriarchs, the promised power
to multiply, can mean. This opens up such a prospect for humanity
today that we can breathe again: all the changes in which man
is involved in this technical age, and everything that men can do
to each other today, do not extend to the source of life and cannot
alter the fact that children are born who are God's creation. This
is what the Bible calls 'blessing': the life-force of which God alone
remains Lord, and which cannot be replaced by a substitute or
destroyed by men. The Bible has to proclaim the God of whom it can
say: *Thou turnest man back to the dust, and sayest 'Turn back, O
children of men!'* (Ps. 90.3).

The second factor which leads to a change is the cry of the
oppressed to God. Here uniquely at the beginning of the Book of
Exodus, the two ways in which God deals with men and which
lie at the root of the whole Bible converge: blessing and deliverance.
The blessing is a pre-personal event; it is what God does for all
living beings and all creatures. The deliverance is specifically
human, and involves a personal relationship between God and man.
God's deliverance throughout the whole Bible can only be described as a two-sided event, an event in the relationship of God
and man, an event which is part of a dialogue. What 'the Lord gives
his own in sleep' is not deliverance or salvation but blessing. But
no one has ever received God's *salvation* while he slept. Here right
at the very beginning of God's history with his people his deliverance can be recognized straightaway as a personal relationship by
the fact that it begins with the oppressed crying to God. In this
cry the plight of the oppressed finds words. This plight and the
cry arising out of it are like bed-rock facts; they are not explained

further. In this respect it is very similar to the cry of Hagar's child when she was driven out into the wilderness (Gen. 21.16-7). *The child lifted up his voice and wept; and God heard the voice of the lad.* This cry of the oppressed slave-workers in Egypt is not yet an expression of repentance; it does not yet stand in the chain of 'guilt—punishment—return of the punished'; it is simply the cry of a tormented creature. It is part of the fact of God's mercy for his suffering creation that this mercy remains unexplained and has the power to recreate. It is the same mercy which, John 3.16 says, moved God to give his Son for this world. It is the same mercy which the Church has to offer to the world today, where the suffering of tormented creatures is still constantly crying out.

These, then, are the two factors which lead to a change: blessing and mercy. Both come from God and together they comprehend all God's activity for his creation. In what follows only the history of the deliverance is taken further; the history of the blessing will only become important and form the theme again when Israel has entered the new land and it is a question of whether those who have been delivered will entrust their changed life in their new land, which previously belonged to other gods and other peoples, to their deliverer, their God of the wilderness. Not till the Book of Deuteronomy will the idea of blessing occupy a central position again.

God's mercy comes to men in their distress not in action but by word of mouth first of all. And the first word which enters that situation of distress from another dimension is the word of encouragement. The history of deliverance begins with good news. The deliverer is not only concerned that the one who cries out in distress should become silent; he desires rather to change the lament into praise. Therefore he does not simply conjure the suffering person's pain away, but he creates a personal bond, he speaks to him.

Deliverance can be given totally different meanings. Everyone, whether as an individual or as a member of a community, has experience of what we commonly call deliverance. The experience of deliverance is fundamentally different, however, depending whether it is experienced as a personal or impersonal event. If the latter is the case then we say 'I escaped once again'. In war there are coarser expressions to describe this. But if a man experiences deliverance as something personal, then linked with the experience of deliverance is a deliverer, who can speak to him and be addressed by him in return.

The statement at the beginning of the book of Exodus, that the Israelites cried to God in their distress and that he heard them and said to them 'I have heard your cry and will help you', establishes the personal character of the deliverance for the whole Bible of Old and New Testaments. Deliverance and salvation in the Bible exist only in the context of a personal encounter. That is why the history of God's salvation begins with a message. In the proclamation of it, something emerges from the history; the history which could be experienced differently is experienced as deliverance; the face of God appears to those oppressed by racking fear, and the basic fact of distress is met by the basic fact of God's mercy. The deliverance is already taken for granted in the Lord's proclamation: 'I have seen . . . , I have heard . . . , I know . . .' (Ex. 3.7) .This is true of the message of salvation throughout the whole Bible, which proclaims neither an idea about God nor a sentiment about God, but a *fact*. Already the first message at the beginning of the history of Israel had the structure of the 'Gospel'. It has the same structure as the message of the angels to the shepherds on the night of Christ's birth and as the preaching of the Apostles after the resurrection. The basic promise in the Bible is the promise of salvation: it announces something to come, in such a way as to assure those to whom the message is brought that the promise is already realized with God. It is first met here at the beginning of the history of Israel, and from here it extends throughout the whole Bible. The message makes the deliverance an act in time. It is therefore more than simply the experience of a moment, or in this case of the hour in which the fugitives escape from the pursuer. It unites two points of time; the hour of expectation and the hour of solution, the moment of promise and that of fulfilment. The cry of the oppressed found a response, the promise of liberation. Those set free could not only rejoice over this help in time of great distress. They could testify: 'It happened to us, as was told us'. They now see a connection: they have begun to *experience* history.

2 · Moses and the Deliverance

T H E experience of deliverance as the fulfilment of a promise makes them prepare at the same time to entrust their future to their helper. And at the same time as they were led forth they were promised that God would lead them into a good, new land (Ex. 38); they could trust this promise now and follow the God who delivered them. In this way the history of guidance and protection joins the history of salvation.

Inseparable from the message is the messenger who told the Israelites they should be freed. The history of the man responsible for the message of deliverance is described along with the history of that deliverance at the beginning of Exodus. We have already spoken about the point where it was inserted—the point where the measures of oppression reached their climax.

What is now related about Moses in the following chapters (Ex. 2-6) cannot be historically verified: the way in which it is narrated is 'pre-historical' and there are several strands of narrative interwoven. That is why in modern descriptions of this beginning of Israel's history the figure of Moses is understood and valued very differently. One view stresses his importance in very strong language, calling him the founder of religion and seeing in him the great hero of faith of early Israelite history; another view doubts whether he was a historical figure at all and seeks to explain early Israelite history without his personality. This deep cleavage of judgement with regard to the traditions about Moses must make us cautious. We cannot skate over the fact that the tradition of Moses in the Bible has in fact quite a different character from the tradition about David. A historical portrait simply cannot be reconstructed from the tradition about Moses. In dealing with these texts, therefore, the most honest attitude is probably one of extreme caution.

One conclusion, however, seems definite: the subsequent history could not be depicted in the way it is if the beginning did not contain the promise of deliverance to the oppressed Israelites. The fact of deliverance, attested throughout the whole of the Old Testament and again in the New Testament and very definitely regarded as a historical event, is not complete without the promise, apart from which it could never have attained such historical importance. Inseparable from the message is the person who brought it. The verbal character of the deliverance at the beginning (which extends throughout the Bible from this point onwards) demands a mediator of the message. And if we only knew this one thing definitely about Moses, namely that he was this mediator, this would be quite enough to confer on him a decisive importance for the history which is just beginning. It was not, of course, the importance of a 'founder of religion' (this concept does not correspond at all to what is reported in the Bible) or the importance of 'a man of outstanding achievements' measured by our Western standards. Moses was the man who stood between God and the people in the events which made Israel a nation. From this beginning it followed as a matter of course that the mediator had to mediate God's word and God's deed at the same time. Moses was not only the mediator of the promise of deliverance, but also the man through whom God led and preserved his people. As deliverance and preservation necessarily belonged together at the beginning, their continued mediation also belonged together in the office of the mediator. It is this more than any other feature in the tradition about Moses which stamps his office as a natural product of events, and which is therefore particularly authentic: the Moses of whom the book of Exodus speaks has authority only as the mediator of God's word and deed. He has no trace of natural authority or influence, of merit or power. The most frequent and at the same time the most characteristic utterances of this man are complaints!

There could hardly be a clearer expression of the fact that this man Moses was a mediator and that, in fulfilling this office, his sufferings outweigh any power or honour he receives.

It should be pointed out that the office of mediator in the Old

Testament has a well-attested history. One result of this history is that a figure like Moses at the beginning of the national history would have had to be posited even if we had not received such a tradition.

> *Wanderings in the wilderness:* One mediator of word and deed together.
> *Settlement:* The mediators of the deed (the Judges).
> *Period of Kings:* The mediators of the deed (the kings) and of the word (the prophets).
> *Exile:* The mediator in suffering.
> *The fulfilment:* One mediator of word, deed and suffering together.

As in the case of so many men in the Bible, the story of Moses begins with the failure of a personal enterprise. (The name Moses is Egyptian and means 'son', as in the name of the Pharaoh Totmoses = son of Tot; the Egyptian name attests both the historicity of Moses and the fact that he was brought up at court.) His attempt to interfere personally against the oppression of his countrymen in Egypt results in his having to flee. Moses becomes a shepherd like Jacob before him and like David after him. It is there that he is called, as Amos was called from the flock. This account of Moses' call (Ex. 3.1-8), which is fundamental for the whole Old Testament, introduces a series of call-stories running throughout the Old and New Testaments. There is a straight line from Moses' call to the call of Isaiah and the call of Peter. The important features in all these stories are similar. The aim of the call is to send a man on a specific mission. The first point in every case is an encounter with the Holy. It is not a spiritual experience; rather, the senses, chiefly eyes and ears, are involved; they all see or hear something and often bodily contact is mentioned. The call is one of the basic experiences between God and man, which the Bible reports. It is in the truest and deepest sense a miracle. A call from another dimension breaks into the life of a man on earth like a flash of lightning. This call produces something in the life of the person it comes to; it gives a new direction to this life, it makes of this life a work, it changes the destiny of a large community through the work and devotion of the person called. At the same time the call gives the person called ability, courage and steadfastness which are not explicable from the experiences which formerly shaped his life.

What the Bible says of this call which comes to a man in the call-stories of both Old and New Testaments is of the greatest importance for our world. Such a call points in two directions: it binds the life of one individual among millions of people with the one from whom the call comes. The reality of this call shows itself not in any mystic experiences (which are too often a substitute for being called) or in a simple consciousness of being called to do great things, but in decisions, negotiations and actions which determine the way of a group of men. Decisive for these actions is the fact that they are not done for personal glory or with the ego as the final authority, but by the order of one who is himself the absolute, final authority. At the same time the call points in another direction also: it gives the life of the person called connection, proportion and direction. It is not the greatness or outward appearance of the work done that gives meaning to the existence of the person called, but his readiness to embrace the call and his obedience in doing and being what he is called to.

Like so many of those whom God called to a special task Moses resisted the call. He brings God a series of objections (Ex. 3.9-15), each of which must be overcome. One of these objections is: 'If they ask me "Who has sent you?" what am I to answer?' In reply God tells him his name in a memorable paraphrase: 'I am who I am'. The meaning of this sentence is not certain; many explanations have been offered. It could also be translated: 'I will be who I will be'. Clearly this sentence is meant to express what this God means for the one who calls to him. The next possible interpretation is 'I am the one who can be relied on'. The first interpretation can be harmonized with this; 'I am he who remains essentially secret and whom no one can grasp or comprehend from without.' Perhaps it is just this that is intended: the meaning of the sentence in which God here reveals himself to Moses is not to be interpreted in one

fixed way. The sentence is not the actual name of God but an ex-
planatory paraphrase of the name. The actual name 'Jahwe' (Ex.
3.15) remains unexplained to the present day. There is an abundance of attempted explanations, none of which can command complete support as yet. Still it is a real name, a personal name like
Zeus or Odin or Jupiter. It does not quite correspond to our term
'God' (in the Old Testament *elohim*) nor to our term 'Lord' (in the
Old Testament *adonai*), but rather to a name like Jesus. That God
in the Old Testament had a personal name connects the history
reported in this book with the religions of mankind; this name is
one among a plethora of names of deities who are invoked all over
the world. Just as the one through whom God accomplished his
work of salvation for the whole world had an ordinary name common among men, 'Jesus', so in the beginning God revealed himself
to his people in a name which is one among others. His words to
Moses were not about a lofty idea of God, but about an ordinary
name. Already this beginning of revelation contained something
of the condescension and humility of God which was fulfilled in
Jesus Christ. This helps us to understand why the Israelites in later
times did not dare to utter this name any more. Instead, they substituted 'the Lord' everywhere where this name Jahwe stood in the
text. As a result of the vowels of the word for 'Lord' being placed
under the consonants of the name Jahwe the name was pronounced
'Jehovah' by later people who no longer knew the connection.
This pronunciation rested on a mistake; there was never such a
word in Israel.

How the liberation from Egypt took place in detail cannot be
decided from the narrative with certainty. It contains many un-
solved questions and contradictions. Especially difficult for us to
understand is the account of the miracles and plagues in Egypt
(Ex. 7-11) caused by Moses in his struggle with the Pharaoh. It
will be as well to avoid at this point any forced explanations and
simply concede that we are confronted with riddles which we can
no longer solve. A special difficulty lies in the fact that not only
Moses but also the Egyptian magicians possess the power to work
miracles—except that they cannot keep pace with him. We can

only be certain of this: there is a peculiar parallel in the exceptional and prominent way in which miracles are reported about
the mediator of the Old Covenant as of the New. While, however,
the miracles of Jesus are almost totally of the helping, healing and
useful sort, at the beginning of Moses' work stands a whole series
of miracles whose *only* purpose is to hurt, destroy and inflict pain;
they are exclusively weapons against the enemies of God's people.
Only later, out in the desert, do miracles which help, preserve and
protect the people come upon the scene. Such miracles which hurt
the enemies of God's people still occur occasionally later, but never
with such frequency as here at the beginning. It is rooted in the
fact that the Israelites stand over against their enemies in Egypt,
unarmed and defenceless, and have no possibility of doing anything themselves to their enemies. We can no longer tell how far the
plagues described in Ex. 7-11, which bring together every conceivable damage that could be inflicted on land and people, really happened. They are described in a way which is not meant to be historical in our sense of the term, and which should not be taken
to be. We cannot, however, simply explain all these narratives as
pure fantasy. We must at present be content with the fact that
these chapters in the story of Moses belong to the dark places of
the Bible, to which we no longer have access.

The description of the liberation from Egypt has, however, other
features which we can fully understand. When Moses returned to
Egypt after his call, to declare the message of liberation to his
people, he gathered the people together, told them what God had
said and showed them his authority. When Moses had stood before
God he had asked, 'Will you trust me?'; and now he stands before
his people and says to them, 'The Lord has espoused the cause of
Israel; he has seen our distress!' The reaction of the people to this
is reported as follows: 'They bowed their heads and worshipped'
(Ex. 4.29-31). This is why deliverance comes first of all by word of
mouth, as a message to those who are to be delivered. They are to
say 'yes' to this personally. Behind everything which will happen
from now on stands this 'yes', affirming the message. In everything
that God plans for this people, in everything that he does for them

and in everything to which he calls them he desires their free 'yes'.
Here, right at the beginning of the history of God with his people, is
evidence that God's dealings with men desire the dignity of human
existence, the nobility of the free decision. He honours men with
a true partnership. Here is an exposition of how God created man
in his own image: he created him in such a way that he can say a
free open 'yes' to him, and this always leaves open the other possibility that he can refuse to say 'yes' to God. In exactly the same
way Joshua will once again ask the nation after it has reached
the promised land, the destination of the journey now about to
begin, 'Choose this day whom you will serve, the God who has led
you thus far or the gods of this new land whom your fathers once
served!' And in the same way Jesus of Nazareth will ask his disciples, when he sees that many have left him, 'Will you too go
away?' At every turning point of the journey which God makes
with his people, there stands in some form or other amid constantly
changing circumstances the question which desires a free decision.

God wills it so, although he knows that the time will come when
the free acceptance of God's call will be shaken, assailed or even
shattered. The Bible sees this in all soberness and the first, joyful
assent to the message which Moses brought is quickly followed by
the first setback. Moses' first negotiation with Pharaoh miscarried;
it only resulted in the Israelites being oppressed more severely. The
anger of the scourged and beaten Israelites is directed against
Moses: 'You put into Pharaoh's hands the weapons he is now using
against us!' Here for the first time we hear Moses speaking in a way
which will constantly recur, up to the end of his active life. These
are words which inspire us with fear, words not only of complaint
but accusations against God: O Lord, why has thou done evil to
this people? Why didst thou ever send me? For since I came to
Pharaoh to speak in thy name, he has done evil to this people,
and thou has not delivered thy people at all (Ex. 5.22-3).

Moses stands alone and powerless between God and the people.
He is bitterly attacked by his fellow countrymen and he feels de-
serted by God. When he turns to God out of this hopeless loneliness
and powerlessness and speaks to him this conversation is something

very different from what we understand by prayer; our criteria are inapplicable. It is a conversation with God which is passionate, direct and full of emotion, which we should for once allow to move us without seeking to judge it. If we do this, it will, I think, become clear that here is a man who knows himself in a living, direct personal relationship with God, and that here God is being taken perfectly seriously. Accusation of God, which meets us clearly for the first time here, has in the Bible an importance which is not to be overlooked. We often meet it in the complaints of the people, in individual psalm-laments, and as such it found powerful expression in the book of Job. Besides this there is the distinctive accusation of God made in the distress of their office by those called to be mediators. There is a direct line from the complaint of Moses and the complaints of the prophets to Jeremiah, in whose case it assumed an especially powerful and terrifying aspect, and finally to the cry of the Saviour on the Cross. This complaint of the mediator from Moses onwards throughout the Bible is a strong, clear indication that the calls are not fantasy or religious enthusiasm but hard reality, which sent the person called on a journey which he certainly did not seek or devise for himself. Here if anywhere, in these words of complaint and accusation from the person called, we can trace the presence of the Other, to whom these words are addressed in loneliness and powerlessness. Moreover this line which runs right through the Bible can destroy our illusion that a man who is prepared to live his life with God can always be saintly, humble and patient. Where God's words penetrate a man's life and are taken seriously there are certain to be struggles and remonstrations and defeat; doubt and temptation also inevitably occur. What happened in the first abortive negotiation with Pharaoh continues after the nation has escaped from Egypt and has taken the first steps to freedom. At the moment when the fugitives perceive they are pursued there is again rebellion against Moses; again Moses is alone between God and the people facing deadly peril, and again he cries to God.

The miracle which lays the foundation of the nation's history takes place in face of the murmurings of the people and the mediator's lone cries to God. But it takes place. If we speak of the deliver-

ance of the Israelites at the Sea of Reeds as a miracle we must not
understand it according to our modern idea of miracle. The
Israelites at that time did not understand their passage across the
arm of the sea's bed and the destruction of their pursuers at the
same spot where they crossed over as an event contrary to the law
of Nature, because they had no concept or idea of a law of Nature.
The decisive facts for them were these: the sea retreated at the
moment when their lives were in the greatest danger and snatched
away the Egyptians at the moment when they had almost over-
taken them in their flight. The question whether we are dealing
with a natural or a 'supernatural' event here is quite immaterial
for the later significance of this act of deliverance by God. The
important thing was that God was at work here, that he fulfilled
his promise of deliverance and that he was present as the deliverer
in the hour of greatest need.

Accordingly, a hymn of praise is introduced—it could hardly be
otherwise—after this point, a hymn which praises the deliverer
(Ex. 15.1, 21):

> Sing to the Lord for he has triumphed gloriously;
> The horse and his rider he has thrown into the sea.

This song about God's act of deliverance at the hour of greatest
need begins the account of the history of the Israelites as a nation.
In spite of everything that has happened and in spite of everything
still to come this remains the basic note. Israel has experienced God's
deliverance as he promised. Never again is this forgotten. Even in
deepest despair as a nation and as individuals they can remember
'our fathers hoped in thee and thou didst help them'. Their confession of faith in him 'who brought us out of the land of Egypt'
is to be found, from this time onwards, throughout every conversation with this God and in every appeal to him, through many
centuries. The message of the Old Testament, like that of the New
Testament, is in origin and essence a message of the deliverance
and the deliverer. All that is said about God and all that they cry
out to him goes back ultimately to the one firm, unshakeable fact
at the beginning : he delivered us.

3 · *Through the Wilderness*

T H E account of the origin of the Passover Festival (Ex. 12-3) is
very detailed and really quite inappropriate in the tension preced-
ing the departure from Egypt. The Passover is probably a very old,
pre-Israelitic shepherd-festival. In connection with the departure
from Egypt it becomes a totally new and different festival. A festival
of nature becomes a festival of history, the festival of recurrent
change becomes the anniversary of a single occurrence. The customs
of the festival, which definitely had quite another meaning once,
are very closely connected with the experiences of the departure
from Egypt. The festival is meant to remind them continuously
of the circumstances of the flight. 'In this manner you shall eat it :
your loins girded, your sandals on your feet and your staff in your
hand. You shall eat it in haste, for it is the Lord's Passover!'
Throughout the world festivals which come round every year are
always expressions of a settled way of life. Here for once this basic
rule is broken : this festival, which is indeed Israel's main festival,
is intended as a continual reminder of that departure in the past
and—in addition—to prepare them for departure in the future.
The Israelites celebrated this festival for the first time when they
were abandoning a settled way of life and leaving the flesh-pots of
Egypt. They never excluded the possibility of God calling them to a
new departure. They must never forget that not only the settled
life and the peace of dwelling securely belonged to their history
with God but also the departure into the wilderness, into the completely unknown, into a hard, nomadic existence. This reminder
of the departure woven into the Passover Festival ('you shall eat
it in haste') witnesses to the fact that the Israelites preserved the
memory of their early, hard times on the journey through the
wilderness as an intrinsic piece of their past. It speaks also of the
fact that even when they had been settled for hundreds of years
they never completely lost sight of the possibility of a fresh departure into another wilderness.

Consequently it is only to be expected that the traditions of the

wanderings in the wilderness had a fundamental significance for
the life of the people. The account of the wanderings in the wilderness, comprising Ex. 16-8 and Num. 10-36, supplies the framework for the large interpolation of the law. If the account is read
straight through without interruption the strongly pronounced
sameness of themes is inescapable. It is constantly concerned with
the same things: hunger, thirst, weariness. Alongside are accounts
of encounters with enemies, but these conflicts are still peripheral;
it is only in the next period that they become central. It is stated
repeatedly that these nomads were on the point of starvation, or
were dying with thirst and could proceed no further because of
weariness. And every time something then happened which made
it possible for them to journey on.[1]

We have removed God's activity and our religious discourse from
reality at its hardest and most brutal for too long. We have spoken
about God too long in a manner which is applicable to pulpit and
pew, lecture room or book, but in a way which is never heard where
people are hungry, thirsty and weary to the point of death. We
must say most emphatically, even at the risk of being misunderstood, that where there is hunger and thirst and exhaustion all
theoretical discourse or reflection about God is done away with.
Only something which meets these elementary needs is of any
avail. Very many of the theological problems which can be important for a man sitting quietly at a table in a warm room in between
fixed meal times resolve themselves into nothing. Only the reality
of the living God is important here; not a reality on a higher plane
above my sufferings but a reality *in* the hunger of the hungry, *in*
the thirst of the thirsty and *in* the fatigue of the exhausted. At times
like these people cannot help giving vent to their grief. One cannot
blame the man dying with thirst if he groans, or the man who is
collapsing if he despairs. And it is so here; these stories of the
journey through the wilderness are permeated with grumbling,

[1] If I may be allowed a personal word here: the first time I understood
these parts of the Old Testament, this section of the history of God with
his people, was after the experience of the last war and subsequent
captivity. And I feel compelled to pass something of this on.

complaints and accusations. How we have learnt by experience in concentration camps what it means to long after the 'fleshpots of Egypt'! The days when we could smile at this are passed. The writer can still see two soldiers walking with great strides through the dirty sand of the camp, talking with faces transfigured of their mealtimes at home. One simply cannot understand all this unless one has experienced it for oneself. And many have forgotten again too quickly. But those who have been out there in the midst of brutal, basic needs and who have known a piece of bread or a plate of soup mean preservation from starvation, and equally preservation by God, will not forget so quickly. They have realized what it was that never let the Israelites forget the time in the wilderness.

It is quite a simple difference but it cannot be understood theoretically. God can preserve human life in two different ways. The normal way in normal times is that of allowing the corn to grow, the fruit to ripen and the cattle to procreate and multiply for food. That is the way of blessing. We heard of it in the patriarchal stories. There is however, the other possibility of being preserved by God in the wilderness of this world, where the fields and meadows of blessing are far away. This preservation is really a series of deliverances, as those know who ask in the morning 'Where shall I sleep tonight?' and who do not see how they are to pay for their next meal; who dream of food and who lie down to sleep on a clay floor tired out. But the man who has no knowledge of God's saving preservation does not really know God. The Israelites rebelled against God on their journey through the wildnerness and cursed their liberation from Egypt. They vented the anger of their despair on Moses and wanted to return on numerous occasions. And yet on this journey through the wilderness they met God so that they could never forget later when better times came. And again—as in the deliverance at the beginning—this remained uppermost: God did help. And when they were at the end of their tether once more—then, at that precise moment, a miracle occurred: the water from the rock, the quails and the manna.

After the Israelites had departed from Sinai as described at the end of Num. 10 nothing else occurred during the rest of the journey

such as had happened when they left Egypt. Chapter 11 begins:
'the people however, murmured. . . .' and it continues as it had from
the beginning, but in the people's complaints there is a very distinctive new note. It is true they now have the manna, but it is
always the same and gradually they grow tired of it. What had once
been to them the gift of God to preserve their life is now a monotonous diet of which they are weary. Instead of thinking of the
saving act of God they now say 'If only we had meat to eat! we
remember the fish we used to eat for nothing in Egypt, the cucum-
bers, the melons, the leeks, the onions and the garlic. But now our
strength is dried up; and there is nothing at all but this manna to
look at!'

At this point the manna is described. 'The manna was like
coriander seed, and its appearance like that of bdellium' (Ex. 11.7).
It is not certain what it actually was; it is taken to be either a plant
or animal (plant-lice) secretion, or the seed of a fruit, which can be
carried over a large area by the wind. At any rate a product of
nature, as the story indicates, is meant.

Moses, touched by the murmuring of the people, lifts up his
voice and complains. One can feel in the words that, in spite of his
anger at this grumbling, he recognizes something justified in it. They
are staggering words: *Why hast thou dealt ill with thy servant?*
And why have I not found favour in thy sight, that thou dost
lay the burden of all this people upon me? Did I conceive all this
people? Did I bring them forth that thou shouldst say to me 'Carry
them in your bosom, as a nurse carries the sucking child, to the
land which thou didst swear to give their fathers?' Where am I to
get meat to give to all this people? For they weep before me and
say, 'Give us meat, that we may eat'. I am not able to carry all this
people alone, the burden is too heavy for me. If thou wilt deal thus
with me, kill me at once, if I find favour in thy sight, that I may
not see my wretchedness (Num. 1.11-15).

In these words we meet for the first time in the Bible the responsibility of a leader. Political responsibility is given expression, one
might say—an expression which indicates the basic features of
political responsibility right up to the present day. If one does not

know what it is like to tread the razor's edge between the murmurings of the people who want to have it better (they do not want
bread but meat, they want a higher standard of living) and the
duty to plan for the future; and if one has never discovered, when
torn this way and that between the two, that the burden of being
responsible for a nation is in fact a burden which is too heavy for
one man, then one does not know what political responsibility is.
Something in this word of Moses is clearly reminiscent of the patriarchal stories; the words of complaint point to the fact that the
(political) leader's task is really derived from that of the parent. In
the Joseph stories all political authority is derived from the parent's
authority. Here Moses complains: 'I am not the father of the whole
nation that this burden should be demanded of me!' One suspects that behind this word of complaint is an event of historical
importance: the transition from the family which had as its head
the eldest, the father, to the nomadic group which needed a fresh
leadership of a different sort: the leader who had to bring enlarged
groups of many families to one destination. These words have yet
another importance. Moses is so overwhelmed by the burden of his
office that he thinks it is no longer possible to hold out under it.
'Let me then rather die', he begs God. These words of despair
announce something quite new: here is a man who longs for death
not for any personal reason but because the burden of the office
laid upon him is impossibly heavy. There is here the first presentiment that in certain circumstances a man must die for the sake of
his office when it is one which affects others. There is still no sign
of the view that this would be death *for* others; but the first presentiment of the fact that a mission to the whole touches the borders
of death is emerging. We shall be reminded of this place when,
at the end of the history that begins with the deliverance from
Egypt, we hear of the servant of God (Moses too is called this!)
of whom it is said: 'Upon him was the chastisement that made us
whole'. This correspondence between the complaint of Moses, the
servant of God at the beginning, and the suffering of the servant
of God at the end, which is faintly hinted at, is not accidental; they
are stations on the same road.

The same cause, the murmuring of the people at the monotonous and niggardly food of the wilderness, resulted on another occasion in punishment by God, a plague of serpents (Num. 21). Again Moses is in the middle. The people come to him repentantly and ask him to intercede with God for them, that the plague might be brought to an end. And Moses interceded with God for the disobedient. It did not, however, turn out as might have been expected according to the rest of the history of the wilderness-journey, namely that God was moved by the entreaties of Moses and removed the plague. God prefers to allow Moses to lift up a bronze serpent, and fasten it to a pole. Whoever looked upon the bronze serpent continued to live in spite of having been bitten by serpents. A change in God's delivering and preserving activity on behalf of his people is indicated here: the act of preservation does not occur simply automatically for all (as e.g. in the gift of manna); rather, the individuals who are struck by the plague are required to believe that the sign erected by God through Moses can preserve them from death. God's saving activity, which in the early period always included the whole nation and in which everybody shared insofar as he belonged to the nation, is here for the first time directed to the individual. For the first time the possibility of a division arising *within* the people with respect to God's saving activity is hinted at. It can be accepted or rejected. This line is continued in the prophets, particularly clearly in Isaiah's demand for faith. This possibility of a cleavage within the people of God is allowed because God's help does not come to the people directly (in the destruction of all serpents) but indirectly in the manner of a symbol. The symbol, the bronze serpent, is not *itself* the help; the power of this symbol is not immediately apparent; the help of God is concealed in it. Understood in this way the fact that the story of the bronze serpent is taken up in the New Testament (John 3.14) is very significant. The salvation offered the world in Jesus of Nazareth is concealed in his person; the kingly rule which he brings is hidden in poverty and powerlessness. He can only point to it, and those who meet him are asked whether they trust God to help the world in this way, through this Jesus of Nazareth and through his suffering on the Cross.

It is important that the question to the individual, whether he can believe what God does in his work of salvation or not, is already firmly planted in the early period of Israel's history, in the wandering in the wilderness. It will extend throughout the whole Bible from now onwards. *And as Moses lifted up the serpent in the wilderness so must the Son of Man be lifted up that whosoever believes in him may have eternal life.*

4 · Joshua and the Struggle for the Promised Land

W H E N the Israelites were promised deliverance from Egypt they were also promised a new homeland at the same time, 'a good, fair land, flowing with milk and honey'. This is clearly not an objective description of Palestine. It had a more favourable climate in those days because it was more wooded than today, but even then it was a bare, poverty stricken country. It is a 'land, flowing with milk and honey' only as seen by men living in the desert, just as a poor room appears exceptionally fine to a man in prison. The fact that the Israelites preserved this description of the object of their longing and continued to use it in their confession of faith when they had become settled, is one indication that they never forgot how this land had appeared from the outside, from the standpoint of hungry, thirsty men. This promised land did not await the incoming tribes of Israel like the garden which God prepared for men in the beginning to dwell there. The land was already occupied and it had first to be fought for. When the Israelites reached the promised land they were in no sense at their destination. Not only did the land so definitely promised by God still need to be settled, but also the most difficult task awaited them. This first great promise has to be worked for, like all the promises of God as long as we are still on this earth. No promise of God is a transfer back to Paradise. When the Israelites had been delivered from the Egyptians they found themselves in the wilderness; when Jesus of Nazareth had completed the work of redemption and had died and risen again, his disciples were anguished and helpless. When the Israelites reached the Jordan, the land of promise was closed to them and inaccessible.

It took many generations—probably two hundred years—before the Israelites in Palestine could form a state. Finally, however, the day arrived when Israel possessed the land. In the later account of this long period of many setbacks, many serious threats and only quite slow advances it is this final outcome—it is our land at last ! —which is overwhelmingly important. The account of Israel's occupation has been moulded by this final outcome. According to the Book of Joshua the confederacy of the Israelite tribes starting from Moab crossed the Jordan, captured Jericho, conquered the land, took possession of the entire South after a great battle at Gibeon (Josh. 10) and of the entire North after a great battle by the waters of Merom (Josh. 11). Then Joshua divided the whole land among the tribes by lot, (Josh. 13-21). After the two and a half tribes whose territory was east of the Jordan had returned there, the book closes with an exhortation from Joshua to the whole of Israel (Josh. 23) and with the ratification of the covenant at Shechem. This is one of the most important passages in the Old Testament where the scholarship of recent years has led to the almost unanimous conclusion that the account has grown out of the sequel; the lines of what happened have been so simplified and shortened that we can no longer perceive the actual course of events.

Beside the Book of Joshua there is another account of the settlement of the Israelites—the first chapter of the Book of Judges. It is only a very abbreviated and thoroughly fragmentary description : it sounds like an extract of an account which must once have been much more extensive and detailed. If one compares this fragment in Judg. 1 with the account of the Book of Joshua then every reader must surely feel that it sounds quite different. It is by no means the story of one success after another, but the settlement of the land proceeds only very laboriously and with many failures. It is repeatedly said in this chapter : ... *but he could not drive out the inhabitants of the plain because they had chariots of iron.*

... *but the people of Benjamin did not drive out the Jebusites who dwelt in Jerusalem; ... but the Canaanites persisted in dwelling in that land* (Judg. 1.19, 21, 27). According to this chapter (Judg. 2) the occupation of the land was by no means smooth or complete in the beginning; on the contrary the Israelite tribes could only establish themselves here and there among the inhabitants of the land; quite a considerable portion of the land, however, remained in the power of the Canaanites. Another difference between Judges and Joshua is equally important: according to the former the tribes did not proceed *en masse*, but individually and indeed from different places. That this account is nearer to the historical facts than the account of Joshua is in fact suggested by several other passages and contexts of the Old Testament.

In solving this question of what actually happened when the Israelites entered Palestine the excavations in Palestine are important. There is need of a detailed description of biblical archaeology which has become so important in recent years. It is often presented from a very one sided point of view as if the excavations have simply confirmed once and for all that the Bible was right all the time; this is, indeed, true in many cases, but it is far from being so in every instance. As far as the account of the occupation in the Book of Joshua is concerned, one cannot say that the excavations in Palestine have confirmed it in every case. If the process of subduing the land west of the Jordan had been so smooth and straight forward as is pictured here and if the whole of the land west of the Jordan had really been subdued in *one* generation or a few years, this would of necessity have been clearly indicated by the excavations. This has not yet happened. In the subjugation of the city of Ai, which is reported in Josh. 8, it is certain as a result of excavations that at the time of the occupation there was no inhabited city there. The name 'Ai' (in Hebrew *Haaj*) means 'the place of ruins' and everything points to the fact that there was only a place of ruins there at that time. There is a third consideration; in the passage quoted above, Judg. 1.19, reference is made to the iron chariots of the Canaanites. The Canaanite cities far excelled the Israelite tribes which came from the steppe in military technique; that the Israelites could have conquered the whole of Canaan in one heavy onslaught remains highly improbable according to all that we know of the period, whereas the account in Judg. 1 corresponds completely with the historical facts as we know them.

As Albrecht Alt, the famous Old Testament scholar from Leipzig who died a short while ago, has shown, it can be assumed that the entry of the Israelites into Canaan proceeded more slowly and peacefully than appears from the Book of Joshua. The tribes probably advanced gradually from quite different places—not into the plains, of course, with their strongly defended cities, but to the partly unoccupied heights. The battles in the earliest period would have been defensive rather than offensive—which does not correspond at all with the Book of Joshua. The individual tribes and groups of tribes first took possession of the land which was still free in unoccupied areas but later came into conflict with the settled inhabitants, and then out of this developed the battles. We probably gain a better picture of these battles through the song of Deborah, which belongs to a later period (Judg. 5), than through the descriptions of the fighting in the Book of Joshua. If this assumption is wholly or partly correct, the picture of the occupation which we are given by the Book of Joshua is altered very significantly in another place also. It is often reported that the Israelites after a victory put the ban into operation against the defeated town, that is they killed everything that was alive in that city. No judgement should be passed on this mode of procedure at this point but it should be admitted that it is very repellent. If the account of the occupation given here is right the ban cannot in fact have been enforced very often. The ban, too, springs from seeing events according to their outcome. Moreover, the ban originated from the view that the Canaanites who had been left living among or near the Israelites threatened the faith of God's people with deadly danger and contributed a great deal to religious syncretism (Baal worship) among the Israelites. The view taken of this danger was probably responsible for the schematizing of the account of the occupation of the land also.

The change which the picture of the Israelite occupation undergoes, if this is so, is considerable in relation to the Book of Joshua. Everyone who has busied himself with the beginnings of the Israelites in Canaan has to face the question quite personally whether he can simply rely on the account of the Book of Joshua as before or whether he should follow the critical and historical work on the Bible at this point. The account of the history of God's people is not altered in any major way at all. What the Book of Joshua then describes is, of course, not the history of the conquest in a single generation after the crossing of the Jordan, but the final result—the land which God had promised them when he brought them out of the land of Egypt has become the new homeland of Israel—of a very much longer and very much more arduous occupation.

The Book of Joshua continues to retain its important place in the Old Testament when seen in this way. In spite of the above strictures the book is not perhaps historically worthless; except that the historical estimates and references are not correct as to the day. To mention only one point here: in Josh. 13-21, in which the division of the land is described, scholars in recent decades have discovered a whole series of valuable historical documents which stem from different periods and are of real importance for the geography and history of the tribes and the kingdoms.

For the continuance of God's dealing with this people the beginning and the end of the book are the most important. The Book of Joshua begins with a promise and warning to Joshua (Josh. 1. 1-9) One sees here very clearly that Joshua is not Moses. The office of Moses was unique. Joshua is his successor. He must be warned: 'Be strong and of good courage! Be not frightened, neither be dismayed!' As so often in history, a man who had a tremendous, unique mission dies. Another must take over his work, a man with fewer gifts and lesser abilities. Moses' succession by Joshua is the chief example of this in the Bible. What point does the Bible make in this case? It does not, at any rate, think it important that the successor should take his predecessor as his model and that Joshua should emulate the example of Moses. The Bible knows nothing of the concept of 'model' and 'model behaviour'; this is a characteristic

of Greek thought and, stemming from this, of idealism. Nor does the
Bible think it important that Joshua should use his small powers
and abilities to accomplish as much as possible and achieve the
utmost of which he is capable. For the Bible the important thing is
that this man Joshua stood firm. The question posed by his life and
work is not whether he achieved much or little, whether he is far
behind the example of Moses or not. It is whether he holds fast to the
promise and the command of God or not. That is the reason for the
warning at the beginning: *turn not from it to the right hand or to
the left that you may have good success wherever you go* (Josh. 1.7).
The conclusion of the book (Josh. 24) corresponds to this beginning.
Joshua summons the elders among the tribes to an assembly of all
the tribes at Shechem in order to set a choice before the nation.
This choice is concerned with only one thing—whether the tribes
which are now settled in the land intend to remain loyal to Jahwe,
the God who brought them out of Egypt and promised them this
land. The description of Joshua's question and the people's answer
in the assembly at Shechem is a biblical prototype for what we call a
creed or confession of faith.

An explanation as to our use of the term must be given first.
We are accustomed to speak of a creed or confession as a series of
statements. This designation of a series of sentences as a creed is
inexact: these sentences are concerned with *what* a person confesses. The creed in the real sense is the *act* of confessing. If the
statements are detached from the act, then they become something
else, an explanation of principle or a programme. One may not
separate the sentences with which an individual or group confesses
his or its faith from the situation in which this faith is professed.
The Nicene Creed, for example, cannot be understood at all without
the discussion which preceded it. It can, indeed, be continued today
and repeated or recited in church, but it is not a credal confession
in the strict sense because our situation has changed so much from
that of the Nicenaean days. A great part of present day discussion
about the relation of the Lutheran and Reformed confessions is
futile for this very reason; the mistake is made of acting as if these
statements, cut off from the situation of the person confessing his

faith, were still a creed in the same way although our situation is undoubtedly different from that in the sixteenth century. That this is so is shown by the fact that the congregations of our day have no interest at all in the discussion about Lutheran or Reformed confessions; this is an indirect but very clear indication that the statements of a credal confession cannot be detached with impunity from the situation of the person making the confession. Moreover, talk of 'taking a stand' on a creed or confession points to this misunderstanding : one can take a stand on a point of view but not on a creed.

What a credal confession really is can best be shown by two passages in the Bible : John 6 and Josh. 24. The act of making a confession is the same in all important points in these two chapters. The most important characteristic of the credal confession lies in the fact that it is an answer to a question. Jesus, seeing that many have gone away from him, asks his disciples : 'Will you also go away?' (John 6.67). Joshua asks the people of Israel who face the choice of serving either the gods of Canaan or the God who had led them through the wilderness : 'Choose therefore today whom you will serve ...' (Josh. 24.15). A further important characteristic of the credal confession is the fact that the making of the confession is an act of free choice. Only as such has it value; and is really a confession. Thirdly, some event must always have preceded the confession. In John 6 it is what the disciples have heard and experienced on their journey with Jesus up to this point. In Josh. 24 it is the mighty acts of God on behalf of his people. In other words, the credal confession is never simply the expression of a theoretical conviction. It is not a true confession if it only affirms a doctrine and is not at the same time something which has been experienced. One can never confess one's faith in a theory of God but only in God's activity. This is the question put to the Israelites by Joshua here. But in the course of asking them Joshua at the same time makes a confession of faith in Jahwe, the God of Israel, for himself personally and for his family : *Choose this day ... but as for me and my house, we will serve the Lord.*

Two things are important about this. First, it is indicated here

that from now on, since Israel is no more a closed unit on
the march but each man goes his separate way to his own dwelling,
the decision of the whole people no longer *ipso facto* covers the
decision of every individual member of the people. Now it is possible for an individual to decide for himself alone. The decision of
the individual begins to acquire an importance second only to that
of the whole people. From these words of Joshua a line points to the
time when it will be of vital importance for the nation that when
the nation or its representative, the king, makes a wrong decision,
a decision against God, there are individuals or perhaps only one
individual who confess their faith in God and his activity.

Secondly, in the promise and warning at the beginning Joshua
was not expected to emulate the example of Moses, nor was the
highest possible achievement demanded. He accomplished what was
entrusted to him and expected of him in declaring to the coming
generation that it was of paramount importance to hold fast to
God—to what God had done, and to what God had promised. He
knew from his own life's work that this trust was no easy matter.
He knew that the powers of a man often do not stretch to this and
he promised nothing to those who followed him. *You cannot serve
the Lord; for he is a holy God* (Josh. 24.19). He says to them that
the punishment of the disobedient will devolve on them all. In the
face of this possibility the people reply *Nay; but we will serve the
Lord*. Now Joshua has only to establish that they are witnesses
of their own statement. 'Your confession of faith now binds you.
You have now to stand by your word, come what will.'

In this last scene of the assembly at Shechem (Josh. 24) a moment
which is equally important in every genuine confession receives
expression: a confession of faith is no private matter, not under
any circumstances. It takes place before witnesses. It is a promise
which now unites the one who made it with the one whom he
promised to serve, and also with those who have said 'Yes' with him
and who keep their word. The decisive feature of this confessional
bond, however, is what Joshua now says to the people who confess
their faith: 'You have not bound yourselves by means of your own
power or your own ability. It is a holy God to whom you have

bound yourselves by your word. In your own strength you will fail. You can only say "Yes" if you look this possibility of failure clearly in the face. Then you can say "Yes" to this God. He is a holy God.'

There is a peculiar, close correspondence in the New Testament to this last scene. When the disciples affirmed their loyalty in the face of Jesus' declaration that they would betray him, then Jesus said, 'You will all fail me'. And yet he accepted their loyalty. His Church was born through failure, and it has always been so. Because every genuine confession of faith leads to this dividing line at some point or other, it is always more than, and different from, the series of statements in which the belief is contained.

5 · The Judges and Inspired Leadership

O N E of the assumptions of our political thinking is that every power must have a form which lends it permanence. This continuity can take very different forms: hereditary monarchy, a constitutional division of power, or some other form. But for a group of men to be unacquainted with any definite authority possessing such continuous power is impossible in our world; we could not imagine it.

In the Book of Judges in the Old Testament we have the record of a unique intermediary form of the exercise of power: it stands in between the patriarchal form of the tribal elders and the form of the state which came into being with the monarchy. It was only possible for a short period and only as long as the tribes were still comparatively small in number and formed a closed unit. In this transitional period, however, we meet it so clearly in a series of figures and events that behind it a historically important period becomes recognizable.

It is the time of inspired or 'charismatic' leadership. If one of the tribes or a group of tribes were hard pressed by an enemy—usually one of the Canaanite city states—then a man arose in one of these tribes who drew together his kinsmen and neighbouring families, perhaps even several tribes, into a common enterprise and led the body gathered in this way against the enemy. In most cases this sudden conglomeration of forces took the enemy by surprise; the body of desperate men under a leader possessed by a sense of his mission was able to overcome far superior odds, and the danger was averted once more. The most surprising thing, however, was what happened next. The victory was not followed up. It was sufficient that the enemy had been repelled. No attempt was made to besiege his cities or to capture them. After they had been defeated and driven back they were allowed to escape. The quickly levied Israelite militia disbanded again equally quickly. At the command 'To your tents, Israel!' every man went to his village again, to his own hearth. The leader did the same. He had fulfilled his mission; the enemy had been driven back; he went back to his father's house, to his cattle and his land, as if nothing had happened. He was no different than he had been before. His status was unchanged.

How was this possible? These men were 'judges' in the sense that they brought about justice or deliverance. They were simply helpers inspired by God. One passage describes the period of the judges as a whole. It is a description from the standpoint of a very different period; it gives only the broad outlines. If the Israelites were disobedient once more, *the anger of the Lord was kindled against Israel and he gave them over to plunderers, who plundered them ... ; and they were in sore straits. Then the Lord raised up judges, who saved them out of the power of those who plundered them* (Judg. 2.14-16). What is generally an 'Either-Or' for the thought of modern man—whether to fold one's arms and pray or to set to work and act energetically when in distress—is here absolutely inseparable. To cry to God when in distress creates the atmosphere without which the rise of the judges would be impossible; the judge who rouses himself and others to take action from time to time would be nowhere and could do nothing without the hope of a change arising from their supplication. Where prayer is taken seriously it can never stand in opposition to courageous action —far from it!

The connecting link between the cry of the people and their

distress and the rise of the judge was his call. Once more we run up against this experience which is so important for the Bible. When discussing the call of Moses we saw that the call is intrinsically one which changes in the course of history. We now look further: even in the same period, at the same point in time, the call can take place in wholly different ways. There are not two identical calls in the Book of Judges. Let us consider two calls which are considerably different from each other, although they are calls to the same activity: the call of Gideon (Judg. 6) and the call of Saul (I Sam. 11; although Saul later became king, I Sam. 11 has in every way the character of Judges). We have already referred to the wonderful story of Gideon's call. A messenger of God comes to him and confirms him as the one through whom God will deliver his people from their present distress—their oppression by the Midianites. The call is here an actual story, told in great detail, similar to a great extent to the patriarchal stories, in which the coming of a messenger of God to men is reported. In the case of Saul it is quite different. For him his mission is, so to speak, a surprise. Only the point of departure is the same in both; Saul, like Gideon, is at work in the fields on his father's farm. He was coming from the field with the team of oxen when he heard about the messengers from the city of Jabesh, who had come to ask for help from the surrounding tribes in their very great need. The enemies, the Ammonites, are so powerful that no one dares oppose them. *Then the spirit of God came mightily upon Saul when he heard these words, and his anger was greatly kindled. He took a yoke of oxen, and cut them in pieces and sent them throughout all the territory of Israel by the hand of messengers* ... (I Sam. 11.6-7). The general summons to military service in this wild and certainly primitive form succeeds in bringing Israel's military force together, and the Ammonites are defeated contrary to all expectations.

The call is experienced quite differently by each of the different men who are called to act as deliverers when times of great need arise, but one thing is always the same: as a result of this call the spirit of God comes upon them. This is the first important passage in the Bible in which the word 'spirit', God's spirit, has real significance. The term 'spirit' is very far removed from what this same word means in the language of the educated today in our country. What is meant by it will become clear from the context of the history of the judges; but it is very difficult to paraphrase the term. It is an active, purposeful force, which comes without explanation and remains without explanation; which can only be attributed to God. It has nothing to do with a special region of the spiritual. It has a direct effect upon actual history. It accomplishes something in that family and the tribe follow this individual who has been called, although he has no visible authority at all, but is simply a son of the soil. This force, however, is recognized by the one who has become leader through it as God's force, in that he personally claims no responsibility for its amazing power. When he has done his work in the strength of it he again becomes what he was before. In this, too, he affirms that the deliverance was not his but God's work.

This leadership of the spirit is an indication for all later times that what has happened before in our world can happen again : a visible historical work, which no might of man's own could establish, can be accomplished in the power of the spirit.

The work of the judges is in every case a work of liberation. If the spirit of God makes this work possible then it is assumed that God will help at that very point where men are wrongly oppressed by those in power. From this time onwards struggles for freedom have always had a special connection with God's activity. But almost always in world history such a liberation has resulted in power being redistributed to the advantage of the freed. There seems to be an inevitable law here, rather like a force of gravity inherent in power. The exercise of power aroused in the fight for freedom seems to contain a gravitational force which inevitably leads to a new grouping of power, which can at any moment cross over into oppression of others in order to make the newly won freedom secure. Time and time again this has proved to be the result of revolutions.

The charismatic leadership in Israel is a historical sign that this law is not inevitable. Here for once—even if for only a short period and in a small area—the liberating force did not make capital out of this to effect a redistribution of power. Here for once—and now the word can be risked—there was 'pure inspiration'. For inspiration in the real and truest sense of the word is what filled the judges and compelled them to do what they did. An inspiration at all events of which the inspiration of idealism is only a feeble copy, though it should be added that what was called inspiration in Germany in the eighteenth and nineteenth century grew out of the same roots as the inspiration of which the Book of Judges speaks. In Judges also it is definitely a thing of youth, the mission of an individual to the whole, the bold, daring deed which draws its strength purely from within, and which could never have come into being simply through calculated resolve, because it scorns all calculation and is bound to defy all computation. If this inspiration of eighteenth and nineteenth century idealism experienced such a terrible collapse in the Germany of the twentieth century, this is— seen purely historically—quite definitely due to the fact that this idealism cut itself off, at first gradually and then radically, from the native soil of faith. There is complete justification for conceding to the sceptical trend of the twentieth century that idealism rooted in a philosophy cut off from faith or in politics is a glittering illusion.

The inspiration, however, which is meant in the Book of Judges always remains a possibility where God and his activity are taken seriously. It is true that the period of the judges was a limited period. The judges were replaced by the kings, and the act of anointing took the place of endowment with the spirit. But important elements of this same inspiration subsequently reappeared with the prophets, especially in the fact that the office of prophet never became a permanent, hard and fast institution, but every prophet was called anew; he had no means of power at his disposal, he stood quite independently and had to begin from scratch. The prophets gained from their office just about as little personal advantage as the judges. The office of the prophets was radically different only in that they were called by God not to fight for freedom but to preach a message of judgement. Moreover, endowment with the spirit was not spoken of among the prophets so that the term inspiration does not strictly apply to them. The appearance of prophecy as a whole, however, shows that in the endowment of the judges with the spirit for a particular work something had begun which would now continue, even if in quite different forms, in the history of God with his people. The figures of the judges in the Old Testament seem to indicate to the Church of today that there must constantly be deeds in the power of the spirit of God without institutional guarantees. Furthermore these stories of the judges warn us above all against placing too much confidence in the institutions of the Church. A church must become torpid and die if everything that is to take place in it must already have been planned and confirmed beforehand. There must be room in every church for a free working of the spirit which still blows where it will.

If there should be anyone among the readers of this book who has read the Book of Judges thoroughly more than once, he could raise an objection against the picture given here of the work of the judges: namely, he could point to the places in which mention is made of the office of judge as lasting a lifetime, and thus forming apparently a permanent stable institution. It is said, for instance, of the Judge Tola: 'he judged Israel twenty-three years. Then he died and was buried in Shamir. After him arose Jair the Gileadite, who judged Israel twenty-two years' (Judg. 10.2-3). It is assumed that here two offices have been combined at a later date, although in fact they have only the name in common. In the one office the judging related to external politics (helping the people to victory against their enemies), in the other to internal politics and thus what we call judging today. Such judges had already existed in the early period and there was apparently at any given time a man entrusted specially with the traditions of justice for all the tribes; perhaps he was also the highest authority in difficult cases of justice. A brief list of such judges (who apparently held the office for a lifetime) is contained in Judg. 10.1-5 and 12.8-15. In the middle of this stands the story of Jephthah (10.6-12.7), a story in the series of genuine judge-stories or deliverer-stories. The simplest explanation of this unusual fact is that Jephthah really belonged to both series. He was one of the deliverers appointed by God, who drove back Israel's enemies in a particular crisis and was then appointed to the office of judge which he held right up to his death. The convergence of both series in the person of Jephthah also helps to explain why these two different series of judges were later made into one series so that it appears that deliverers like Gideon were also judges for a lifetime. Samson appears a little strangely (Judg. 13-16) among the other judges. The stories concerning him have a strong legendary character; many of them resemble picaresque stories. The story of Samson catching foxes in order to tie faggots to their tails and then chase them into the cornfields of the Philistines has certainly provoked many loud laughs when told in the family circle at eventide. The last of the Samson stories, however, rises to true greatness : the prisoner of the Philistines and in fetters, the hero is still able, even in death, to bury a great number of the enemy, who are intoxicated with victory, under the house whose supporting pillars he brings crashing down by means of his revived strength.

The Book of Judges is a book of youthful spirits. Most of its figures are young men. More important, it describes a nation's youth, a wild, effervescent and often exuberant period, when they lived for the moment, a period in which inspiration counted more than sober planning, the daring deed born of the moment more than a clever system of government. It was a time in which joking, wild spirits and audacity had their place, and in which the fierce battle (Judg. 5) still had something of play about it, and the melancholy story of the princess who has to die because of a vow and who bewails her virginity on the mountains still has life (Judg. 11).

This, too, then is not lacking in our Bible; the youth of a nation with its merry-making, its unconcern and its inspiration belong to the history of the people of God and has its place in it. It belongs to the Bible so that its voice may be heard by us also. It is just this, of course, which constitutes the wonder of the Bible—it encompasses the whole of human existence before God, no aspect of human life has to be left out. There must be a deep, deplorable misunderstanding of the Bible if the view persists that the message of the Bible as it is proclaimed in church is really for old people or at least

for respectable people who act like grown ups, and that youthful
wild spirits and all effervescence have no place in the Bible. The
Book of Judges, the book of the young, knows nothing of this.
They all belong to the people of God : Gideon who threshes his
father's corn in the wine press and, full of indignation, speaks to
the angels of God about the humiliation of his people; the maiden
Deborah who rouses her oppressed people from lethargy and in-
spires them to fight; Samson who plays many a practical joke on
the enemy with his effervescent strength and who then, after being
severely punished for his rashness, performs his greatest exploit
when in prison and on the point of death; Gideon who finds the
army is too big for the fight for freedom and who surprises and defeats the enemy with only a few men; Jephthah's daughter who
comes to meet her father with a dance; Jotham, the youngest son of
Gideon, who mocks the murderer of his brothers—he is the only
survivor—with the daring fable of the thorn bush; Abimelech who
tries to become king by force but fails.

It would be an excellent thing if these pages of the Bible, the
province of young people, could be affirmed more courageously in
the life of our churches and congregations !

6 · *The Land and the State*

T H E primaeval history was concluded by the story of the tower
whose pinnacle was to reach to heaven and by means of which
those who built it desired to make a name for themselves. In the
history of mankind this impulse to excel and outlive others has
received its most powerful expression in the formation of states.
In the approximately seven thousand years of human history which
we know, the greatest or noblest works of men's hands are the
formations of states, kingdoms and empires.The greatest or noblest
or most powerful men in these seven thousand years have been for
the most part statesmen : leaders, kings, emperors, politicians. The
largest and most lasting buildings of this period have been those
for which the Ziggurat of Babylon was a model, buildings which

represent the state, a category which includes temples also. The narrative of the building of the tower of Babel recognized the inner connection between the overtowering edifice and what it represented.

In the twentieth century this inter-relationship of large buildings and the state is beginning to change. The towers whose pinnacles have grown up to heaven are today no longer exclusively state buildings. The state, on the other hand, can no longer be represented simply by a large building. We cannot clearly recognize or clearly express the essence of this change yet; but that something is changing can no longer be denied. The nature of the state is changing right down to its foundations. In the historical books of the Old Testament in the narrower sense—that is in the Books of Joshua, Judges, Samuel and Kings—we are given a full, clear and detailed picture of how in one part of our earth a body of nomads became a state. This fact alone makes the historical books of the Old Testament important for our time: we can look from the last stage of a development to its beginning and we shall in this way be better able to understand what is happening today and to take the necessary steps more confidently. There is another consideration also: the state has always, for as long as we find it in human history, existed only in relation to a church or a religion. Here, too, since the French Revolution the way has been prepared for a change. For an understanding of this situation it is important to get to know the earliest stages of this opposition of State and Church. Attention to these early stages will show, for example, whether any valid principle about the relation of Church and State can be laid down for all times and all places. To anticipate the answer: the historical books of the Old Testament will show that this is not possible. We shall see that God speaks and deals differently with his people in the different sections of the history of the people of Israel. The forms of government, the kinds of wars, the relation of internal and external politics, change, and one cannot say that the one is according to God's will and the other contrary to it. In all these changes the clear lines of God's will for his people, of his relationship to the other nations and of the relation of the members and groups within the nations to each other, will emerge. Above all these historical books of the Old Testament are the ones that can demonstrate conclusively that there is no space, no area, no region in the corporate life of man into which the will of God for man does not reach, to help, to explain and to direct.

7 · The Writing of the Historical Books

A T the beginning of the collection of the five books of Moses, the Pentateuch, stands a hymn of praise, the creed of those who were saved at the Sea of Reeds and who saw in this and their consequent liberation from Egypt the beginning of their history. At the beginning of the collection of the historical books (Josh. to II Kings) stands a confession of sin. In other words, during the Babylonian exile after the complete collapse of the Israelite-Jewish state a great change took place among those who survived—whether in Judaea or in Babylon is not certain. They were confronted with the fact that the prophets whose message had been rejected and unheeded had been proved right. The judgement they had proclaimed had taken place. God *had* to act so, the destruction of the state was deserved, there was only one possibility for the future: acceptance of their guilt. This step was taken with complete conviction by the survivors. They admitted now that the nation and the kings had taken a perverse path, they excused themselves no more. They admitted too, that they—every generation anew—had been warned by the prophets that God had troubled himself with them for the last time. This, basically, was the way they now looked at the history of their nation. But this confession of the nation's past guilt also made possible a new hope. Possibly God still had some plans for his people if only they would really return to him. For this reason, because they still had some hopes for the future, they compiled their nation's previous history, while they gave to the traditions which were to hand a framework which would pass on to future generations a knowledge of the truths they had gained through the collapse.

In this way the Deuteronomic history, so called after Deuteronomy, the fifth Book of Moses, came into being; its basis, the Deuteronomic law, had been proclaimed as the foundation stone of King Josiah's reform shortly before the collapse. The 'Deuteronomic School', in which the great historical work originated, was able to attach itself to this law, for it was an attempt to return to the nation's foundations which had been laid at the time of the deliverance from Egypt and the wanderings in the wilderness. The law which is contained in the fifth Book of Moses (Deut. 12-26) is in the form of a reminder and a warning, which sets before the people of God a great Either-Or, a decision. The sentence which is specially characteristic of this book is the conditional clause, '*If* you will obey the will of God ... *then* he will allow you to live in the land, *then* he will send you blessing, *then* it will go well with you'. Those who survive the catastrophe are confronted with the fact that Israel had not fulfilled that condition. Their interest in the past therefore is directed above all to this one point: how did they come to this false path? Who failed? Where are the weak spots? Where in their long history of disobedience and apostasy are the rays of hope for a return to God?

This point of view shines clearly and steadily throughout the whole work: as, for example, in Judg. 2, in which the pattern of events in the period of the judges is described synoptically; in the speeches which a leader makes every so often; and above all in the judgements passed on individual kings, which, taken together, show that only quite a few in the series of kings followed the path of obedience—most turned aside from it. The sentences in which this is stated are almost word for word the same. The synopsis of the whole history or a single section of the history, which recur at intervals throughout the whole work, allow us to recognize a typical, stylized language, namely the Deuteronomic style. This makes it possible in many places, though not all, to recognize where the author or authors, and thus the Deuteronomic school, is speaking, and where other, older sources which were at the disposal of the school in collecting the old traditions are speaking.

The documents which were at the disposal of the collectors for their work differed greatly in type and value. Clearly, many historical documents were lost in the destruction of Samaria and Jerusalem and had disappeared. Moreover, there are almost no historical accounts from the earliest period when the Israelite tribes entered the land; these only begin with the rise of the monarchy. Chronicles were kept at the courts of the kings and these are the basis, at least in part, of the Books of Samuel and Kings. In addition there are reports and notes of a different kind. With this in mind, therefore, it is quite understandable that in the Deuteronomic work of history there are many parts which are historically very exact and reliable, while other parts, especially if early, should not be accepted as historically accurate without further question; this is particularly true of the Book of Joshua.

Deuteronomy was placed at the front of this work as an introduction, although it also marked the conclusion of the Pentateuch, the five Books of Moses. In a special sense this book occupies a central position among the historical Books of the Old Testament. It is the connecting link between the Pentateuch and the historical work. Both are fastened together in such a way that the death of Moses is reported at the end of Deuteronomy—this shows that Deuteronomy clearly and of necessity belongs to the Pentateuch—while the speeches of Deuteronomy introduce the historical account.

V · THE MONARCHY

1 · The Brilliance and Tragedy of Kingship

NOWADAYS if one buys a newspaper in Paris, Warsaw, Rome or Chicago, one of the headlines on the front page will on many days of the year contain names which are known throughout the world, in all parts of the earth and in all the large cities of the world. This fact points to one of the outstanding features of our time, which in spite of all the differences and oppositions of men today, is united in giving pride of place to political matters. This pre-eminence is not as unanimous today as it was about fifty years ago, but it is still here. 'The political', politics as a special domain of life, a special institution with its own customs and laws, its own language, its own expression and symbols, began in most parts of the world with kingship. In our world kingship is the basic form and classical expression of the exercise of power among men. The chief words for power—the wielding of it and the area of it—have in most languages developed from kingship. The fact that the rule of God has chiefly been called kingship or kingly rule, as in the Old and New Testaments, is particularly significant. In the Bible the view is expressed that there cannot be anything higher than the king. The king is the head, the ruler *par excellence*. This understanding of kingship is still basically the same even today. No name for a ruler which would give expression to a higher rule than that of king has ever gained sway. There did come a time when the name of king was no longer sufficient. When the rulers of the Mesopotamian basin conquered other kings and added their kingdoms to their own they were more than kings; but the difficulty of finding a name for this higher rule revealed itself in the name which they proposed: king of kings. Roman rule was responsible for the origin of the ruler's title 'emperor' (*Caesar*), which was taken up as *Kaiser* in Germany and persisted up to the beginning of the twentieth century. Today, however, it is clear that this title was not capable of replacing or supplanting that of king. Nowhere on earth has God been spoken of as an emperor. The strangely fascinating force which the words king and queen have retained (from fairy tales to the present day) even among the bourgeoisie of the technical age has never transferred itself to the word emperor. The same is true of derivative uses of the titles king and queen and for the adjective kingly. The king is the embodiment *par excellence* of ruling in the thought of many thousands of years.

In the Bible the origin of kingship in Israel is described for us in the four Books of Kings (I and II Sam., I and II Kings). There are not very many places in the world where the beginnings of kingship are historically recognizable. For this reason alone this part of the Old Testament is of importance. The account of the origin of kingship in Israel however, derives its essential tension from the question, 'How can a nation have a king if it recognizes God as its Lord?' (and that is, for that world, as its king). This alternative is no longer intelligible to us; we ask why should it be so difficult? The king is lord of the political sphere, God is Lord in the religious sphere! It is precisely at this point, however, that the difficulty arises, because these two spheres are inseparable in the world of the Old Testament. The rise of kingship at that time really jeopardized the rule of God. The Israelites only needed to look at the great neighbouring kingdoms, in which the king was exalted to a height of almost or complete divinity and in which he was addressed as God and honoured in a way befitting the only God. It was not at all surprising, therefore, that the kingship in Israel prevailed only after a hard struggle. There was a tendency towards a radical rejection of kingship for fear that the rule of God might be impugned. The Israelite tribes had had a patriarchal system of government until then, only the elders of the tribe having a permanent pre-eminence; their authority, however, was only the extended authority of the father. In all concerns affecting several or all tribes the elders came together to take council in common. All such business depended on the agreement of all or the majority. Thus in this respect a strictly democratic constitution was in force. Kingship necessarily brought a complete change. It is understandable that strong opposition was raised. Later kingship attained such great importance for Israel that it was considered the beginning of the nation's most important period. In the latest account of Israelite history, the work of the Chronicler, this importance—seen from a great distance—has so increased that everything that happened before the monarchy appears simply as an overture to the real history which began with the monarchy. What began with the monarchy was not only a new political era but a new chapter in the history of salvation. The king enters into a special relationship with God, he is God's anointed, the *mashiah* (Messiah), and a special promise is made by God to the royal house (II Sam. 7). This is based on the fact that the importance of the king did not come to an end with the end of the monarchy. The expectation of another king, the Messiah, was based on the old promise to the king. The message of the New Testament cannot be understood without the previous history of the Israelitic monarchy. Two of the chief ideas of the New Testament, the 'Christ' (=Messiah) and the 'kingdom of heaven' (really: the kingly rule of God) presuppose the monarchy in Israel and its history.

In view of the monarchy's importance it is especially noteworthy that the origin of kingship and the Old Testament is described in such a way that in this account the opposition which a certain group raised to the introduction of kingship can still be clearly recognized. The account in I Sam. 8-12 is not homogeneous. It is a compilation of different traditions. One of these traditions is outspokenly critical of the kingship; another accepts it gladly as a gift of God, at a time when the nation was being increasingly hard-pressed by external enemies. Both of these traditions can be recognized quite clearly by their very different language and by many other idiosyncrasies. This distinction of different strands or traditions or sources in the account of the origin of the monarchy is particularly important here. A superficial judgement would say that only one of these two reports can be right! At all events one can say with some probability that only one of these traditions comes nearest to historical truth. More important, however, is the fact that only both lines together, the one favouring *and* the one opposing the monarchy, correctly portray the total situation at the time the monarchy came into being. It is an excellent proof of greater historical accuracy that the tendency that was hostile to the monarchy was not suppressed or smothered, but was preserved in this way for later generations: the kingship *was* God's gift at a difficult period; the anointing of the king was at God's command and therefore the monarchy had God's promise; *but* at the same time this gift of kingship was fraught with dangers and temptations from the very beginning. The hostile part in the account of the origin of kingship corresponds to the final judgement on the monarchy: namely, that it was largely to blame for turning Israel aside to disobedience. This discordant judgement on the rise of the monarchy in Israel had an important consequence for the history of the kings in Israel. Israel never came to the point of bestowing divine honours on the king as neighbouring countries did; the king in Israel belonged to man's side, not God's side. This received its clearest expression in the fact that, from the first to the last king, there was a critical authority which would, if necessary, oppose the king in the name of God: the voice of the prophet.

That in this one place, as distinct from the divine kingship of Canaan, Assyro-Babylon and Egypt, the king remained man had far reaching consequences in the history of the West. The Roman empire stood quite definitely in the line of oriental divine kings. The opposition of the Christian Church to the divine worship of the emperor, an opposition which finally destroyed the emperor's position, had its roots in the denial of divine kingship by the old people of God. This limitation on human powers was taken over and maintained by the Christian Church: its opposition to the divine worship of the emperor destroyed one of the greatest attempts of mankind to make the political element absolute and to give to human authority at its head the character of something absolute, totalitarian and divine and to make it the ultimate authority. It is quite understandable that at the end of the age of Constantine the same attempt was made, in the form of totalitarian states, to make the political element absolute. And when the Church of Christ once more opposed this absolutism of the state at the cost of its life this was a continuation of the rejection of divine kingship in the Old Testament. Something happened here which cannot be reversed by any force in the world. Here, once and for all, the political element, the rule of men over men, is limited by the criticism which no state in the world at any time can or should completely ignore: a criticism which somehow or other gives expression to the fact that the authority of the state—whatever it may be—is never the ultimate authority.

This constitutes the abiding importance of the history of kingship in Israel which began so brilliantly and ended so tragically: from the moment of its origin it was never without criticism and at its end stands the expectation of another king. In this way God's approval of the state, human rule and politics is clearly expressed but equally clearly, too, God's rejection of a state which sets itself up as absolute.

2 · The History of the Kings

T H E history of the kings of Israel in the Old Testament is a powerful, self-contained drama held together by tremendous tensions. It deserves a special account devoted to it; but only a few of the main lines can be indicated here. This drama could, in fact, be described more accurately as a tragedy, a powerful tragedy in three acts. The first act (*c*.1005-926) comprises the history of the first three kings, Saul, David and Solomon. The scene of this first act is the whole of Palestine. Its central point is the one and only great, prosperous period of Israel's history, the time of the Davidic empire. At that time—and only at that time—Israel was master of the whole of Palestine, the country was at peace and flourished in its youthful vigour. The second act comprises the history of the divided kingdom after the death of Solomon up to the fall of Samaria (926-722). Its scene is the northern kingdom of Israel, and at its centre stand two sets of wars—externally against the Aramaeans and internally between prophet and king, chiefly Elijah at the beginning, Amos and Hosea at the end.

The third act contains the history of the southern kingdom of Judah, beginning like that of the northern kingdom of Israel with the division of the kingdom. It only becomes the history of Israel with the dissolution of the northern kingdom, when it takes over some of the traditions of the northern kingdom (722-587), until this half of the kingdom also collapsed and Jerusalem was captured and destroyed (587). The dominant feature of this third act, as far as external politics go, is the gradual submission to Assyrian rule and the last attempt at political recovery with the collapse of the Assyrian empire; in the realm of internal politics the central events are the reform of King Josiah in 622, which was connected with this political recovery and the programme of which is preserved for us in Deuteronomy, and the activity of the great prophets Isaiah and Micah at the beginning of this period, and of Jeremiah at the end.

If one desired to depict the history of the monarchical period by means of a graph, one would have to draw a curve rising steeply upwards at the beginning to a point which was never reached later. It would have to remain about this point in Solomon's time, apart from a slight fall, only to sink sharply after the death of Solomon with the division of the kingdom. A significant rise is observable in Israel in the time of Jeroboam II (787-747) and in Judah in Uzziah's time (785-747); from then on it goes steeply downwards to the destruction of Samaria (722). Under Josiah (639-609) the surviving state of Judah, had a time of external, as well as internal, recovery once more; this gave rise to the greatest hopes. Then, however, from the battle of Megiddo, in which Josiah opposing the Pharaoh Necho was defeated and fell, the graph plunged quickly downwards until the destruction of Jerusalem and the exile.

But this one line would not be enough, of course, to depict the actual history of this nation. At the very least another line would have to be added, namely the remarkable line of prophecy which we do not meet with in any other nation in the history of the world. This line accompanies the line of political events—from the pinnacle to the collapse—but at the same time points to yet another dimension, whose existence cuts right across the political history and which cannot be drawn into the tragic collapse, which points to something other, something new and is itself the beginning of something else which will survive the collapse and grow.

However, what are these two lines except a poor expedient to help us explain a little what happened at that time! In actual fact the history which stretches from the call of Saul to be king and the capture of the last king Zedekiah, who tried to flee from Jerusalem as it was falling, cannot be simplified in this way; it cannot be contained in lines but is as complex and difficult to grasp as all actual history. The history of Israel may serve as a particularly good example of the fact that the history of a nation really has some of the characteristics of the history of a living being. It is not only a constructional aid but it corresponds to reality if we see the history of a nation in terms of youth, maturity and old age. The life of a nation is actually the life of an 'individual', an inseparable entity. A nation has its time as a man has his time. This can be perceived in the history of Israel with unique force and clarity. It must, however, also be said that the history of a nation can never be completely contained in a historical description any more than the life of an individual can be contained in a biography. There remains so much that is difficult to grasp, so much that is without connection, so much that is inexplicable and does not fit into any picture, that a description of the whole cannot be more than a feeble attempt. Here, however, we are concerned with a period of the history of God with his people which is at the same time a period of history such as a historian, for whom God is only a hypothesis, can describe. It would be surprising if everything did not remain a complete mystery!

3 · King Saul

W E are told very little, unfortunately, about Saul and his reign in the account of the Book of Kings. It strikes one immediately that the events concerning the origin of the monarchy (I Sam. 8-12) take up more room than the account of Saul's reign itself (13-15). The little that we are told of Saul's reign presents a dark, obscure picture. It is quite overshadowed by the conflict between Samuel and Saul, which is in turn very difficult to understand, seeing that Samuel anointed Saul king and Saul's faults which are recorded are not really sufficient justification for this serious quarrel.

A word must be said next about Samuel. The first two Books of Kings are named after him; in the first part in the first of these books his figure is central, it projects itself far into the history of the first two kings. Samuel must have been an important man for that period of transition to the monarchy. But what we have recorded about him remains remarkably unclear and iridescent. To come straight to the point : we do not know who and what Samuel actually was. Recorded tradition speaks of him as a priest. He was handed over as a boy to the shrine at Shilo and was instructed in the duties of a priest by Eli. Later he celebrates the sacrificial meal in Mizpah, and still later the offering of sacrifice is his prerogative alone (I Sam. 15), as seer (9-10), as prophet (3.19-21) and also as judge (7). It is very questionable whether he actually united all these offices in his own person; which of these offices he actually held we can no longer tell from the recorded tradition. All we can say is that in what we are told about Samuel the transitional character of that period stands out clearly. According to the accounts we possess many lines converge in his person, but we can no longer separate them clearly from each other. Probably the transition from seer to prophet was completed in his person and his life time. The seer had more to do with private life, the prophet with public, national life. In I Sam. 9.9 it is clearly stated that 'those who were previously called seers were now called prophets'. The transition from seer to prophet takes place before our very eyes in the beautiful story, told with great artistry, of how Saul is anointed king (I Sam. 9-10). It pre-supposes that Samuel was well known as a seer, who was sought out in times of personal difficulties and who gave advice in return for payment; for example, on this occasion he was asked where they should search for the lost asses. But when, in the continuation of

the story, Samuel was commanded by God to anoint as king of
Israel the farmer's son, Saul, who should come to him, then Samuel's
office changes also: he is acting now on the direct instruction of
God for the whole people of Israel and thus the transition from
seer to prophet is complete. In any case this narrative reflects a
historical fact: with the rise of the monarchy the prophet replaced
the seer. It is, moreover, quite possible that this change was completed in the person of Samuel.

This story of Saul's anointing by Samuel agrees in one further
point with the narrative in I Sam. 8, where the people come to
Samuel with their request for a king and Samuel yields, although
he sees in it an open lack of trust in God's rule over the people,
as he repeats very emphatically on his departure from the people
in chapter 12. These two chapters are clearly written from the
standpoint of a much later period, which already looks back on a
history in which the kings have been rejected. But behind it one
can still perceive that Samuel played his part in the founding of the
monarchy in Israel, as I Sam. 9-10 assert.

Only these two facts, that Samuel was a seer who subsequently
became a prophet, and that he played an important part in the rise
of kingship can be taken as at all certain—plus the fact that he
subsequently had a serious quarrel with the first king.

The beautiful story of Samuel's birth and youth in the first three
chapters is important and valuable for its own sake. The story of
God and his people in the Old Testament has three important intro-
ductions to new sections: the beginning of the patriarchal history
(Gen. 12), the beginning of the nation's history (Ex. 1) and the
beginning of the history of the kings (I Sam. 1). At all three points
the story is about the birth of a child: for all God's dealings in
history presuppose the birth of a child. At the beginning of the
history of the kings the mother occupies the centre of the narrative.
The mother who is in despair because she has not received a child;
who weeps in the sanctuary before God and implores him for a child;
the mother who is promised by the priest that her prayer will be
heard, who believes this promise and through it finds happiness
once more. The introduction of the New Testament, also, will con-

cern the birth of a child. And once again a mother will sing a hymn of praise.

It has already been pointed out in the account of the history of the judges that Saul, although he was the anointed king, really belonged more to the series of 'charismatic leaders'. The liberation of the city of Jabesh in Gilead, which was the most probable historical cause for Saul being called to be king, has all the characteristics of the history of the judges. A farmer's son is possessed by God's spirit to meet the serious threat to an Israelite town from a far stronger enemy; he takes command of the levy of the Israelite tribes by virtue of this call and he succeeds in liberating the town. If the story does not now continue exactly as the stories of the judges with the army disbanding and the leader returning to his own home and work, but if, instead, the assembled nation goes to Gilgal and there, at the sanctuary, summons Saul to be king, there is a definite reason for this in the foreign politics of the time. The Philistines, who had entered Palestine about the same time as the Israelites and—probably after being displaced from Egypt—had occupied the southern coastal strip (the modern Gaza strip), had become such a threatening force for the Israelites that their previous manner of repelling the enemy, the charismatic leadership, no longer seemed sufficient to meet this threat. A permanent institution of defence to stabilize the power in the hands of one man seemed the only solution. Therefore the Israelites demanded that they should have a king like other nations.

Saul's battles against the Philistines and other enemies of Israel are, as it happens, the most important feature in the brief account we are given of his reign. But it is almost painful to read these stories: Saul cannot undertake anything without something unexpected and senseless working against him. On the occasion of the first great decisive battle against the Philistines, Samuel fails to arrive in time to offer his necessary sacrifice before the battle. The waiting is unbearable; the men leave Saul because the chances of victory continually grow smaller with the delay. Then Saul offers the sacrifice himself, and at that very moment of course Samuel arrives and tells him he must pay a very heavy penalty for his rather minor offence.

In a further battle Saul succeeds in inflicting a heavy defeat on the Philistines through a daring surprise attack of his son, Jonathan. But Jonathan, unsuspecting, breaks a food regulation (about abstinence) which Saul had proclaimed. Here again Saul was too harsh and asks for Jonathan to be executed, an act which was only prevented by the opposition of the army. The people used this opportunity to enrich themselves with the spoils. After his battle with the Amalekites Saul does not carry out the ban (I Sam. 15) and for that reason he is rejected by Samuel. From this moment on Saul has forfeited the kingship as far as Samuel is concerned. He anoints another as king—the young David—in response to God's command. The rest of what is reported about Saul is a story of fatal decline and deterioration: his sinking in morbid melancholy, his unhappy rivalry with David, his recognition of the hopelessness of his position which finally brings him to have the ghost of Samuel entreated by a witch in order that he might still obtain some word of advice. This last desperate attempt brings him nothing but the confirmation of his rejection.

Saul is like a rejected, condemned man, who suspects his fate but does not turn aside. Unyielding, he meets the Philistines in a last battle on Mount Gilboa. It is a terrible battle. Saul sees three of his sons fall. He himself is severely wounded by an arrow. In order not to be taken prisoner by the enemy he falls on his sword. His armour bearer dies with him.

This dark and depressing picture of the first Israelite king has a symbolic significance. Israel's monarchy as a whole is depicted in Saul rather than in David. A single feature serves to underline this: the last king, Zedekiah, goes to his enemy, Jeremiah, when Jerusalem was already surrounded by the Babylonians and was already beyond rescuing—Jeremiah who had prophesied his downfall and whom he had imprisoned. He goes to him with the same question with which Saul had gone to the witch of Endor and receives the same answer. The fate of the Israelite kingship has already been darkly hinted at in its first representative. It is, however, also probable that this picture has deliberately been drawn so darkly and that a great deal of the positive, bright and telling things which could have been said about Saul's reign has been omitted. One can in fact still say, in spite of all Saul's failures, that he knew he was God's servant in his regal office and that he remained true to his Lord. It cannot be denied that he was a brave man and a noble one, who only sank so deeply into melancholy and despair because he took his task with deadly seriousness. In spite of all his mistakes, even with regard to David, a kingly man is recognizable.

4 · King David

I F we leave the path of King Saul, as we find it in the first Book of Samuel, for the path of David, it is like stepping out of a dark narrow room into the light of day. Here is the path of a king such as a nation can only wish for, a path of success and splendour, the path of a purposeful, strong man, a man who attracted the spontaneous good will of many people, and who could find a way out of the most difficult situation, a king who was also a singer and who radiated joy and strength. We shall see later that this is only one side of King David and his reign. There is another side and the Bible does not pass over it in silence. Nevertheless, the picture of this king— and this king alone, of all the kings of Israel and Judah—is predominantly a radiant one of a happy king, loved by his people and victorious, a king of whom his nation's songs will still be telling hundreds of years later, and who always remained for his people the ideal king.

The story of David's rise from the house of his father Jesse to the throne of the two kingdoms, Judah and Israel, belongs to the most valuable of the historical accounts in the Old Testament, and indeed to the most distinguished pieces of historical writing in antiquity. It probably arose at the court of David directly after the events it relates, written by a man from the circle closest to David, who had personal experience of these events. The priest Abiathar is thought to be the author by some commentators.

David's rise is described in three phases. In the first phase (I Sam. 16-20) David is at Saul's court, he becomes Jonathan's friend and Saul gives him one of his daughters in marriage. At first he rises in the favour of the king and then in the favour of the people. In the second phase David is fleeing from Saul; he becomes leader of a guerilla group and has many adventures (I Sam. 21-30). After the death of Saul and his son (I Sam. 31) David becomes king of Judah and subsequently king over the whole of Israel (II Sam. 1-5).

In each of these phases a historical experience of Israel is being described. If it is true that the life of a nation has something in common with the life of the individual, then one may say that in these three phases of David's rise we have a picture of how Israel reached maturity. What the developing king experiences in these three phases is the entry of the young nation of Israel upon maturity and its transition to manhood.

The first phase is characterized by the gaining of a friend and the establishment of a family. These two steps to maturity are to be found wherever life is whole and healthy. Here in the story of David as a young man the fact that both these things take place at the king's court, in view of the whole nation, in close proximity to the throne and in the bosom of the royal family, gives them special prominence. Consequently, there seems little resemblance to everyday life; everything seems to take place on a loftier plane, in an ideal world of beauty and splendour, far above the daily routine. This is exactly what is meant by royalty in our fairy tales: the king's castle, the prince and princess, the nobles, the magnificence and splendour; for the king-motif in our fairy tales draws life from the historical experience lying behind it, namely the experience of kingship in its earliest form. Right up to the present day people remember such kingship with longing, and even in the middle of the twentieth century a coronation, the birth of a prince or princess or a royal wedding, is turned into an event of world importance, in which millions of people in all parts of the world take an interest.

In fairy tales connected with royalty there is one theme which frequently occurs and which has obviously held a particular fascination for people of many periods: the rise of a young man from the lowliness of a very simple, poor life to the royal sphere, like the shepherd boy who rescues the princess and then becomes king. It is precisely this motif which stands at the beginning of the history of the Israelite monarchy. This had already been the case with Saul, who had come straight from his father's farm to become the deliverer of a city and then king. So now in David's case also. He used to look after his father's flock and through an heroic deed in a fight he attracts the attention of the king, who takes him off to his court. David becomes an attendant at the king's court. The group of stories which relate this belongs quite closely to the genre of sagas dealing with heroes and knights, such as are to be found among many peoples. In these the young man who comes from the healthiest stock of the people distinguishes himself at the court of the king, wins general favour and somehow embodies in his radiant, daring and dare-devil youth the soul, the desire and the longing of the people; he wins their hearts forthwith. In David's life and deeds at the court of King Saul, his friendship with Jonathan obviously occupied first place. It is described in such brilliant colours and with such sensitivity that this episode alone is a jewel in the history of Israel's kings. There is nothing belonging to man which does not find a place somehow in the Bible. The friendship of two young men has received a wonderful tribute in the story of David and Jonathan.

There is a good reason for this happening at this particular point in the Bible. We should be inclined to take it for granted that such a thing as the friendship of two young men had been a common occurrence at all times and in all places. Thus it may strike us as remarkable that this is a new experience at that time for the young people of Israel. Before the time of the kings every young man and maiden grew up in their own family, which lived as a closed unit in one place. They mixed with hardly anyone except relatives, brothers and sisters, cousins and others who belonged to the 'father's house'. They met young people of other families·at the festivals, on military expeditions or when travelling. That young men of quite different families and tribes should live together for a longer period only happened on a greater scale for the first time at the king's court, where they were educated as attendants for the service of the king. Thus, the friendship of David and Jonathan reflects in fact the first experience of this new possibility in human relationships: friendship. Linguistic usage reflects this late development of friendship in all societies: Hebrew, for instance, has no word of its own for 'friend'.

The most lovely testimony to the friendship of David and Jonathan is David's lament for the death of Saul and Jonathan: *I am distressed for you my brother Jonathan; very pleasant have you been to me; your love to me was wonderful, passing the love of women* (II Sam. 1.17-27). Much more could be said about such a friendship. Here it will be enough to suggest that in this matter too we should listen to the Bible carefully. A whole series of later passages dealing with friendship are still to come. We are certainly not mistaken in seeing this fragile and valuable picture of friendship as threatened by serious danger in our time. The Bible has the power to indicate in a unique way the sources and the nature of true friendship. It is actively concerned to preserve and renew this precious gift.

How David won the king's daughter, and of their love and marriage, we unfortunately know very little. But it is a common theme of fairy tales for the attendant at the king's court to win the king's daughter by an unsurpassed act of heroism (I Sam. 18.17-30). Signs of the king's jealousy and distress already overshadowed the episode, however; the king desires to rid himself of the up and coming hero by setting him an impossible task. How the insignificant attendant subsequently triumphed in spite of this and compelled the jealous king to give him his daughter is another frequent feature of fairy tales. But behind the fairy tale motif is a genuine solid fact: the feeling, which reaches far back into the springtime of the human race, that the best and truest way to find a wife is by a strong, bold deed which is performed for her sake. Modern man still retains this feeling. It is the significant and almost necessary completion of this when the wife later rescues the husband from mortal danger (I Sam. 19.8-17) by a clever, bold deed. This reflects a healthy, youthful interpretation and experience of marriage in a young nation. Thus, then, David won a friend and a wife, the necessary foundation of a firm and loyal group to root and support his life in love.

The second phase begins with the flight of David from the king's court. Without his friend and his wife he would probably have been killed. A series of fortunate accidents, which will continue unbroken till David is king, begins at this point. He not only has to flee from the king's court but he also has to flee from the area ruled by Saul, because otherwise his life is not safe. David becomes an adventurer, an outlaw. Again we are reminded of the stories from the corresponding period of our own history in which this is a common theme: the exile from the king's court who has to resort to a life of adventure. It is clearly a wild life that David leads in these years with a band of wild companions. He succeeds in many bold daring actions; he goes boldly to his death many a time, and time and time again he has, as the saying goes, 'the devil's own luck'. But in all his detours he never loses sight of his objective. He can even risk being sold into slavery to the Philistines, the deadly enemies of Israel, with his band of men; but he cheats his Philistine overlord on all hands and uses his men to turn things to the advantage of his own people. On one occasion the situation was extremely difficult; David had to join the army in an expedition against Saul. If he had actually been forced to engage in battle against the Israelites then his calling and his future among his own people would have been ruined. At the last moment, however, when the army was already drawn up in battle array the commander of the Philistines sent him home, because he thought that as a Judaean David was too unreliable (I Sam. 29).

The period of his adventures had its very serious side in the opposition of Saul. Rivalry, the struggle of one man against another for the right to rule, is the parallel to the motif of friendship at the king's court. The earliest and simplest form of the struggle for power, experienced by every nation at some time or other, is the duel. Here, however, the position is complicated by the fact that one of the rivals is the king. The king, as God's anointed, may not be touched. David sticks to this without deviating. Several times he has the opportunity to kill Saul, but he never does. Here for the first time David reveals himself as a man of intelligence whose thinking is not marked by pettiness. By his consideration for Saul and by respecting his immunity he lays the basis for his later kingship. This feature gives the whole of the second phase of David's rise a unique suspense: David himself lives a life in which he is responsible to no-one but himself in the truest sense of that phrase; he lives a wild, lawless life. At the same time, however, in defending himself against Saul's relentless pursuit, he sets up a powerful new law, an obligation which he voluntarily binds himself to honour; by recognizing a boundary protecting the ruler's position and securing it against any brutal attack. David's restraint lays the basis for what the Reformation called 'the authorities'. The position of a nation's leader is recognized as permanently secured. Even the man whose life is threatened by the king and who is pursued by him has no right to use force against him. There is one qualification: David respects Saul as God's anointed. Saul is not immune through the kingship as such, but because he had been confirmed in this office by God. The law which David sets up by his restraint, therefore, is only valid and important insofar as the position of the one in authority stands in a clear relation to God which has been given historical expression.

The third phase of David's rise revolves round his installation as king. After Saul had fallen with his sons in the battle on Mount Gilboa, David settles in the Judaean city of Hebron. It is baldly reported that the men of Judah made him king (II Sam. 2.1-7). Meanwhile Abner, Saul's army commander, sets up one of Saul's sons, Ishbaal, as king over the northern tribes, that is over Israel. Immediately the rivalry of two men, Saul and David, becomes a rivalry between the two parts of Israel which had been united under the rule of Saul. Consequently an extremely dangerous position arises. The small war which now begins between north and south threatens to cripple the Israelite tribes completely in view of the Philistinian victory. For David the position is almost hopeless. But within quite a short time through an extremely astute move he succeeds in bringing about a state of affairs in which the northern tribes themselves consider it the best policy to invite him to become king over them as well (II Sam. 5.1-5).

David crowns this extremely astute strategy by a daring surprise attack on the stronghold of Jerusalem, which up till then, including the period of Saul's rule, had remained in the hands of the Jebusites, a Canaanite tribe, and had acted as a barrier between the territory of the northern tribes and the land of Judah. He enlarged the stronghold of Zion and made it his residence, the city of David as he himself called it. Through its naturally advantageous position and equally through its situation midway between Judah and Benjamin, Jerusalem was very well suited to being the capital. David now had the basis on which he could build his kingdom. The basic facts need a little explanation. Up to now we have spoken of the monarchy as if it were of a constant, unchanging power and scope. But even at that time it included a number of different types of rule and it could assume very different forms. In fact the form of the monarchy in the first three kings was different each time in an important respect. When the Israelites came to Samuel and said to him, 'We too want to have a king like the other nations!' they could have been thinking of three different types of monarchy among their neighbours. In the great empires to the north and south there had existed an absolute monarchy from time immemorial, based on the divine sonship of the king. Then there was the city monarchy of the Canaanite city-kings: these kings were vassals in spite of their relative independence. This city monarchy too had a strong absolutist character; the king was the God's representative and played an important part in the worship. In fact these city kings were rather like a reproduction of the great kings, on a considerably smaller scale. There was another type of monarchy, however, in neighbouring lands such as Moab and Edom. This was formerly a constitutional monarchy; a list of Edomite kings is contained in Gen. 36.31-9, from which it follows that there the monarchy was not at first hereditary. It was probably this sort of monarchy that the Israelites thought of when they made their request to Samuel to give them a king.

As we have already seen, the rule of Saul was a transitional type between the charismatic leadership and the monarchy proper. Saul himself probably never thought of a dynasty; it was only his army commander, Abner, after his death, who tried to make one of Saul's sons king—but without success. We are never told anything about Saul's position as king having anything but external political functions. His task was to conduct Israel's wars. In all probability there was not yet any central government of the country under the king in Saul's time.

David's kingship represents something quite new. He is, in fact, corresponding to the way he became king, a threefold king; that is, he unites three different types of kingship in his person. First of all he is elected king by Judah. This is clearly a type of constitutional monarchy. Two events accompany his installation as king here: the divine designation (that is, it must be certain through some event or other that God desires to have this man as king; this is confirmed through the anointing which must be undertaken by a man of God) and the acclamation of the people (that is, this man chosen by God must be called to be king by the people). David is king of Israel in a second way. At the point where it is recorded that the northern tribes called David to be king it is expressly stated: 'The king David made a covenant with them in Hebron before the Lord'. This is a transfer of the kingship of the northern tribes to the person of David. David is, therefore, king of Israel by a personal union. (This will become important later; after Solomon's death and Rehoboam's statement of policy the northern tribes recall this covenant relationship to which they have a right in fact according to their previous history.) And David is king in yet a third way, however: through the capture of Jerusalem he has personally become master and lord of this city. He is then king of Jerusalem in a way similar to the Canaanite city kings. This means that David is king of Jerusalem as the city's master; none of the tribes, neither Judah nor the northern tribes, can raise any claim to this city. Thus David has a residence where no one can contest his right, which is in fact his own personal property. This made it possible to found a dynasty whose seat was this Jerusalem, the city acquired by David.

After the capture of Jerusalem David added to this political foundation of his kingdom yet another important tie which was calculated to hold the tribes together. His first task on becoming king of all Israel had 'to be the war against the Philistines. It is reported that the Philistines felt themselves threatened by the new Israelite king and marched against him. In two battles David inflicted such a heavy defeat on them that the country now had peace for the first time. David then did something which, next to the strengthening of the external politics of the kingdom of Israel, was the most important action of his reign: he brought the ark of God to Jerusalem.

In the Book of Samuel, there is a highly individual and in many respects strange account of this ark. With great literary skill the story of the ark has been connected with the story of the beginning of Israel's kingship. The history of Samuel's youth in the first chapters of the first Book of Samuel terminates in an announcement of judgement on the house of the priest Eli. Eli was the priest of the temple at Shilo, and the ark of God stood in Shilo. It was Israel's old portable shrine from the days of the wanderings in the wilderness. The oldest traditions of the people were connected with this ark. The judgement prophesied by Samuel fell upon the house of Eli through a victory of the Philistines over Israel. The ark fell into the hands of the Philistines, the sons of Eli fell in battle and Eli himself was so struck by the news of the disaster that he fell dead from his seat. The fate of the ark among the Philistines—how it brought bad luck on the enemy and was finally returned by them—is described further at the beginning of I Sam. 4-6. It was brought to Kiriath-Jearim: there it remained standing without playing any important part at first as far as Israel was concerned. The narrative of the ark is not continued again till the second Book of Samuel. David recognizes the importance of the ark. He desires to attach his new kingdom quite deliberately to the old traditions of Israel. In a festal procession accompanied by ancient rites which had already become obsolete by David's day he brings the ark to Jerusalem. It becomes the central shrine of the whole nation once more. This transfer of the ark to Jerusalem was of the highest importance for the course of the young kingdom. It meant that Israel's past, the time of poverty, slavery and wandering in the wilderness, was affirmed, that the faith of their fathers was to be preserved in spite of their changed way of life, and that David understood his royal position and the power of the growing kingdom to be a continuation of the old promises to the patriarchs.

It is not accidental that the new kingdom receives a new promise at this juncture. In II Sam. 7, one of the most important chapters in the history of the kings, it is related that King David, after he had built the palace, planned to build a temple, a house of God for the ark. He had no desire to carry out this plan just as he himself might choose, however, so he asked the prophet Nathan. At first the prophet agreed with him. But in the night a word of the Lord forbidding the king to build a temple came to Nathan. The design of the king is now reversed in a unique way. David is not to build God a house; he is not a God who can be enclosed in a house. But he, God, will build David a house, he will promise David's house (house and family are the same word in Hebrew) that they shall remain on the throne: *Thy throne shall stand forever*. The promise, that the kingdom should remain with David's house for all time, signifies two things: a dynasty of the house of David was established with divine confirmation, and God's history with his people was linked with a single house among his people. This promise of Nathan to David stands, in fact, in the centre of Israel's history. It is the final point of the arc which began with the promise that they would be led out of Egypt into the promised land. It is the first point of a new arc which extends from this moment when the Davidic dynasty was established to the collapse of this same dynasty and its rule, and from there to the expectation of another king of the house of David and finally to its fulfilment in Jesus of Nazareth, the son of David.

5 · The Reign of David

II Sam. 7 stands in the centre of two great connected historical accounts. It is preceded by the history of David's rise (I Sam. 16-II Sam. 5); it is followed by the history of David's reign, which, from the beginning, has as its goal the transition to Solomon's reign (II Sam. 9-20 and I Kings 1-2). Consequently scholars have called it the history of the succession to David. What was said of the history of David's rise is true here to an even greater extent: it is a work of great historical descriptive powers, drawing the lines with a surprising precision and above all objective in a way which can be asserted of the best historical writing of the world's literature. There is one further point to be noticed: surprisingly little mention is made of God in the story of the succession to David. If one compares this with a section of the Deuteronomic history, for instance Judg. 2, the difference is striking. There God is mentioned in almost every sentence, here almost not at all. What is the reason? The history of the succession to David originated at the court of Solomon; it is moulded by a definite political point of view and has a political purpose: it wants to prove that Solomon is really the rightful successor to the throne of David and to explain how this succession came about. We said at the very beginning of this section that with the monarchy politics as a special province of life became important for Israel. This is indicated by the fact that political events and contexts can now be spoken about quite 'objectively', that is in a manner corresponding with the facts, without every event always having to be connected with God in some special way. It is enough if at critical turning points God is referred to as the one from whom all history proceeds and in whose hands all the threads of history converge (II Sam. 11.27; 12.24; 17.14). The Deuteronomic history, on the contrary, sets out quite deliberately to be a theological interpretation of history; it aims to call men back to God while describing history at the same time. The difference, therefore, between speaking explicitly about God's activity in history and describing historical sequences objectively, with all mention of God and his activity dropping out of the picture completely, is a difference which exists within the Bible! But it is only a purely objective historical description that can give expression to the fact that it is *God* who directs history and is its Lord.

The story of the succession to David takes as its starting point an apparently unimportant episode at the end of the account de-

scribing how the ark was brought to Jerusalem. David dances before
the ark of the covenant and Michal, the queen, takes offence. As a
result of words with which, in her proud anger, she attacks David
on his return home she remains childless. Hence the heir to the
throne cannot come from her, the king's daughter and David's first
wife. The mother of the heir to the throne is Bathsheba. David's
army commander, Joab, a brave and excellent soldier, fights a brilliant campaign against the Ammonites and at the same time against
the Syrians, their helpers. David himself—this proves that something has changed—stays in Jerusalem. Next year Joab marches
against the Ammonites once more while David remains in the
palace on Zion. From the roof of his palace he catches sight of a
very beautiful woman and desires her. He learns that she is the
wife of one of his officers, Uriah. And now it is reported with un-
impeachable objectivity how David, in order to possess the woman,
had Uriah sent by his commander Joab to a particularly dangerous
position, where he is killed. Thereupon David takes the woman
Bathsheba for himself. At the end of this report stands the short
sentence: 'But the thing that David had done displeased the Lord'
(II Sam. 11.27). The hour had come for the kings to be introduced
to the prophetic office. The king had misused his power to do
something low and despicable. The worst feature was that, as king,
he could not be punished. If this action of David's had been passed
over, then the Israelite kingship would at that moment have slipped
into oriental absolutism, the anointing would have been degraded
to a formality and the change would have been possible only
through the overthrow of David's house.

There was no authority able to step in to oppose what David had
done. David alone held the supreme power. Then God sent his messenger, the prophet Nathan. He brings before David a case of the
rich man who takes away the solitary lamb of the poor man in
order to set it before his guests; the rich man desires to spare his
own numerous sheep and cattle. *Then the anger of David burned
fiercely against the man and he said to Nathan, 'As the Lord lives,
the man who has done this deserves to die . . .'* Nathan said
David, 'You are the man!'* In explaining this charge he tells the

king of his guilt without fear or awe, bluntly calling a spade a spade, and to his face. Then as God had commanded him he declares to David his punishment: 'Thus says the Lord, "Behold I will raise up evil against you out of your own house".' With the speed and force of a stroke of lightning the living God's word of wrath strikes here in the middle of the history of the prosperous, divinely anointed king David, who is successful in all he does and wise. In this one word of the prophet Nathan at this instant we see prophecy at the first moment of its emergence in what is essentially its fully developed form. What happened at this moment will now—without any important changes—accompany the path of the kings of Israel to the bitter end. From here on, to the last word of the last prophet to the last king, the prophetic word consists of the same two basic ingredients: the charge, which points simply to the fact of guilt, and the announcement of judgement, the punishment of God for this guilt.

The moment when Nathan came before David and said to him, 'You are the man!' belongs to the decisive events of the Old Testament. In this account a person who is quite unfamiliar with the Bible may recognize why the Old Testament was written and why it belongs to the Bible of Christianity. This moment can show why the coming of another king was necessary, but it can also make clear why the Old Testament belongs to the account of the mighty acts of God. The Church of Jesus Christ, too, must allow itself to say this with ever renewed freshness, and it must learn from the hardness and stubborness reported here in this narrative that the hour may come when it receives the same command: to oppose the misuse of power with all severity and boldness, disregarding its own interest, come what may. And it must be added here that the Church has often missed this moment. Once and for all, clearly and unconditionally it is asserted in the first hour of prophecy: where there is such a misuse of power, where a 'poor man' is overpowered by a 'rich man', God is on the side of the poor. This is something which has never altered, and here too the fact that the 'rich man' is the anointed man of God makes no difference. Unfortunately it has not often been realized in the history of the Christian Church that if Jesus of Nazareth sets himself on the side of the poor and is conscious of being sent to the lost, the sick and the outcasts, the background of Old Testament prophecy is necessary to understand this properly and to appreciate its consequences for the status of the Church in the world.

What is this event going to mean for King David? It certainly cannot be inferred from what immediately follows. David bows to the accusation of the prophet Nathan and acknowledges his guilt. This is a great thing for the king. It would have been easy for him to silence the accusation of the prophet. But if he had done this Nathan could not promise him the forgiveness of God. This means first and foremost: 'You shall not die'. Forgiveness in the Old Testament often means repeal of the death penalty; the future which had been forfeited is restored to the guilty party. This does not mean complete freedom from punishment, however. The forgiveness of God in the Old Testament is compatible with the imposition of a punishment whose affirmation and acceptance is at the same time the acceptance of forgiveness. So it is here. The child which is born to David by Bathsheba dies. But this is not, in fact, the whole punishment; the child's death is only the grim sign of what God means by allowing David to continue living and continue being king. Nathan's first declaration of judgement is confirmed.

These events take place at the peak of David's reign. II Sam. 8 tells of David's wars and of the installation of his officials in the districts of Israel. David is lord of a remarkable kingdom, internally and externally secure, a kingdom such as had never existed before or since in the small area and the poor land of Palestine. There was only one respect in which the king was unfortunate: in his family. His house, his family, is the recipient of the promise, but this promise certainly does not mean that everything goes smoothly in his house. The following part of II Samuel, like the second part of I Samuel, is concerned chiefly with a struggle between rivals: David's son Absalom rebels against his father. It began with Amnon, the first born son of David, who was marked out as heir to the throne, forcing his half-sister Tamar. David had to suffer what he himself had inflicted on others. It reveals that he is weak at this point: 'he did not want to hurt his son Amnon, because he was his first born son' (II Sam. 13.21).[1] But Absalom, Tamar's brother, 'hated Amnon because he had ravished his sister'. He waited a long time for his opportunity. At a sheep-shearing festival to which he invited all the king's sons he had Amnon murdered by his servants. He himself fled out of the country. After a time there was a reconciliation. The king is weak to this son also. He is a handsome man of great charm, like David in his youth; success in his dealings with people comes his way too often and too easily. Hence it comes about that he seeks to seize the sovereign power for himself. He prepares systematically for an insurrection. At the city gate he intercepts the people who come to the king to have their disputes settled and gets them on his side. This is the description given: 'So Absalom stole the hearts of the men of Israel.' He set on foot a conspiracy and had himself proclaimed king in Hebron and a great part of the population supported him. David had to flee from Jerusalem, 'the city of David', pursued by insults, a bitter path (II Sam. 15). On this path, however, something that his youth had made bright and strong returns to David: the loyalty of a friend. Not only his commander in chief, Joab, but also a Philistinian commander with his troops, whom David had given permission to leave, stood by him: 'Wherever my lord the king shall be, whether for death or for life, there also will your servant be'. David crosses the Jordan back to Machanaim. There too he finds friends who stand by him in his hour of need. Absalom pursues him and is defeated in a terrible battle by the superior commander, Joab. Absalom, who is riding on a mule, gets his head caught in the branches of an oak tree and is killed by Joab. Again David is unequal to the situation: he indulges in inordinate and unworthy grief for the son who has deceived and tricked him. He has to be severely checked by Joab in order that he may show himself to the people who have remained true to him. The hour is so critical that even now it has almost come to a revolt on the part of the northern tribes. Immediately afterwards the Benjamite Ziba makes another attempt to rebel, with the detachment of the northern tribes

[1] These words occur in the LXX and Vulgate *(Translator)*.

from David as its goal. It is thanks only to Joab's decisiveness and
stubborn determination that this rebellion also is nipped in the
bud.

The events at the king's court in the last years of David brought
little satisfaction. David was crippled by the heavy blows within
his family. He had become a weak, old man. Hateful intrigues and
rivals' quarrels grew up round the question of the succession:
Solomon, a son of Bathsheba, emerged from them as the heir to
the throne. In these struggles yet another son of David's, Adonijah,
who had already been invited to be king by one faction, had to lose
his life. He is not the only one. Joab also, the most daring and honest
man of David's day, was a victim of this strife between factions and
was murdered. At last Solomon was firmly established on the
throne; the country had peace again, but there was something
oppressive about it, reminiscent of the peace of the grave. This
question forces itself eventually upon every reader of this gripping
and moving story of the succession to David: will this kingship
have a good end? But that is not the sole impression that remains.
At the end there stands before us the figure of David—the figure
of a man. Little of his glamour remains. At any rate, he will not be
remembered by his people in the way he is described in this powerful historical work. The man who compiled this chronicle of events
at the king's court has ventured to give a mercilessly objective report. He has not tried to make anything out of David. He has left
him as he was; a man with his good and bad sides and quite often a
weak man. Not a trace of ruler-worship or royal exaltation! That
God is God and we are men is taken seriously by this historical
document. It is a sober statement of the fact that in our world
even distinguished men are like other men in the main. This narrative of the succession to David which says very little about God is
situated at the very heart of the Bible however, in that, like the
whole Bible, it is very unfriendly to all human exaltation. For it
knows that all human exaltation detracts from God's honour. This
then is the real positive value of this story: with unforgettable
seriousness it declares that if God had something in mind for this
people and intended to journey with them, if God gave the house

of David a promise and a position of great importance for the future, then in this history it is God who disposes. The great thing that is happening here is God's activity. The greatness appropriate to this activity does not belong to men or to David. If anyone is to be praised here then it is God.

It is this assertion which gives the history of the succession its importance in the Bible of Christianity. This royal history points inexorably to the next king. Few stories of the Old Testament point to the future so clearly as this one with its final question 'What is the result of this kingship?' Furthermore it has something to say to Christianity also about the treatment of heroes and great and famous men in the course of God's journey with his people. It would be better for the Church of Christ if it had more often spoken with this unsparing objectivity of the leading Christian personalities and the key figures of church history. There is, unfortunately, too much idealizing, too much human exaltation and too much trust in human greatness. It would be an excellent thing if we took with us from this account of the history of David the reminder that Israel was able to speak of its greatest king in this way. It was able to speak of him in such a way because it gave the glory to God who is the Lord of history and who could achieve something great even through David, a very imperfect tool.

6 · *Solomon in his Glory*

T H E account of Solomon given by the Book of Kings (I Kings 3-11) stands out by its peculiarly stiff, formal and impersonal style. There is no longer any trace of the human intimacy and passion found in the narratives of David and Saul. This style is probably a true reflection of his reign. It is apparently a new type of kingship, different from that of David, nearer to absolutism, a kingship which needed to make itself seen and felt by a brilliant display of power and glamour. Solomon was the first to maintain a court which sought to be like those of the oriental kings, with a great harem, a great crowd of servants and magnificent buildings and large-scale expenditure. In this way an estrangement between king and people arose quite involuntarily. A great distance separated the king and the simple Judaean farmer; the king was surrounded by a court ceremonial that hardly allowed him to come into contact with the people any more. The king had now become His Majesty.

Politically Solomon was able to maintain the kingdom of David about the height it had reached under his father; although, it is true, towards the end of his reign the structure of the kingdom was torn in two and it crumbled away at the edges. There was always another row of bordering, tributary territories, so that the king still disposed of what was a remarkable kingdom for the people of that time.

In domestic politics Solomon took a measure which brought him a great deal of money, it is true, but which had a disastrous effect on the future; the military service to which all the Israelite tribes were liable when an enemy threatened was extended by Solomon into peace time—and he waged very few wars it seems—to supply forced labour. In doing this Solomon overstepped the competence of a king in Israel. Now there was forced labour in their own land! This measure could only be put into effect by means of an extensive organization. Solomon divided the land into twelve districts, and introduced officials and overseers. It was the beginning of an organized state, which in its centralized structure was the very opposite of the old tribal confederacy and its patriarchal arrangements. The king's officials, who naturally possessed royal privileges, constituted a new propertied class. Thus there entered Israel, for the first time since its foundation, two classes opposed to each other. More must be said about this class later when we come to the prophets.

Solomon made an important contribution in the area we today call 'cultural'. In his period, and chiefly through his court, an independent cultural life developed in Israel. He was a great builder; the centre of his life's work was the building of the temple at Jerusalem, which occupies the largest part of the account of Solomon (I Kings 5-8) and the building of the new royal palace on Zion. Apart from this, however, Solomon built a great deal else. In

I Kings 9.19 and 10.26 mention is made of 'chariot cities' which Solomon planned for the chariots and horses. In the following verses there is a detailed description of the import of horses from Egypt and of their export through the king's traders. One of the most valuable results of the excavations in Palestine has been the discovery at Megiddo of such a 'chariot city' belonging to Solomon. The foundations of the horses's stalls are well preserved; the individual horse-boxes separated from one another by posts can still be recognized, and even individual stone mangers are still preserved. These stables are laid out on such a large scale and so carefully that the statements in I Kings 10 are fully confirmed. By means of one such discovery as that of Solomon's stables the period of Israel's kings is suddenly brought into the clear light of historical reality. A person today can step from his car and walk along the passage-way between the horse boxes where Solomon's horses stood and his officers shouted to the servants to harness the horses! Recently traces of an important copper-iron industry have been found. There are furnaces for smelting and plant for refining, going back to Solomon's time probably. In I Kings 9.26 it is recorded that Solomon built ships in Ezion-geber near Elath on the Sea of Reeds, and that he equipped fleets which carried chiefly gold and precious metals to Palestine. This Ezion-geber has now almost certainly been discovered (by the American archaeologist Nelson Glueck); on the same spot were copper mines and copper kilns. As a result of these new discoveries the surprisingly swift rise from Saul to David and from David to Solomon with his riches and splendour is more understandable. Up till then Palestine had been a purely agricultural country; under Solomon Israel became a country with important commercial and industrial undertakings. This great boom declined rapidly, of course, with the division of the kingdom after Solomon's death. But that Israel really did reach a height of prosperity at the time of Solomon can no longer be doubted as a result of recent discoveries.

Almost always corresponding to such an increase in commerce and industry is an increase in cultural activity also. Solomon has gone down in history as the wise king. The story of his judgement

(I Kings 3.16-28) describes his wisdom. Judging was one of the areas in which wisdom was specially able to develop in the ancient world and was particularly valued. The Queen of Sheba (South Arabia) visited Solomon because she was attracted by the reputation of his riches and his wisdom: 'she came to test him with riddles', and she soon discovered that he could give an answer to all the questions which she put to him. We have stumbled here on a very old and primitive type of 'intellectual conversation' practised throughout the world. The asking of riddles and the solving of them is an early form of knowledge where knowledge is surrounded by play, play in a much higher and nobler sense of course than we generally give the word. This game of asking and answering riddles was the form of intellectual competition which once occupied something like the place in men's social life that book reading occupies today. Reading detective novels is for well-educated people today a very similar form of participation in a riddle game.

A third way in which Solomon exercised his wisdom was in composing maxims and songs and fables about animals or plants (I Kings 5.9-14). This is one of the surprisingly precise notes, small but pregnant with truth, in the historical books of the Old Testament which provide us with the key to unknown territories. Now at last as the result of research into folk lore it has become clear very recently that what is stated in this small note corresponds closely to an early form of pre-literary proverbial wisdom which gave birth to the following forms: riddles, maxims, songs and stories or fables of animals and plants. Only a little of all this is contained in the Bible itself; but what has been preserved fully confirms this estimate of Solomon's wisdom. We can be certain of this—that in Israel under the first kings a vigorous proverbial wisdom flourished. It was a pre-literary proverbial wisdom, sometimes expressed in quite small unities such as the forms mentioned above. We must picture to ourselves a great number and variety of songs, sayings, riddles, stories and fables; there is not necessarily any exaggeration when it is said of Solomon: 'he composed three thousand proverbs and his songs were one thousand and five'. They had their place in the life of the people in assemblies and festivals, village gatherings and festival evenings, on journeys and above all in the social life of the king's court, where this pre-literary proverbial wisdom was consciously fostered and concentrated for the first time.

In this proverbial wisdom they were also glad to learn from one another, as already indicated for example by the visit of the Queen of Sheba. In Egypt the art of making proverbs had already existed for thousands of years and it is no wonder therefore that Israel's close commercial connections with Egypt led to a cultural exchange also. In particular, Israel took over a great number of Egyptian proverbs, as the Book of Proverbs which has been preserved in the Bible still shows. In that first fine spring of cultural activity in Israel it became clear that wisdom had international currency and that people were willing and anxious to learn from other nations in this field. The international, universal character of knowledge has its roots here.

In another respect, however, the assimilation of foreign values must have led to severe conflicts. Attached to Solomon's court was a large harem to which foreign princesses also belonged. It was under-standable that in a foreign land they continued to worship the gods of their own country; but Solomon let them build shrines for the gods of their country in the environs of Jerusalem and that must have given great offence to the simple Judaeans who were loyal to their God. The later judgement of the Deuteronomist, which can be clearly heard through the language of chapter 11, was probably justified in that Solomon himself must inevitably have been drawn into these foreign cults. This was an attack on and a threat to the pure, loyal worship of Jahwe. There was a further factor, too; Solomon had to import a whole crowd of foreign, above all Tyrian, craftsmen for his numerous buildings, especially for the building of the temple. Art and religion met in their handiwork. The motifs with which they decorated the walls of the temple, the style and form of the vessels which were manufactured by them for use in the temple and its cult—all this could not help but import foreign elements into Israelite worship. Perhaps this infiltration of foreign elements into Israel's worship as a result of Solomon's temple was much more insidious than the present account permits us to see.

In the last part of I Kings 11 three sections begin with the words: God 'raised up an adversary against Solomon ...'. Solomon's idolatry will have a greater effect on the future than all the economic and cultural splendour which his reign did in fact bring. The building of Solomon's kingdom did not stand on any very firm foundation. It needed only one attack for all Solomon's glory to suffer a sudden collapse. There is one further point about Solomon's reign to be noticed: during his long reign the word of a prophet never came to him. This is very unusual, since otherwise throughout the whole period of the monarchy the line of kings is accompanied by a line of prophets. Only once, right at the end, does there come a prophet's word, the word of the prophet Ahijah announcing the division of the kingdom to Jeroboam. Jeroboam was still a taskmaster of Solomon's at that time. All the more unusual that no prophet's word came to Solomon. Corresponding with this is the fact that we are told more than once of a direct conversation between God and Solomon; thus, at the beginning where God allows Solomon a wish (I Kings 3), and in the temple consecration prayer (I Kings 8), in which a conversation is carried on. Does this mean that somewhere behind all this stands the fact that Solomon aspired to a form of the kingship in which the king had a more direct connection with God than ordinary men had? Is there here a case of a deliberate encroachment of the oriental 'divine son kingship', which has been concealed as much as possible by the later accounts? This cannot be excluded. This much at any rate can be said: this period of Israel's greatest wealth and great cultural vigour belongs to one of its most dangerous and critical periods.

7 · The Kingdom Divided

T H E reign of the first three kings in Israel spans something less than a hundred years: the second period, the time in which northern Israel was an independent kingdom covers exactly two hundred years. In these two hundred years twenty kings ruled in Israel: on average a king had ten years of rule (in Judah in the same period there are twelve kings). There is a definite reason for this frequent change of kings in the northern kingdom. It is explained by what happened when the northern kingdom separated from the southern kingdom.

How the division came about is described in I Kings 12. Solomon's domestic policies were behind it. Solomon had not only called up the Israelite tribes for military service, but also for forced labour in peace time. He had set up a system of compulsory labour as a result of which every adult Israelite had to become part of a labour-pool for a definite period. This was the other side of Solomon's wealth and splendour: the compulsory labour of the Israelite citizens. Revolts against this had already begun while Solomon was still alive. Jeroboam one of the northern Israelite overseers appointed to superintend the workmen, made an attempt to revolt. The revolt was crushed but Jeroboam himself escaped and fled to Egypt. In this insurrection of Jeroboam a prophet Ahijah from Shilo played a decisive part. It is related (I Kings 11.29-40) that he went to meet Jeroboam on an open field one day; there he tore a new garment which he was wearing into twelve pieces and gave ten of these to Jeroboam. Jeroboam is to retain ten of the tribes of Israel, only two are to be left to the house of David. Once more, therefore, as with the first two kings, a word from God on the lips of a prophet heralds the beginning of a new reign. The dissection of the large, rich Solomonic kingdom takes place at God's command and the division is grounded on the failure of the great, wise and mighty king Solomon at the decisive point: in obedience to God. The beginning of the history should be recalled at this point (I Kings 3). There in a dream God allows Solomon to make a wish. He does not ask for wealth or a long life, but for 'a wise and discerning (i.e. attentive) mind' and this request pleases God so well that he grants him the other. At the end, however, it has to be said that Solomon failed at the decisive point so that his work could have no permanence. 'What is man that thou art mindful of him, and the son of man that thou dost care for him?'

As long as Solomon was ruler it was possible to avoid a split.
Immediately Rehoboam, Solomon's son and heir, succeeded to the
throne the break came. How it came about is a perfectly classic
example of an erroneous political decision. David and Solomon
were kings of Israel only by their personal union, on the basis of a
covenant. Thus the covenant had to be renewed with the new king
Rehoboam. This was to take place in Shechem, the place where
Joshua had held the general assembly of the tribes. The northern
tribes attached a condition to the renewal of the covenant. 'Your
father made our yoke heavy. Now therefore lighten the hard service of your father!' First of all Rehoboam took council with the
elders who had served his father Solomon. They advised him to
accede to the demand and offered reasons for their advice by suggesting that if he gave way on this point the union could only be
strengthened. Then, however, Rehoboam took council with the
young men who had grown up with him at court. They could only
lose by any relaxation of the demands on the northern tribes. There
are very clear traces here of the growth at Solomon's court of a
new ruling class which has lost the old feeling of the brotherhood
of the whole people and seeks deliberately to live on the work of the
lower classes. They advised Rehoboam to do the opposite and to
increase the demands upon the northern tribes still further. He
should answer like this: 'My father chastised you with whips but
I will chastise you with scorpions!' Rehoboam followed the advice
of the young men; the result was that the northern tribes dissolved
their personal union with the king of Judah. The proverb with
which the division was completed has been handed down:

> What portion have we in David?
> We have no inheritance in the son of Jesse.
> To your tents, O Israel!
> Look now to your own house, David (I Kings 12.16)

This division was final. The two parts never came together again.
This immediately brought about an important change in Israel's
worship. The northern tribes made Jeroboam king over Israel. He
saw his kingdom threatened by the fact that Jerusalem had become

the central sanctuary for all the tribes since David had had the ark brought to Jerusalem and by the fact that people went therefore to Jerusalem to the great festivals, even from the most northerly part of Israel. Jeroboam must have feared, with justice, that Jerusalem would always remain the capital and this could have political consequences. Accordingly, in two cities of the northern kingdom, in Bethel and Dan, he created two new principal sanctuaries for Israel and set up images of bulls in both : 'Behold your gods, Israel, who brought you out of the land of Egypt!' The bulls were probably not intended to be images of God in the strictest sense, but only pedestals or supports for the throne of God, so that the commandment not to make images was not directly broken; apart from this the formula used to install the bulls makes it clear that Jeroboam continued to hold fast to Jahwe, the God who had brought Israel out of Egypt. The facts of the case have been made to seem much coarser by people of later times speaking of bull-worship and Jeroboam's idolatry. But the bull is for Canaan an ancient, traditional symbol of divine fertility; through the images of the bulls, even if they were only intended as pedestals to God's throne, Canaanite elements must have forced their way into Israel's worship almost of necessity. In addition, there was the double nature of the bull-images which tended to obscure the absolute oneness of God; this was very dangerous in a totally polytheistic environment. It is very understandable, therefore, in view of the establishment of these new centres for Israel's worship that in northern Israel a life and death struggle soon flared up around the question whether Jahwe alone was the God of Israel, a struggle against the gradual permeation of worship by infiltrations from the indigenous religion of Canaan.

The record of this struggle occupies a considerable amount of space in the Books of Kings. In fact the Deuteronomic historian is more interested in this controversy than in the purely political events of the period. We learn very little from his work about the wars, about the change of ruling houses in northern Israel, about this whole period of the Israelite monarchy. For large sections of these 200 years only quite scanty data have come down to us in the

Books of Kings; the length of the kings' reigns in Israel and Judah, a little about the wars, about the changing of ruling houses in northern Israel, about battles between Judah and Israel and only very seldom a detailed description of foreign or domestic affairs. We have to take into account the fact that in these two hundred years much that was important took place which we shall never know anything about. If the majority of the kings in this period receive a simple negative judgement, then we must see in this too a certain one-sidedness, because the historical work which is our only avenue to these times lays down very strict criteria which are limited to a small number of events. Probably this is especially true in the case of the Israelite king, Ahab. He is of interest to the account in the Book of Kings only in the discussion connected with Elijah, and thus he fairs very badly. But probably Ahab was a very able ruler, one of the most active kings of Israel who had great importance for the history of Israel. From the names of his sons, who all had the name of Jahwe, it can be inferred that he was at least willing to remain true to the God of his fathers. That he worshipped only Baal, as the Book of Kings says in its summary judgement, would be difficult to support. The description of the opposition between Ahab and Elijah is right in that Ahab did not come out sufficiently radically and clearly against the influences of Baal worship at critical junctures, and in that Ahab himself—just like David— made serious mistakes in the course of his reign. Nevertheless, we are not by any means given a complete picture of the reign of this king.

8 · Elijah and the Remnant

T H E stories of Elijah and Elisha take up a specially large amount of space in the Books of Kings. They extend from I Kings 17 to II Kings 9, and are only seldom interrupted by historical information. In them for the first time we see the history of prophecy in greater fullness by the side of the history of the monarchy. A prophet was already standing next to the first king; the prophet

Nathan played an important part in the life of David; Jeroboam is promised the rule of the ten tribes by a prophet. The same prophet, Ahijah from Shilo, later announced God's judgement to Jeroboam (I Kings 14.1-18). On several occasions we are told of prophets who interfered with the course of history (I Kings 12.21-4; 13; 14.1-18; 16.1-4). Now, however, in the fight between Ahab and Elijah, comes the first big difference between king and prophet—at any rate, the first of which we possess a detailed description.

Something must first be said about the style of this history. Among the stories of Elijah are some which correspond exactly to the descriptions of later prophecy. This is specially true of the account of Naboth's vineyard (I Kings 21). In the centre of this story stands a word of Elijah to Ahab, which in its sharpness and pregnant brevity has probably been preserved exactly as it was spoken at the time. Alongside it, however, are descriptions of his activities which sound so completely different that the question must be raised whether it is really the same Elijah. The story of God's judgement on Carmel (I Kings 18.20-40) belongs to the second block; likewise, the story of Elijah's ascension into heaven (II Kings 2.1-12). The first story, specially its conclusion when Elijah slays the priests of Baal (18.40), is not easy for the Christian Church today to listen to as a part of the Bible. It is not the gruesomeness of this act as such that is repellent—gruesome deeds are reported more than once in the Old Testament, they belong to another age with different standards—but the fact that here a prophet not only announces God's judgement but executes it with his own hands. It should first be simply established that this is the only time this happens in the history of prophecy. A further difficulty lies in the fact that God's judgement on Carmel is concerned with a sacrifice, and therefore the system of worship. Apart from this story, the prophets whom the Old Testament describes do not have anything to do so directly with sacrifice, which is the business of the priests. In this respect also, therefore, this story is exceptional among the usual accounts of the prophets. For this and many other reasons quite a different explanation of this story has been suggested by Old Testament scholars. It will be given here with the express warning that this is only a possibility, and makes no claims to give the absolute truth. It is suggested that the story of God's judgement on Carmel does not intend to describe a solitary historic event, involving the individual Ahab, Elijah and the priests of Baal; rather it represents the continuing struggle between Jahwe and Baal, which raged at that time in Israel. The participants in this story are, then, not intended to be individuals but representatives. Ahab represents the Israel at that time, of which Elijah once said, 'How long are you going to halt on both sides?' This would explain why the position of Ahab in the whole proceeding was so remarkably passive and hesitant, so unlike a king. Elijah represents zeal for Jahwe, the company of those who remained faithful to Jahwe in Israel at that time, and the priests of Baal represent Canaanite religion. The story describes the struggle of the minority who trusted in Jahwe against the superior force of the indigenous Baal religion and the indecision and neutrality of the majority. The battle is decided through the intervention of God, who reveals himself to his people as the Mighty One, the Helper. Thus Baal worship is defeated and the few who maintain their trust in Jahwe gain the victory.

The story of Elijah's ascension belongs to the group of Elisha stories at the beginning of the second Book of Kings. It is true to an even greater degree of the Elisha stories that they represent a type of narrative which cannot be accepted as a historical record as it stands. A simple observation may serve to make this clear. If we compare what we are told of the prophet Elisha with what the Book of Isaiah says about the prophet Isaiah, then in comparison with Elisha, Isaiah is a simple, straightforward man, possessing only the word which had been entrusted to him, a man not marked by resourceful action or miraculous powers; in fact, apart from his preaching, nothing special. Elisha, on the other hand, must have been a powerful man who performed a great number of striking miracles, ranging from the very small to the very great, according to the narrative in II Kings 6 : he is able to bring an axe head which has fallen into the water to the surface again, and a whole army is struck with blindness at his request. In explaining this story something must be said which will cause offence to many a reader. If Isaiah is represented in the Old Testament as such a simple, straightforward man, so powerless and very ordinary, while Elisha is a powerful man by reason of his great number of miraculous deeds, then this must be attributed to the style of writing. From everything that we know of the history of prophecy we simply cannot accept that Elisha was so much more forceful, spiritually powerful and effective than Isaiah, Amos or Jeremiah. The account we are given of these, the written prophets, is one of extreme objectivity, rigour and simplicity. The narratives of the prophet Elisha are of a completely different sort. We must not hesitate to call them legends—at least in part. They are pious, edifying narratives, which originated in the small circle of Elijah's and Elisha's disciples, who are mentioned several times in the Elisha stories; they were related within the group in order to honour and commemorate the master. Those readers who object to the word 'legend' may be asked to read once through II Kings 6.8-23, quietly and with an open mind. Hardly anyone is familiar with this story. Its similarity with legends from the early Middle Ages or the early Church cannot be mistaken. If one tries to explain it as a historical description of historical events, then the result is bound to be something cramped or unreal. If one reads it as a legend, however, which transmits in a simple legendary way something of the activity of the man of God as this man lived on in the thoughts of his group of disciples, then it gains a meaning and a value for us also. There is a profound meaning of great beauty in the way this legend tells how the man of God went out from a beleaguered city right through the middle of the enemy who had been struck blind, and pointed his trembling servants to the hosts of God who surround him with protection: 'Fear not! For those who are with us are more than those who are with them!' Elisha is able to lead the blinded army of the enemy into the centre of the King of Israel's troops in Samaria; but instead of their being destroyed there the man of God ensures that they are served with food and drink and then allowed to depart in peace.

The whole of this narrative bears the stamp of a legend so clearly

and unmistakably that it is surely better to concede this openly
instead of passing over such stories in the Bible in embarrassed
silence. Why shouldn't there be a place for legends also in our Bible?
Why should we not simply concede that Elisha as a historical
figure seems remote to us—unlike the written prophets—and we
can now recognize only the legendary trappings with which his
figure has been clothed? There are, too, stories of Elisha which are
quite different, such as the story of the Syrian Namaan's healing
(II Kings 5); it should not be denied, however, that alongside these
clear and simple narratives many of the miracle stories are intended
as legends and should be regarded by us as such. But it is not possible to draw a hard and fast boundary between the legends and
straightforward records. The reader of this highly unique group of
stories, the like of which is not to be met with again, even in this
Testament, must be content with the fact that straightforward
records and legends pass over into one another here. This also
applies to the story of Elijah's ascension which cannot be classified
in any simple way. We may be certain that this story also has
legendary traits; but it should remain an open question, what actually happened on the occasion of Elijah's departure from Elisha.

The historical figure of the prophet Elijah stands out clearly
from a series of other narratives. The appearance of a prophet at
that time who relied only on God and his message in opposing the
king and queen, and who acted as God's representative, made a
deep impression on the minds of the people, and cannot be omitted
from the general course of Israel's history. Elijah was given a remarkable nick-name, 'Chariots of Israel and its horsemen'. (II Kings
2.12; in II Kings 13.14, Elisha also is so named.) This name which,
we can confidently infer, really transmits what Elijah signifies for
his contemporaries, shows us an important development in early
Israel. The judges were the divinely appointed deliverers of Israel.
The kings took their place; the first kings were anointed by the
command of God because God had appointed them to rescue Israel
from its enemies. But already the early history of the monarchy
has shown that the kings were not only deliverers of the people;
they could also seriously endanger the whole nation by their dis-

obedience. New ways and new means of deliverance were needed when this happened. It was to meet such a danger that God sent the prophets to be the new and quite different agents of help and deliverance. This is how the name of Elijah, 'Chariots of Israel and its horsemen', is to be understood. This name is evidence that in Israel at that time there must still have been a small group who recognized what sort of help the nation needed to repel the threat of Canaanite syncretism and who believed that the prophet was the one whom God had sent to his people as a 'trusty shield and weapon'.

The occasion of Elijah's appearance on the scene was the Baal-cult which the daughter of the Tyrian king, Jezebel, the wife of King Ahab, had introduced. The reproach already levelled against Solomon in the Book of Kings—namely that the daughters of foreign kings in his harem were allowed to erect sanctuaries of their religion in Jerusalem—was especially dangerous in the case of the Tyrian king's daughter because the religion and worship of her own city were very similar to the religion and worship of the earlier inhabitants of northern Israel and lived on under cover. Quite definitely, the popular religion of Israel at that time was strongly influenced by the native religion of the country, in which nature deities, the *baalim*, played an important part. We can form some idea of what happened from the way in which in German lands, after they had been Christianized, a distinctive, syncretistic religion arose, responsible for certain quite strong features in German religion. In the figures of many saints fairly clearly recognizable features of Germanic gods lived on. In the belief in witches and ghosts much older and much deeper strands, reaching right back into animism, continued to exist and to be active under cover. They survive even to the present day in some parts—chiefly in North Germany. From this comparison it can be estimated what a powerful, spiritual struggle was waged at that time in Israel under the kings.

The God whom Israel acknowledged in its confession of faith, 'Jahwe is our God', was a God of history, the deliverer in the wilderness, the helper in battle. It was hardly conceivable that when

Canaan was occupied he could become a God of settled farmers overnight; for such a God's activity and sway were a completely different matter. The land had its gods who had belonged for thousands of years to the hills, the fields, the woods, the rivers and springs, and who were at home among them. The prosperity of the state, the fertility of the cattle, the coming of the rain, the constancy of the springs—all this was in the minds of Canaan's population inalienably linked with the worship of the gods of the land, its own 'lords' (*baal* means 'lord'). It was very understandable that the incoming Israelites asked whether it would not be wise and beneficial if now, in the territory of the new land and its gods, room were made for worship of the gods of the land on a limited scale, side by side with the worship of Jahwe, the God of the wilderness. Or, however, if they were convinced that at least Jahwe alone ought to be worshipped, they thought that at any rate something of the forms of worship as it was practised in Canaan ought to be taken over. One result of taking over the old centres of worship was that almost as a matter of course something of their usages was also transferred into the new worship. But it was at this very point that a great danger lay. The smallest compromise with the Baal religion of the land could lead to its slow and gradual but irresistible resurgence. Thus the faith of Israel in the God who had delivered it from Egypt would be slowly undermined. This could not happen without a struggle, and in this struggle the issue was simply whether Israel would remain faithful to its God or not. There was only an Either-Or.

Involved in this struggle was Elijah. It is clear from the account of one of Elijah's encounters with God (I Kings 19), which is very closely connected with God's revelation to Moses (Ex. 19), that Elijah wanted to bring his own times into connection with Israel's origins and early history in the wilderness and to link them with the work of Moses. Elijah fled from Jezebel into the wilderness and almost died there. He is sent on his way to Horeb, the mountain of God in the wilderness-period, by a messenger of God. There on Horeb he spends a night in a cave and God reveals himself to him. He goes before Elijah in a storm, in an earthquake, in a fire, but each time it is said that God was not in it. This shows Elijah that the normal ways in which God appeared in the wilderness and during the wanderings and conquest are now past; he comes in a different way now, 'in a quiet gentle whisper'. The expression could also be translated 'in a low whispering voice'. The sequel shows that this in itself is not the revelation, but only a preparation for it; it is the silence into which a word now comes. It is true we cannot explain this unique story of a revelation with complete finality, but it probably points to a change in the history of God's dealings with his people. Elijah is being shown that perhaps the history of his people will not be determined by the powerful, elemental manifestations of God, whose truth is attested chiefly by their power to frighten, but by the quiet word which makes its way without violence and which God's messenger has to deliver.

The first word which comes to Elijah out of the stillness is a question, 'What are you doing here, Elijah?' And the answer of the prophet, who in his lonely fight for the exclusive worship of Jahwe despairs of his extremely difficult task, is a complaint. It is the first complaint of a prophet in the Old Testament. We think back to the complaints of Moses and recognize the line which leads from Elijah to the later prophets, above all to the laments of Jeremiah and finally to the cries from Gethsemane. The cry here is, 'Israel has forsaken thee'. This is the new situation to which the prophets address themselves; that is the new crisis into which they are sent as deliverers and which they, as the messengers in the front line, have to experience, from the complaint of Elijah on Horeb to the tears of Jesus over Jerusalem.

Yet a further factor which characterizes the coming period appears here for the first time. At the end of his answer to the complaint of Elijah God gives a promise for the future: 'Yet seven thousand will I leave in Israel; all who have not bowed the knee to Baal'. God can no longer deliver his people now by liberating them from their enemies; it is against his own people who have forsaken him that he must take steps. Accordingly Elijah is commanded to anoint Jehu and Hasael. Jehu will rise up as a revolutionary against the godless royal house; Hasael, a Syrian, is confirmed and strengthened by a prophet of Israel in his battles against Israel! Thus the decisive issue in the future will concern loyalty to Jahwe. A division between the faithful and those who turned from God is no longer avoidable and the promise of God therefore can no longer be applied to the whole nation without division but only to a remnant. Much later Isaiah will give one of his sons the name 'A remnant will return' (*Shearjashub*). It is this same promise which is here given to Elijah. Here in Elijah begins the gradual separation of the people of God who are faithful from the people of God who are simply Israelites by birth; here are the first traces of the equation of the Church with those who put their trust in God.

9 · *The Nature of Prophecy*

T H I S story of Elijah on Horeb is fully in the tradition of prophecy as we know it from the books of the prophets. (That it is an early form of prophecy is indicated by the fact that *inter alia* Elijah's commission to anoint Jehu and Hasael is a direct interference in political events. The transition from charismatic leadership to early prophecy can be recognized here.)

The story—wonderfully well told—of Naboth's vineyard (I King 21) is also fully in line with the later major prophets. It stands midway between Nathan's word to David (I Sam. 12) and the words of Amos. These three points are joined by a straight line: the prophetic word has exactly the same character in all three places. Thus, this story is such a direct and vital reflection on the unparalleled situation at the court of Ahab and his queen that we certainly have before us in this chapter, an authentic, historical tradition.

The influence of the Tyrian king's daughter, Jezebel, could not be limited to matters of worship; worship was connected too closely with politics at that time for that to have been possible. Jezebel brought with her a basically different understanding of the kingship. The Canaanite city king was in his province a great king on a small scale; his rule was absolutist and the most important thing about his relationship with those beneath him was not brotherhood but domination. Ahab wants Naboth's vineyard which borders on his palace. He offers Naboth full compensation but Naboth is unwilling to part with the land of his fathers. According to ancient Israelite law Naboth was quite justified in this refusal, and Ahab knew it. It vexes him greatly, however, that he does not possess the vineyard, although he knows quite well that even as king he is not justified in taking away an Israelite farmer's inherited property. The land has been lent to Israel by God and every Israelite has a right to his inheritence, a right direct from God. Now Jezebel intervenes. A marvellous scene! She demands: 'Do you now govern Israel?' In other words, to her way of thinking, he is no proper king who acquiesces in such a situation. If the farmer is so stubborn as to refuse the king's offer he deserves what is coming to him. Jezebel takes the matter in hand. She procures false witnesses who bring a false charge against Naboth: 'You have cursed God and the king!' That was enough. Naboth was put to death by stoning; the king had the right to confiscate the goods of a man condemned to death. The king let it happen, and the officials who were used for this judicial murder obeyed the authorities. With this the case seems to be ended. This is the moment for the messenger of God.

His opposition to the king was an act of God bringing deliverance to his people. Through the sin of the king God's people as such were seriously threatened. If a single deed of this sort succeeded and if the people of God let it pass, then something would have proved stronger than God's activity and law. A great deal depends here on the first encroachment which a king is willing to allow (exactly as in David's case!); for such an act marks out a path from which it is difficult to turn back. It was very important that someone was there to oppose the first encroachment. The office of God's messenger as one of intervention can be recognized especially clearly on this occasion. He must intervene wherever there is ultimate injustice, where God's law is disregarded and the law is abused to perpetrate a murder—if none of those whose task it is to safeguard justice steps in. Throughout the Old Testament the task of

the prophets is to intervene at a point where one of the established
authorities fails. For this very reason prophecy is not itself an established authority, but whenever such a moment as this has arrived
the messenger is summoned by God. This is an indication of something very important for prophecy. It is just not true that prophecy
is concerned with the 'prophesying' of the future first and foremost. The pronouncement of judgement on Ahab is only secondary
and additional. The primary task is to intervene at a moment when
it is necessary for the reasons stated above. Prophecy always has to
do with the present, first and foremost. The message of the prophets
is a word addressed to the present situation of an individual or a
community; this word to the present takes its validity or necessity
from the future. The future will demonstrate the necessity of the
word spoken in the present.

Elijah opposed Ahab with these words : *Have you killed and also
taken possession? Therefore thus says the Lord: 'In the place where
dogs licked up the blood of Naboth shall dogs lick your own blood'*
(I Kings 21.19). We have before us in this word the basic form of
prophetic utterance in all its purity. The word consists of two parts,
an accusation ('You have . . .') and a declaration of punishment or
judgement. Between the two stands the 'messenger's formula', like
a link binding the two parts together : 'Therefore thus says the
Lord'. The first sentence does nothing except establish a fact. The
word points like a finger to an obvious fact which anyone could
prove for himself and needs no sort of prophetic gifts—except that
even in this specific situation no one dares to draw the king's attention to this bare fact. The second part declares that Ahab will meet
a violent death. It is in this sentence, in this declaration of judgement, that he is a messenger; he had neither the ability nor the
right to say this of his own accord. The declaration of punishment
is joined with a sign : Ahab will meet a violent end on the very
spot where Naboth had to die. This sign is sufficient to show Ahab
the connection between his death and the death of Naboth, the
connection of guilt and punishment.

Prophecy as a whole is concerned with preserving this connection. The people of Israel promised God to remain faithful to him

(Josh. 24). A covenant has been made between the people and God. It was clear from the first that there would be lack of faith and disobedience on the people's part. Therefore, provision was made to enable them to return to God when they had gone wrong. If, however, the people as a whole or their representative, the king, committed a serious sin and nothing happened, then the connection between the activity of God and man was broken at this point. This makes it seem as if a man could do what he wanted if only he had the power to succeed, and as if all talk of God's intervention, of loyalty to the covenant, of obedience and punishment were simply pious words. Prophecy is concerned with the reality of the relationship between God and man, with the reality of God's activity.

At the time of Elijah the Syrian empire with its capital, Damascus, the foundation of which was recorded in Solomon's time, was Israel's most dangerous enemy. The wars with Aramaea (the name given to the Syrian empire by the Book of Kings) lasted approximately a hundred years—with varying results. They only ended when the Assyrian empire became so strong that, after oppressing and weakening Syria, it conquered and destroyed Aramaea and Israel almost at the same time.

In the chapter which follows the story of Naboth's vineyard we are given a description of an episode from the Aramaean war about the year 852. The king of Judah, Jeoshaphat, visits Ahab the king of Israel; they decide upon a united expedition against the Aramaeans. Before the army sets out the king of Judah asks the king of Israel, 'Enquire of the Lord first!'—and now there takes place a very peculiar scene, quite foreign to our way of thinking and feeling. The king of Israel has the prophets who belong to his court, about 400 men, summoned, and asks them, 'Shall I go to battle against Ramoth-Gilead, or shall I forbear?' The prophets give the answer the king wants, 'Go up; for the Lord will give it into the hand of the king'. This answer is not enough for the king of Judah. Apparently he is suspicious. He asks, 'Is there not here another prophet of the Lord of whom we may inquire?' The king of Israel answers, 'There is yet ... Michaiah, the son of Imlah; but I hate him, for he never prophesies good concerning me'. While this Michaiah is being brought and the two kings are sitting on raised thrones at the gate in their armour, ready for battle, the four hundred prophets make every effort to reinforce their oracle. One of them makes himself iron horns and acts out how the king will destroy the Syrians, while the others continue to repeat the oracle. Meanwhile Michaiah is brought. The messenger who brings him tries, even while they are on the way, to influence him so that he should say the right thing by telling him the others had unanimously prophesied success. Michaiah replies, 'What the Lord says to me, that will I speak'. When he stands before the two kings and is questioned, he says in fact the same as all the others. Evidently no one had expected that, and now the king presses Michaiah to tell him nothing but the truth. For the first time Michaiah now says what had really been laid upon him : he prophesies a heavy defeat. He is struck by the spokesman of the prophets of success and thrown into prison by the king. He is to remain there until the army returns in safety. The army goes to war in spite of Michaiah's warning; Ahab is seriously wounded but bravely keeps himself propped up in his chariot facing the Syrians until evening. Then he dies. The news spreads through the army and it disperses. The corpse of the king is brought to Samaria on his chariot; the king is buried. 'And they washed the chariot by the pool of Samaria, and the dogs licked up his blood ... according to the word of the Lord which he had spoken' (I Kings 22.38).

In this story we are confronted by a phenomenon of great importance for prophecy in Israel, which belonged to it from now on right up to the last prophets before its disappearance: the opposition of prophecy of success and prophecy of doom. It must have existed long before this story, otherwise Jehoshaphat of Judah's obvious suspicion of the prophets of success in spite of their numbers and noise would be unintelligible. We know very little about these prophets of success who apparently existed before the early monarchy. We know them principally only from the descriptions which reject them out of hand; perhaps we are not given enough information about them in the Old Testament because next to nothing was said about them except negatively. A few recurrent features can be clearly recognized.

In the Elijah and Elisha stories reference is made to schools of prophets. Elisha is Elijah's disciple and successor. Mention is also made of anointing to the prophetic office; and groups of prophets, who live together, maintain a strong tradition amongst themselves and form a distinct class, are spoken of. It could be that such groups or schools of prophets were attached to certain sanctuaries with quite definite functions there. Unfortunately the Old Testament displays no recognition of this, at least directly. One trend of present-day Old Testament scholarship regards this so called 'cult prophecy' as very important; in this connection the opinion is also advanced that most or all of the prophets leaving literary evidence were actually cult prophets, although there is no direct tradition to this effect. The attempt has been made, for example, to explain the call of Isaiah (Isa. 6) as a cultic experience, belonging to cultic prophecy. There have, it is certain, been exaggerations and much pure fantasy in this recent discovery of cult prophecy; but it is true that such a cultic prophecy did exist in Israel at the sanctuaries of Canaan, at which these cult prophets had definite cultic functions. We shall have more to say later about its possible nature.

The most important difference between these cult prophets and the prophets who are described in the Old Testament as the *true* prophets sent by God is not simply that the one group prophesied only success and the others only doom. This only emerged in the course of time as the strongest palpable difference. It is that the cult prophets had a permanent position, whereas the prophets like Michaiah ben Imlah, Amos and Jeremiah were called by God at a particular point of time. They were subsequently silent for a long period until a fresh call came, or they came forward on just one specific occasion for a short time and then resumed their former occupation. This was what happened in the case of Amos, who in opposing the high priest Amaziah emphasized, 'I am no prophet or prophet's son' (= prophet's disciple). This, then, is the important difference: to be a prophet in the true sense one had to be called specially by God; to be a prophet in the style of the cult prophet one had to belong to a group, which formed something like a school where one grew into the tradition of the group by studying and serving.

It is easy to understand why such groups of prophets were established chiefly in the residences of the kings and at the royal sanctuaries. Here they had the special task—so much, at least, we know quite definitely from a number of accounts—of answering the questions put to them by the king and king's officials when important political decisions had to be taken. In the case of the first kings the oracle would be consulted through a priest on these occasions. Evidently, this custom of consulting an oracle gradually fell into disuse and its place was taken by the custom of consulting the court prophet or prophets. These court prophets must have had their place at the courts of Israelite kings over a long period of time. We meet them from Ahab onwards, but probably they already existed at the court of David, where the seer Gad is perhaps their forerunner. They continued right up to the last king of Judah, Zedekiah; Hananiah, the opponent of Jeremiah, was employed by him. As they had a permanent position they must have lived on the proceeds of their occupation, and they were certainly maintained at court by the king. It is understandable therefore that—especially as a group—they quite naturally tended to prophesy success for the king. This is only human and an alternative was hardly possible. But herein lay the great danger that they would prophesy something that was not really a message from God but was based on human considerations. And this was often the case according to the account of the Book of Kings and the prophetic books.

This, however, led to such encounters as we find described in I Kings 22 and frequently elsewhere: one prophet stands against another, both claim to speak in the name of God, but the one contradicts the other. It is the shattering picture of the Church which is divided in itself, the tragic drama of the servants of God who are at loggerheads and so are found not worth believing in the eyes of the world.

It must be said here, once and for all, that although today in the twentieth century a Church of Christ has openly opposed a Church of Christ more than once for all the world to see, and although 'religious wars' have taken place and do take place, this is unavoidable at certain junctures of history. If, as at the time of National Socialism, a group in the Church passes over in silence or approves open crimes on the part of the state authorities, the Church in such a country can only be saved by a life and a death conflict with this group (which continues to hold its religious services in the name of God) on the question whether it still speaks and acts in the name of God. There are moments—as the moment which this chapter (I Kings 22) describes—in which action in the name of God is possible only *against* the prevailing trend in the Church.

The first eight chapters of II Kings consist almost exclusively of stories about prophets. Reference has already been made to some of these stories, but there is one which ought to be mentioned again at this point. An important group of the Elijah-Elisha stories has to do with the private sphere of their personal life. Here we come across the same difference which we found between the seers and the prophets (cf. what was said about I Sam. 9ff). The men of God in the early period obviously had the home, the family, for the scene of their activity; the mission to the nation as a whole and its leaders came into the foreground only gradually in the case of some prophets with the result that we know virtually only those who spoke to Israel, to the kings and to those called to lead. The Elijah-Elisha stories mark the transition clearly. Words and actions which concern national history occupy only a small part of the picture. And even within this group of stories the theme is only partly concerned with the political aspect of the nation's destiny. Many of these stories speak of the countryside and its crops and above all of the coming of the rain. Standing in a close relation to these narratives is the largest group of Elijah-Elisha stories which are concerned with personal destiny. Quite clearly we have to do with an earlier strand of 'prophecy' here, an activity of the men of God who ought not to be called prophets really, who were active in the sphere of the family (prior to the rise of history), to whom men in great distress came, who were widely known and of whom stories which often passed into the fantastic were related. Thus it was related of Elijah (I Kings 17.7-24) how he created meal and oil in abundance for a widow who was starving and raised her son from the dead; of Elisha how he made unwholesome water drinkable, supplied water to the army when it was almost dying with thirst and promised a child to a childless woman; several miracles connected with food are recorded of him, one of which (II Kings 4.42-4) quite surprisingly resembles the feeding of the 5,000 in the New Testament. It is told how both Elijah and Elisha raised a dead child and also how Elisha recovered a field for the child's mother.

In between all this stands the story of Naaman, the Syrian, a commander who is ill with leprosy. His wife has a servant girl who had been captured as booty during a Syrian raid into Israel when she was a little girl. And, as often in the Bible, a very small insignificant person shows the great and mighty the way to salvation. She tells her mistress of the man of God, Elisha, who would have the power to heal the leprosy. When Naaman finally comes to Elisha, Elisha has word sent to him by a messenger that he should bathe in the Jordan seven times, then he would be clean. To the commander this instruction seems an insult and he turns back homewards in anger. It is the servants once more who have the stronger faith and persuade him to do what Elisha had suggested. The story concludes with a valuable and impressive picture of religious belief at that time: the Syrian commander is, as a servant of the king, bound to worship the God of his country and its royal house, but from now on he must honour the God of Elisha by whose power he was healed. He asks Elisha therefore for a load of soil— as much as two mules could carry—in order that he might be able to honour Israel's God in his homeland on this patch of earth brought from the land which is now his holy land too. It is a first indication pointing into the far distant future—pointing to the power of salvation which is to go forth from this land one day. Naaman is an officer of Israel's most dangerous enemy. This did not prevent the prophet Elisha, who was zealous for Israel's God, from helping Naaman in his suffering without regard to the fact that the enemy's fighting strength would be increased if he were healed. We hear in the distance the words of the Saviour.

There is still one final word to be said about this large group of Elijah-Elisha stories. They stand in many respects very much on the fringe of our Bible. They contain much that is offensive from the standpoint of the New Testament; many of these stories have quite definite legendary characteristics. But, on the other hand, these stories contain striking resemblances to a whole series of Gospel motifs. The most important types of stories used to relate Jesus' deeds are to be found here: healing (leprosy), miracles of feeding, raising of the dead, helping the poor. Nowhere else in the Bible except in these two places does all this occur together. This is a very remarkable fact which has barely been noticed until now. What conclusions can be drawn from this we cannot say; it may be reserved for later generations to recognize the connections here. Only one thing can be assumed as probable. The man of God who dealt with the personal suffering of those stricken by poverty and misfortune, and who helped them without regard to their person, and to whom men came in their need, did not manifest himself in Israel only in the two cases of Elijah and Elisha. There were probably such people later also, who were at work quite unobtrusively, even if we hear nothing further about them. The possibility that many of the later prophets were active in this direction is not excluded, although we hear nothing of it. This, however, is certain: the healing and help of the Saviour, as related for us in the gospels, has its roots deep in the history of the Old Covenant; it is a continuation of what God wanted to establish and develop in this nation. In his activity as the Saviour also Jesus of Nazareth fulfils and perfects what God has been doing for this nation from the beginning.

For us, however, who are seeking today to understand the Bible as a whole once more, and to let the Old Testament speak to our present situation and work on it, it is a specially encouraging sign to find that there is meaning in listening to the Old Testament even in the parts which we find difficult to approach and where we —rightly—find much to repel us. We shall be wise not to suppress our critical faculties, but to state openly once and for all where we feel obliged to part company. It will, however, be wise in this case not to make any general judgements, but to wait until the

passages of the Old Testament which seem to have nothing further
to say to us also begin to speak afresh.

10 · The Death of a Nation

T H E decisive influence in the section of royal history which now
follows is still the activity of Elijah and Elisha. In II Kings 9-10
the revolution of Jehu is reported. Jehu is anointed king by a
disciple of Elisha (II Kings 9.1-15); he exterminates the house of
Ahab in a wild revolution; he attacks them as worshippers of Baal
and attempts a reformation in the sense of pure Jahwe worship—
but it does not lead to any real change in Israel. A parallel revolution in Judah, however, brings a reforming king to power—Jehoash
of Judah. Northern Israel, it is true, experiences a period of political
eminence and economic prosperity under one of the following kings,
Jeroboam II; but this final period of prosperity does not last long
and already carries the seeds of destruction within it. About ten
years after the death of Jeroboam II an Assyrian army under
Tiglathpileser IV (745-727) attacked Israel. Tribute had to be paid,
provinces were lost, the kings changed in rapid succession and in
the year 721 Samaria fell after a long, heroic resistance. The greater
part of the population of Israel was deported, foreign settlers were
brought in and the kingdom of Israel became the Assyrian province
of Samaria. Northern Israel's independence as a state was brought
to an end for all time.

There is a detailed report of only one event from this section of
Israel's history: the revolution of Jehu (II Kings 9-10). It should
not be passed over simply on the grounds that we as Christians
can only read it in our Bibles with horror. Jehu, a commander in
the army of the Israelite king, is anointed king by a disciple of
Elisha. We are given a wonderful description of the scene. The
officers of the king are sitting at a banquet when Elisha's envoy
comes to them and says he has a message for Jehu. Jehu goes with
him, they go into the house and the prophet's disciple anoints
Jehu with the express command to exterminate the house of Ahab

and likewise Baal worship in the land. Jehu goes back to the officers. They ask, 'Why did this mad fellow come to you?' And as Jehu tells them, at first hesitantly, the officers hail him as king. Now follows the terrible drama of the bloody revolution of Jehu. Like a wild hunter he rides furiously with his men to the place where Joram, the king of Israel, is recovering from the wound he had received in the battle against the Aramaeans; with him is Ahaziah, the king of Judah. Both the account of the meeting between Jehu and the kings, which is presented with such skill, and the description of the course of the revolution, derive their whole drama from the words of greeting which are exchanged. It can hardly be reproduced in English. When, for example, the king sends to Jehu to enquire how things stand and receives no reply, he knows that Jehu's coming means treason. But it is too late to think of flight. Both kings fall, pierced by the weapons of their own soldiers. A terrible scene of murder follows—beginning with Ahab's sons and ending with the priests of Baal, who are murdered in the act of offering sacrifice. In the midst of it all, Jezebel, proud and unbroken to the last, is killed.

If one has read the story of this bloody revolution to the end, revolution which was brought about through an anointing in the name of Jahwe and which also swept away a royal family with all its members in the name of Jahwe, and which exterminated Baal worship by brutal force, one cannot avoid asking: was it really God's will? There is no unequivocal answer to this. All this really did happen at God's command; nothing can alter this. Elijah had already been told on Horeb (I Kings 19) that God had chosen Jehu as his instrument. But even within the description of the revolution of Jehu there are indications that this is not the whole of the story. At the end of this account it is said, 'In those days the Lord began to cut off parts of Israel' (II Kings 10.32). Jehu does not receive a judgement of approval in spite of his extermination of Baal worship. 'Jehu was not careful to walk in the law of the Lord with all his heart.' Moreover, Jehu did not succeed in destroying Israel's enemy, Syria; he was defeated and had to pay a heavy tribute. Thus, Jehu was not honoured in later judgement on account of his bloody extermination of Baal worship. There seems to be a suspicion running through the description that this was the end of a road. Such internecine fury was no longer the way by which God's people could be delivered. At the same time—whether intentionally or not —the tendency of that earlier prophecy to think it could save the inheritance of the old days by its destructive zeal for the God of Israel was definitely called in question. Seen in this way, this description of Jehu's revolution could stand in the Bible in all its naked brutality as a warning, or at least as a question.

This, at any rate, is certain : in the northern kingdom, as in the southern kingdom, not many decades before their eclipse a vigorous attempt was made to return to a pure Jahwistic faith and to a pure worship of Jahwe. In the north this happened through the bloody revolution of Jehu. The report of the Book of Kings itself has to concede that it made no decisive difference. This has to be linked with the fact that northern Israel, although it rose once more to glittering heights under Jeroboam II, was completely destroyed with the capture of Samaria in 721 and those deported never returned but were scattered among foreign peoples. In the south this last great attempt at reform took place through a reformation led by the king : the Deuteronomic reform. From this reform, shortly before the collapse of Judah, forces were set in motion which bore fruit later after the catastrophe among the survivors, and which made an important contribution to the creation of something new.

Josiah's reform stands in the middle of the last section of the history of the kings of Israel, namely the history of Judah from the collapse of the northern kingdom to the fall of Jerusalem. A highly unique and also highly significant similarity between the Old and New Testaments calls for comment at this point. In the middle of the New Testament stands a death, in the middle of the Old Testament also stands a death. In the New Testament it is the death of a man; in the Old Testament it is the death of a nation. One of the distinctive features of the Gospels which is often commented on and often emphasized, is the fact that the history of Christ's passion is so emphatically central that it has been said that everything else which the Gospels tell us about Jesus of Nazareth is only an introduction to the story of the passion. It is like that in the historical books of the Old Testament. The great Deuteronomic history (from Joshua to II Kings) is conceived from the point of view of a group of survivors looking back on the nation's catastrophe; the whole work slopes towards this catastrophe. The distinctiveness of the historical writing in the Old Testament consists precisely in this—it takes the end of a nation's history, its collapse, very seriously as God's judgement on this whole history and it sees in it—paradoxical as this seems—the goal of Judah's and Israel's history. The work as a whole sprang out of an affirmation of the nation's death, based on the acknowledgement of guilt. This is what constitutes the uniqueness of this history, and establishes its connection with the 'historical books' of the New Testament, the Gospels, most plainly. Even the nation's pre-history, the story of the patriarchs, is secretly determined by this. We may recall what was said in the account of Abraham. Abraham is the man who has to give up something. With Abraham the whole Israelite-Jewish nation is the nation which has to give up something. It is the history of a nation going to its death, and its climax is the history of the death of the one man who also had to die and whose death was to be the seed of the new people of God.

11 · From the Fall of Samaria to the Fall of Jerusalem

II Kings 18-25 describes the last act of the history of the Israelite-Jewish kingdom, the short period of the independent kingdom of Judah after the collapse of the northern kingdom, with very few dates and facts. We hear in greater detail of King Hezekiah, in whose reign Isaiah was active, and King Josiah, in whose reign Jeremiah lived. These two kings receive a positive judgement from the author of the history. Both carried through a reform of worship, both are praised as upright kings.

At the time of Hezekiah, in the sixth year of whose reign Samaria fell, Jerusalem escaped the same fate only by a hair's breadth. The Assyrian king Sennacherib marched against Judah seven years later

and captured all the fortified cities. Hezekiah surrendered and sent
Sennacherib a large tribute to Lachish, where his camp was. Even
the golden ornaments of the temple's doors and pillars were sacrificed for this tribute. In spite of this Sennacherib sent his commander to Jerusalem to demand the city's unconditional surrender. The
Assyrian commander stood in front of the city at shouting distance.
He tried to convince the men on the walls of the folly of resistance.
The words he speaks are a very remarkable example of how integral
a part of the common life—even between nations—religious faith
was. He knows very well that the soldiers on the wall are being
summoned to persevere by reference to God's help in distress. But
he also knows the weak spot of this faith :

> Do not listen to Hezekiah!
> For he misleads you when he says,
> 'The Lord will deliver us'.
> Has any of the gods of the nations
> ever delivered his land
> out of the hand of the king of Assyria? (II Kings 18.32-4)

After the failure of the first attempt to persuade the city of Jerusalem to surrender, Sennacherib sends a personal message to
Hezekiah repeating the same demand. There follows a scene which
shows that the throne of David is once more occupied by a king of
the sort described in the old promise to the house of David. We
read, 'When Hezekiah received the letter from the hand of the messenger, he went up into the house of the Lord *and spread it before
the Lord*'. Here is a king who has faith in his heavenly Father. In
his greatest need he goes to him and lays before him the cause of his
great grief with strong, simple faiths. 'God alone knows what I
should do with this letter; he alone can help now.' And then in his
distress he pleads to this God for help.

At this critical juncture the prophet Isaiah, the messenger of
judgement, the man of so many words of doom, is the one commissioned to tell the king that his prayer has been heard. The word
with which Isaiah has been commissioned at this hour is, it is true,
a word of doom on this occasion also (II Kings 19.20ff.) but it is

directed against Assyria; he announces to King Hezekiah that the city will be liberated. Sennacherib had in fact to withdraw from Jerusalem—this is said not only here but in an Assyrian chronicler's account of these events—and the city was once more delivered.

Of Hezekiah's son, Manasseh, the Book of Kings has only evil to say. He practised every conceivable manner of idolatry and put an end to all his father's reforms. He is pictured as a violent overlord, who 'shed much innocent blood'. He ruled longer than all the other kings of Judah, 55 years. Probably Judah was almost like an Assyrian province during these years; it is difficult to explain the long undisturbed rule of Manasseh otherwise. The report indicates that prophets rose up against Manasseh and declared God's judgement to him. But the few words concerning his rule are pale and general; we do not know what happened to Judah at that time. His son Amon was murdered after two years. The conspirators were killed by the country folk of Judah and Amon's son, Josiah, became king.

Josiah brought the land of Judah prosperity and greatness once more—for the last time. In the middle of his reign stands a fundamental work of reform, a real reformation which made a decided return to the bases of the old Israel's faith and order. The reform was only possible by casting off the Assyrian yoke. Assyria was shortly to collapse. Simultaneously with the reform of worship and social life Josiah was able to extend the country's borders and to restore to Judah a large part of what was once North Israel. The Davidic Empire seemed to be resurrected in its old glory and purity; the old hopes were roused and it really seemed as if now at last the fate of God's people had taken a turn for the better.

All the more terrible, therefore, the blow which destroyed all their hopes again: the Pharaoh Necho marched through Palestine from the south in order to defend sinking Assyria. Josiah opposed him but was defeated and killed. The two subsequent final decades up to the final collapse are closely connected with the history of the prophet Jeremiah; and Judah's end will be discussed in connection with the work of Jeremiah.

Josiah's reform, although it disintegrated after his death so that little or nothing of it remained, retained its importance. The law book, on the ground of which King Josiah carried through the reform, was the book preserved for us as Deuteronomy. Important movements spread from this book into the future. It was the basis of the Deuteronomic school which collected the traditions of Israel in exile; it gave them a firm foothold in catastrophe, so that they might proceed to repentance and fresh deliberation. We must now discuss this book in greater detail.

The fifth Book of Moses, called Deuteronomy in the Greek translation (the Septuagint), is in the form of a long speech made by Moses to the people of Israel before they crossed the Jordan. The speech links the period of the wilderness with the period of the settlement in Canaan, by means of retrospective reminders, anticipatory exhortations and, above all, by the proclamation of a law (Deut. 12-26) whose spirit is that of the very earliest period. It is the law of Josiah's reformation in the year 622, not long before the end of the state. Old Testament scholarship is almost completely unanimous that we are dealing here with a reforming law which originated in the decades before its discovery in the temple and its proclamation as a great planned reform; it stemmed from the *âm haarets*, the country folk of Judah together with a group of priests. The aim of the reform was a purification of the worship of God from all foreign elements, a definite return to the foundations of Israel's faith; the preaching of the prophets, which for the most part lay idle, was recognized and affirmed. The most important feature of this reform was the centralization of all divine worship at the Temple in Jerusalem; all the 'high places' were to be destroyed because the worship at them was shot through with foreign elements which were harmful to the faith of Israel. Next to this reformation of worship, the primary objective was to expedite a social reform. If the relation of the people to their God was to be set in order again, this must of necessity affect the way men lived together; and thus there runs through the whole Deuteronomic law a strong social emphasis, which had its most important source in the social preaching of the prophets.

There are two themes of social reform which are specially

characteristic, and should be noticed at this point. The first concerns slaves: running throughout the whole law is the warning to treat slaves as persons, to draw them into the life of the family and the religious festivals, and to allow them sufficient holidays. There is, in addition, a law providing for the release, after seven years, of Israelites who have become slaves through debt. The basis of all these laws and warnings is the recollection *Remember that you, too, were a slave in the land of Egypt and that the Lord your God set you free; therefore I give this charge to you this day* (Deut. 15.15). The second concerns the possession of land: the accumulation of many pieces of land by one person, the oppression of small farmers, the abuse of justice by the rich, who apparently legally appropriated for themselves the possessions of the poor, had already been attacked by the prophets with great severity. Now Deuteronomy tries to create a legal basis for a social reform guaranteeing a just division of the land. The reason for this social reform is again a recollection: 'Do not forget,' says Moses to Israel, 'that this land is the gift of your God! Do not forget that you came into this land poor, and that you were not the first to create its civilization; do not forget that you came from the wilderness!' Translated into practical terms, this affirmation of the past means that *all* the nation's families have basically the same share in the land which God had given to his people; no one ought to depart empty-handed, nor should some gain too much and others too little from the possession of the land which was entrusted to all. Thus, from the recognition that the land was a *gift*, which should be divided justly, grew a social programme, which had as its motive the affirmation of God as the real owner of the land and the recognition that the land itself had only been entrusted to the people on loan. Both sides of the Deuteronomic reform, the religious and the social, are thus based unanimously and emphatically on the beginning of the nation's history: the deliverance from Egypt, the journey through the wilderness, the promise and the gift of the land. It is natural therefore that Moses has been made the author of this call to conversion and that this call is portrayed as a speech of Moses at the moment before the entry into the promised land. In this way the whole reform is placed under the authority of Moses. By placing the introductory and concluding speeches, which framed the whole Deuteronomic law, in the mouth of Moses, a definite and emphatic connection with an earlier period, namely that denoted by the name Moses, is achieved. It is not intended by this, however, to make Moses the literary author or historical source of the law. Later still the whole Priestly law is represented as God's revelation to Moses—with exactly the same intention: to tie it firmly to the origin of the nation's history. Under no circumstances should we make our understanding of what is historically 'authentic' or 'unauthentic' the standard in this case.

12 · Deuteronomy: Theses of a Reformation

I N the middle of the introductory speech (Deut. 1-11) stands Israel's confession of faith in one God, its Lord (Deut. 6.4ff.): Hear, O Israel: the Lord our God is one Lord; and you shall love the Lord your God with all your heart and with all your soul and with all your might. Israel's confession of faith in the one God, the so called Shema (=Hear . . .) stretches from the early days of Israel to the present day. It is the creed of Christianity just as much as of the Jewish Synagogue, where it still occupies the centre of every act of divine worship right up to the present day throughout the whole world. It has been of far reaching importance for the history of mankind. The term 'monotheism' has been coined to describe this faith, and the worship of one God has been seen as an unusually highly developed and spiritual worship. This still does not do justice to the real importance of this faith, however. If one compares the faith of Israel in one God with the religions of neighbouring countries the decisive difference is this: in the Canaanite, Babylonian and Egyptian religions the gods have a history of their own. This is what constitutes the substance of myth: it deals with stories of the gods, dramatic episodes between the divine beings—struggles for ascendancy, struggles for areas of power—together with all the drama supplied by the bisexuality of the gods, as in dramas of love and the family with all their accompanying phenomena. What happens between gods and men remains peripheral. In the Babylonian creation-myth, for example, the creation of the earth and of men is only a part of a divine drama, which being on a higher more divine plane is much more important than the creation which results from it.

In the Old Testament the relation of God and his creation, the world, is radically exclusive because he is the one God. He has no history in a separate divine sphere; his only history is with his world and his people. Here lies the real importance of what is called mono-theism—that is, belief in one God. The one God is he who is turned toward the world with his whole being. Consequently it is natural that the science of history as it developed in the western world has its most important source in the Bible and specially in the Old Testament. Out of the Israelites' view that history involved a per-manent, unchanging relationship with the *one* God, whose dealings spanned the heights and depths of human history and linked them together in a meaningful way, was born the ability to understand and interpret the flux of history. Where, as in Egypt and Meso-potamia, the dynasties of the gods change places with the dynasties of kings, a science of history which seeks to interpret the flux of events cannot develop.

The belief in *one* God gives rise to something else: because those who called to God, who prayed to him and praised him have to do only with one God, their call to God is given an absolute, exclusive character which is unattainable where there is always a possibility that perhaps another god is to be invoked, perhaps an-other god can help, if the god invoked refuses to act. This is the reason why the God of Israel, the one God, was invoked even on those occasions when he refused to act, when he apparently did not hear the call. Then the invocation could turn into a complaint against God. But even when it became a complaint against God it remained the only possibility! This is why even in the times of greatest distress, in the times when God was silent, when many or almost all lost confidence in him, the people of Israel still continued to seek him and invoked him *against himself*, until he had mercy again. This is why many individuals found themselves in great travail and cried out against God but refused to abandon him whatever happened.

Hear, O Israel: the Lord our God is one Lord. The drama of the history of the gods became, in Israel, the drama of the history of God in relation to his world, to his people and to those who wrestled with him, and this imparted to this history its unique poetry, intensity and unswerving purpose. It was only on the basis of such a belief that in the time of God's judgement there could arise such an intensive hope—prepared to wait for the turning point, for deliverance and for the One who should come, prepared to wait through centuries of humiliation until the time was fulfilled. Without this belief in *one* God it would never have been seen that the redeemer, Jesus Christ, came not only for his own time and country but at the mid-point of time for the sake of the whole world.

This basic belief of the Old Testament community in the *one* God (in Deut. 6) is preceded in Deut. 5 by a catalogue of the Ten Commandments, the Decalogue, which has been inserted in the midst of Deuteronomy to represent the fundamental principle of the community's life. Deuteronomy, like our catechisms, brings together the fundamental principles on which community life is based: law and faith and the most important elements of worship (esp. Deut. 12, 26). The fact that the Decalogue is recorded twice (Ex. 20 and Deut. 5) tends to be noted mechanically and learnt by heart. But what is the sense of doing this if one does not know what significance the basic Ten Commandments have in these two particular cases? In Ex. 20 the Ten Commandments are the pillar of the revelation of God's will to his people, who have been delivered by God (the foundation-event of their history—Ex. 1-14), and protected by him (Ex. 16-8), and now, ready to serve him, are listening to what God requires of them (Ex. 19-20). In Deut. 5 the Ten Commandments are affirming this same will of God at the end of the nation's history, and are part of the reformation which, in view of the threatening collapse, seeks once more to set before the nation the will of God as revealed at the beginning.

The connection of the two places in which the Decalogue occurs will become still clearer if one notices how Deut. 4-6, which contains the kernel of Israel's faith, is set within a framework of historical reminiscence which binds the present with the events of the beginning. Deut. 1-3 briefly sketches once more the journey following the departure from Sinai up to the arrival in Moab before the Jordan; Deut. 7-10 looks forward to the conquest of Canaan, but constantly links this with what happened in the beginning, from the departure out of Egypt to the making of the covenant and the idolatry at Sinai. Thus, the hour when God's people first understood God's will and bound themselves to it is linked to the present moment when Israel has to decide once more.

The Old Testament constantly emphasizes the particular importance of decision: obedience towards God must be a free decision. The last part of Deuteronomy leads up to the challenge to decide freely, in one of the Old Testament's most beautiful and most powerful passages, both in language and content (Deut. 30.11-20). God's will, set forth in the previously proclaimed laws (Deut. 12-26), is now finally set before the community of God's people as a simple offer springing from the father's love. *For this commandment which I command you this day is not too hard for you, neither is it far off . . . But the word is very near you; it is in your mouth and in your heart, so that you can do it. See, I have set before you this day life and good, death and evil . . . I call heaven and earth to witness against you this day, that I have set before you life and death, blessing and curse; therefore choose life . . . loving the Lord your God, obeying his voice, and cleaving to him.*

In this word it is possible to recognize what the law, the command of God, meant to the community of God under the Old Covenant: the offer of life, success and blessing. The law here has nothing of the character of a threat or limitation, a list of prohibitions, a barrier or wall: on the contrary, it is a clear, attractive way, a way to life, which one may tread with joy and pleasure. This way is not too difficult, for God knows where our limitations and temptations lie. And all the many and varied commands, precepts and warnings constantly lead back to the one single commandment which is at the same time a great and wonderful offer: to cleave to God with trust and vigilance and to obey his words. In conclusion it should be emphasized once more that the affirmation of God's command is an act of free decision: therefore now choose life!

In the law contained in this framework there are some important features which deserve stressing. The first and the last chapters of the law deal with worship. Sacrifices are to be offered at only one single place 'at the place which God will choose'; the Temple at Jerusalem was meant. The basis of this command that the cult should be centralized has already been touched on; it was expected that it would lead to a purification of worship from all the foreign elements which had crept into all the shrines throughout the land. It corresponds in the sphere of the cult to the command to worship the *one* God (Deut. 6): it is a way of putting this command into effect. This limitation of sacrificial offering to the city of Jerusalem had a far reaching result, however. Since the families who lived out in the country could only come to Jerusalem at the great festivals, their opportunity to offer a sacrifice was limited to these few occasions; they could no longer sacrifice on the altar the prescribed part of every beast they killed. Accordingly the killing of beasts at home was released from the law of sacrifice and now became a secular affair (Deut. 12.15: 21-5). That was a tremendous change in the ancient world. For thousands of years the practice of killing domestic animals had been a religious act. There is a similarity here between the reform of Deuteronomy and the Reformation of Christianity in the sixteenth century, which likewise resulted in the radical liberation of whole large areas which had previously been fenced in by the cult.

In the last chapter of the Deuteronomic law a rubric for the offering of the first fruit of the field is given and it illustrates the spirit of the Deuteronomic law particularly well (Deut. 26.1-11). An Israelite farmer comes to the temple with the first fruit of his field in a basket, which the priest takes from him and places in front of the altar. And now the farmer repeats certain words with his offering. It is a confession of faith—to bring these fruits, brought from his field to the shrine, into connection with the mighty acts of God for his people, from the patriarchal history to the gift of the

land. In a way which is surprisingly simple but completely convinc-
ing, this rubric succeeds in bringing the everyday life of an Israelite
farmer into connection with the great line, spanning hundreds of
years, of the history of God with his people—or rather, it succeeds
in blending them into a unity. The farmer himself repeats the 'brief
historical creed' alone before the altar, and as he does so *really and
truly* links the corn in his basket with what God has done for his
people from the beginning, from the deliverance out of Egypt onwards. Whenever he thanks his Lord in heaven for the harvest he
has brought home, the first fruits of which stand there before him
at the altar, his thanksgiving expresses itself in the hymn which
his fathers sang whenever God performed his mighty acts for them.
Here field and church, work and altar, daily round and worship are
equally necessary and equally meaningful in the same world.

What we could learn from this chapter, if only we dared! With
courage and imagination, but with the same simplicity, we could
join the work of modern man in its manifold variety with our creed,
our prayer and our hymns. Men of our day would at last notice
again that worship is concerned with their everyday life and the
realities of their work, to the extent that these are brought into
connection with the mighty acts of God.

There are a great number of commandments in Deut. 12-26 to
which we today should be well advised to pay attention. Luther's
judgement that the laws of the Old Testament are antiquated
Jewish laws and do not therefore concern us should be emphasized
in its positive rather than its negative aspect. It is perfectly true that
we are dealing with the law of a historical people, tied to a
particular period in history. It is also true that these laws do not
concern us insofar as they could not be our laws, because historical
conditions have changed. Luther, however, did not know that the
law of the Jewish people was not complete and entire from the
beginning but only developed gradually, and that within the Old
Testament different stages of the law from different periods have
been recorded. They now describe for us an important part of the
history of God's people, and as such are exceedingly important.
But here and there in these laws tendencies which could be im-

portant for the Christian Church, and for the preaching of the Word, also reveal themselves. Running throughout the Deuteronomic law is a very strong and unmistakable social influence. It manifests itself in many places and in quite different ways but most clearly and frequently in concern for the poor and slaves. It has already been pointed out that this is definitely rooted in the social preaching of the prophets. *For the poor will never cease out of the land; therefore I command you, You shall open wide your hand to your brother, to the needy and to the poor, in the land* (Deut. 15.11). That is one example among many. But among these social laws are some which point to something else. It is recognized that the social question is a question of mutual self-respect and that a great deal depends on guarding the self-respect of the poor and needy. This receives expression even in apparently small details: *When you make your neighbour a loan of any sort, you shall not go into his house to fetch his pledge. You shall stand outside, and the man to whom you make the loan shall bring the pledge out to you* (Deut. 24,10-11). Much social legislation and many expressions of social help and welfare in our day would benefit enormously if there were only a trace of this sensitive consideration for the self-respect of the poor.

The social laws of Deuteronomy radiate a genuine humanity. The above commandment continues: *And if he is a poor man, you shall not sleep in his pledge; when the sun goes down, you shall restore to him the pledge that he may sleep in his cloak and bless you* (Deut. 24.12-13). It is an especially fine feature of the Deuteronomic law that this humaneness extends to respect for animals also (e.g. Deut. 22.4, 6ff.; 25.4). The members of the Israelite nation are expected to observe in surprising detail every need, every want and every distress, however small, in their environment and to interest themselves freely and willingly in this distress, whether it is the difficulty of a widow, the oppression of a slave or the injury of their neighbour's ass. This is the proof of whether they really love God with their whole heart and obey his words. When one reads these commandments of Deuteronomy today at the distance of two thousand years, one is bound to ask whether the Christian

Church has not a great deal still to learn in this respect. It may be that the simple dismissal of these parts of the Old Testament as antiquated Jewish laws has done great damage to the Christian Church, because nowhere in the Bible are general statements about love of one's neighbour related so concretely and specifically, in such a human and intelligible fashion, to the empirical conditions of everyday life, so that one simply cannot evade the issue any longer.

13 · When Your Son Asks You

W E began with the confession of faith in *one* God in the middle of the introductory speech in Deuteronomy. We shall end by describing from the same chapter (Deut. 6) another event which is even more important both in regard to Deuteronomy itself and to the whole Old Testament. The command to worship the *one* God is followed by the exhortation : *And these words shall be upon your heart; and you shall teach them diligently to your children.* Here is another similarity between Deuteronomy and our Catechism : it considers instruction of the children, the coming generation, as particularly important. By 'teach diligently' in the passage just cited, however, we should not think of 'cram'. Towards the end of this same chapter the way in which young people were instructed is described more closely : *When your son asks you in time to come, 'What is the meaning of the testimonies and the statutes and the ordinances which the Lord our God has commanded you?' then you shall say to your son, 'We were Pharaoh's slaves in Egypt; and the Lord brought us out of Egypt . . .'* (Deut. 6.20-1). Then follows the same confession of faith in the mighty acts of God in the midst of his people which we have already met with in the account of the bringing of the first fruits. A very similar situation is described in Josh. 4.21ff : *When your children ask their fathers in time to come, 'What do these stones mean?' then you shall let your children know* . . . There are many other similar passages, describing how the faith of the fathers was passed on to the children. In this there is something that seems of real importance for us : the reason for the instruction is in every case a question of the children, and indeed a question which is very understandable and natural, a *genuine* child's question. As they grow up into the world around them they stumble across something which they do not understand, and they ask their parents about it. Their parents do not give them pious answers but simply report how the events which the children would like explaining came about. In our present efforts to instruct the children in the faith of their fathers this very simple and natural process has been directly reversed in some respects; those who are asking the questions are the parents—or the teachers. A science has actually been made out of how the teachers have to choose the right questions to put to the children in order to teach them what they wish to teach them. This indication alone may serve to show how far we are removed from the simple procedure adopted in the Bible for passing on instruction regarding the mighty acts of God. Does not a great deal depend on the fact that the lives in which the faith of grown-ups is represented are often so rigid and conventional, so little infused by joy and passion that the children are given absolutely no reason by their excursions into this life for asking about worship, the fellowship of the Church, its customs and so on, because it does not seem to them really interesting and important for living?

One thing at any rate is firmly demonstrated by the description in Deuteronomy of the way in which the tradition is passed on to the coming generation. The tradition is genuine and alive, and the questions of the children are a natural growth, attracted by the life of the grown-ups with God. The answers simply describe what happened and what it was like, and the children and young people grow up in to the life of the religious community quite naturally, questioning, listening and taking in. And, it should be added, no instruction, however good, can take the place of what is portrayed here in Deuteronomy—children receiving from their parents the answers to their first questions about God, the Church and its festivals, and the Bible, and being led by those who bring them up and care for them to that reverence of God which compels a man to bow down before him.

VI · THE PROPHETS

1 · The Purpose of Prophecy

WE of the mid-twentieth century should attend to this! It is worth noting that there is hardly a part of the Bible which has been rediscovered so frequently in the course of history and which has, at the same time, failed to be understood by so many for so long. Every prophet in his own time and in his own way has been a foreigner; and the prophetic books have retained something of this quality. There come times when they suddenly emerge from obscurity and begin to speak with force, but then they become silent again for a long time or they are so misunderstood that one cannot form any picture of them. We of the mid-twentieth century, therefore, should give especial attention to this, because in our day a type of man is emerging who has little or nothing in common with the prophets. People are spoken of to-day as 'instruments', meaning by that people who accommodate themselves, whether they like it or not, to the age of the machine, people who are capable of minding a machine, who 'switch on' and then function. This accommodation to the machine was and is unavoidable; we should stop moaning about it. Who would really like the housemaid with the broom, who provoked Luther's famous words about 'her divine service', to take the place again of the housewife with the vacuum cleaner? It is precisely when the changed conditions of human work are fully accepted that it has meaning to pay attention to the part of the Bible which describes the prophets and their work. The prophet is the exact opposite of 'the instrumental man'. He has been called 'the mouthpiece of God'; but that is a very false, misleading picture. The prophets have nothing of an instrument about them, not even an instrument of God. That quite indefinable quality, which constitutes the true life of man, is integral to their existence. That quality is seen in the way love overtakes two people, brings them together, and binds them to each other, and in doing so scorns all institutions, all boundaries and conventions erected by men. Similarly, a prophet suddenly stands before the people or the king with a word from God. The prophets combine, to an unusual degree, the qualities of extreme constraint and extreme freedom, qualities which wherever they are found constitute the distinctive worth of 'what is human'. The prophets and prophecy absolutely refuse to be classified, organized, switched on, numbered or regimented in any way and that is why they emphasized and insisted that the genuine human bond authorized by God should not be broken.

The prophet is the exact opposite of the instrumental man for another reason also; in his life and work everything turns on what is most personal. They are messengers of God's wrath; but it is due to his merciful goodness that instead of judgement itself, the messengers of judgement came. These prophets embody both in their presence and in their words this insoluble opposition and inseparability of love and wrath. They are exponents of God's indictment of his people and bearers of his love to the lost. In the anguish of their cries God suffers for his people. The prophets are also personal in the deepest sense in that for every one of them the whole drama of prophecy is played out between two cries, the cry which they hear and the cry which they pass on. They have no set of doctrines, no system, no axioms; they are sent to pass on what they have received and only this. The real miracle, however, is the *succession* of prophets, which begins side by side with the first king of Israel and runs parallel with the royal history, coming to its end with the last king. Everyone of them is and remains an *individual*. Many stand quite alone, many have a small group around them. None moved the masses. The tension between each one of these individuals and the nation to which they were sent leads to a rupture. This nation is like a part of a mountain that had broken away from its base and slowly turns into a landslide. It is cracked and smashed until everything finally breaks up, and with a crash the whole lot races thundering into the abyss. In the midst of this mountain landslide stand the prophets, one after the other, from the moment when the first crack appeared right up to the last stage of the collapse. They neither can nor should hold themselves aloof from the landslide; they accompany it and sink with it—although they are the only ones who have not lost their connection with the base. All their work seems in vain. They make no difference to the landslide, they have—judged by our standards—no success. They come and call—and their call fades away. The next prophet comes along and the same thing happens. So it goes on for two hundred years, and if one adds the early history of the prophets four hundred years. Looking back one man says of this history of prophecy: *But I thought 'I have laboured in vain, I have spent my strength for nothing and vanity'* (Isa. 49.4). The coherence of this two or four hundred year long history of prophecy lies only with God. The fact that individual prophets repeatedly came, spoke, exhorted, suffered, despaired and became silent admits of no further explanation on the human side. From the human angle this constant succession of the prophets, which never brought the nation to repent, was meaningless. What purpose did it serve? If the mountain had already begun to break up what could all the words of the prophets accomplish? Were they not rather a sign of God's helplessness against a mighty force imminent in history? Why could God not stop the landslide, if it were still *his* people that was slowly crumbling? What was the point of the history of these powerless men who raised their voices in warning but were unable to alter anything basically? If the *secret*, the inexplicable secret, of the majesty of God as the Lord of history breaks into our human life anywhere, it is here in the history of prophecy. One very clear result of this secret is that prophecy cannot be classified as a spiritual or religious phenomenon in comparative religion; it does not fit our normal standards and categories. The pattern of 'rise, development, climax, continuation, result' with which we are familiar and into which we fit such a movement otherwise is not possible here. On the human level the single points of each prophetic appearance do not form a line. Each of the prophets stands at the end where he stood at the beginning, and the next one must begin afresh. The history of prophecy does not produce a counter-movement, which could halt the landslide. At the end of the line of prophets, at the beginning of which Elijah had raised his voice in complaint on Mount Horeb, stands a single defeated man, Jeremiah, who shares in the last collapse and is dragged off by the survivors on the last flight to Egypt, powerless and unwilling. The miracle lies in the *succession* of prophets, this startling paradox of the saving activity of God, which is hidden in the apparently unsuccessful but un-failing attack of messengers of judgement sent with unfailing regularity. Judged in itself and by the standards we have at our disposal, this history cannot make sense. All that can be said of it is what the servant of God said of his apparently fruitless work. The history of prophecy is the strongest pointer within the whole of the Old Testament to another book beyond it. The landslide and the final crash of the mountain is not the end. Out of the collapse grew something new. But this new entity has its roots in the preaching of the prophets. The prophets grow silent one after the other without any of them bringing the people of God to repent-ance. Nevertheless their words were a seed from which something new grew, as the prophet of the exile again says of the word of God which comes to men : *It shall not return to me empty but shall accomplish that which I purpose, and prosper in the thing for which I sent it* (Isa. 55.11).

2 · The Heyday of Prophecy

P R O P H E C Y has its day. In the course of Israel's history its be-ginning and end can be recognized fairly clearly; it has already been noted that it runs parallel to the history of the kings of Israel from beginning to end. It is true the prophets are spoken of both before and after this; but then 'prophet' is being used in a wider sense. Prophecy had a history both before and after; but prophecy in the narrower sense of the word is confined to the period of the monarchy. During this period the appearance of prophets was neither welcome nor regular. For long stretches during the monarchy we hear now and again of single words of the prophets;

but the full cry of prophecy is concentrated at certain points. Here again the prophets have their day, in that their voice is heard especially loudly and frequently at the decisive crises and turning points of history. This fact alone is an infallible sign that the prophetic word grows out of, and issues in, particular historical moments. One cannot detach the word from its context and obtain a valid, timeless wisdom, any more than one can subtract a message from the event it announces.

Israelite history contains four particularly serious crises. In the case of northern Israel there were (1) the war against the Aramaeans in the ninth century, and (2) the threat from Assyria in the eighth century, leading to the destruction of the northern kingdom. At the same time (3) Judah was threatened by Assyria, but was spared as if by a miracle. (4) Judah's final crisis came with the arrival of the Babylonian empire, by whose attacks it was overcome. The prophets grouped themselves round these four crises of Israelite history. At the time of the Aramaean wars Elijah, Michaiah ben Imlah (I Kings 22) and a series of prophets are active in the northern kingdom. The words of these prophets were not gathered together and handed down; all we know of them is what the historical books report.

The first period of written prophecy, approximately the period from 750 to 700, coincides with the zenith of the Assyrian empire. Amos (*c*.750) and Hosea (750-725) were active in the northern kingdom at this time, Isaiah (740-701) and Micah (722-701) in the southern kingdom. The two most important events of this period are the fall of Samaria (721) and the siege of Jerusalem by Sennacherib (701).

The second period of written prophecy, approximately the period from 650 to 600, coincides with the collapse of Assyria and the rise of Babylon. The prophecy of this period also revolved round the two most important events of the time: the destruction of Assyria (612) in Nahum, Habbakuk and Zephaniah, and the destruction of Judah and the capture of Jerusalem (597 and 586) in Jeremiah and Ezekiel.

A third period follows directly on the last event: prophecy in the period of the exile, represented by Ezekiel and Deutero-Isaiah. This period too revolves round an event of world history: the destruction of the Babylonian empire by the rising power of Persia. (Babylon fell in 485.)

The fourth period no longer belongs to prophecy in the strict sense, it is like an echo of what prophecy once was; as in the third period, the time of the exile, the opposition of state and monarchy which had determined the prophets' task was absent. Judah is now a province, one of the provinces of the Persian empire, and the nation of Israel has become the Jewish community in this province. In this fourth period therefore, historical events fall into the background. The new prophecy is only interested in the concerns of the Jewish community. The prophets Haggai and Zechariah, both about 520, and the prophet Malachi about 470, belong to this period. This last recognizable period of prophecy—which is, however, now changing its form—revolves round the restoration after the great collapse. Prophecy has had its day.

The rest of what is transmitted to us in the prophetic books (the Book of Daniel among the major prophecies, the Books of Joel, Obadiah, Jonah, the additions and interpolations in other prophetic books such as Isaiah 24-7, the additions to Zechariah and Deutero-Isaiah) has little to do with the classical prophecy of the pre-exilic period. They are after effects of prophecy from the last centuries before Christ, the period when men were waiting for something new.

Prophecy on the whole, therefore, set against the broad sweep of history, presents itself as the word of God's messengers in times of crisis; it runs parallel with the history of God's people and points to the times of crisis in the great kingdoms of the ancient world.

After a brief survey of these few dates and lines of the history of prophecy in Israel a very definite impression forces itself on one. This history was not fortuitous; what happened belonged necessarily to the whole of history. It cannot be accidental that in the course of Israelite prophecy the important dates of the history of the Near East from the beginning of the Assyrian empire to the Babylonian and Persian empires—which then formed the bridge

from the great empires of the Orient to the empires of the West—
are reflected. Here, behind drama on a very small scale, the drama
which takes place between the God of Israel and his disobedient
people in the small, bare land of Palestine, we trace drama on a
very large scale, the drama of world history. It is world history
whose heights and depths, rises and falls, come from the planning
and activity of the same God who is responsible for the journey of
the small nation of Israel—for the special history leading from
the call of Abraham to the coming of Christ. The history of prophecy demonstrates for all time that the one God who is active in
all events, however small or great, is the same God who directs the
course of history and intervenes in it. Assyrians and Babylonians,
Egyptians, Persians and Syrians, their kings and commanders, their
religion and civilization, meet in the words of the prophets. Pontius
Pilate, Cyrenius, Augustus, Herodes and Antipas have their part
in the history of Christ. And in the same manner, in every period
of church history, what happens in the Church and its fellowship
is never the whole activity of God—for this always reaches out
beyond the Church and comprises all that happens. There is still
this same contrast (which we can no longer grasp) between the
insignificance and smallness of the Church, where God's word is
heard and he is invoked and praised by a small group, and the
vastness of the world. World-shaking events occur outside, there are
great achievements by men who remain outside. Outside, it is not
clear that every activity of God signifies and desires the whole—
the whole world, the whole of humanity, the whole of history. We
must, however, let the history of prophecy continually tell us afresh
that connections *do* exist between what happens among the people
of God, often in such a shabby and poverty stricken fashion, and
the ups and downs of world events which have an appearance of
power. Usually we are not in a position to see these connections,
but they are sometimes suddenly illuminated, as here in prophecy,
to show that God is Lord of all.

3 · The Roots of Prophecy

T H E word prophet (from the Greek *prophetes*) does not mean 'one who sees or says something in advance', but the *pro* has the sense of 'in front of everyone, publicly'. The prophet, then, is one who states or declares something publicly. The Hebrew word (*nabi*) which lies behind the Greek word probably has the same meaning; although some interpret it as 'filled with rapture or enthusiasm'.

In prophecy, which has its roots deep in history, several lines converge. Influence from outside Israel may also have played a part in its birth. One predecessor of the prophet is *the seer*. There is a detailed description in the Bible of a seer called Balaam, who was summoned by Balak, the king of the Moabites, to cripple the army of Israel by a curse, which was however changed by God into a blessing (Num. 22-4). Samuel too is a seer originally (I Sam. 9). Gad is a seer at the court of David (II Sam. 24). Later we come across the seer Ahijah from Shilo (I Kings 14). We find traces of the seer in Elijah and Elisha also. The seer must have been very important in the early period, but we know very little of him. He appears not only in Israel; the seer Balaam, for instance, comes from a long way off, from the Euphrates. We come across the figure of the seer in many nations and many religions.

Another root of prophecy is the *ecstatic figure*. Religious ecstasy also is a widespread phenomenon in both primitive and civilized religion. A particularly clear example of a word of God heard and spoken in ecstasy occurs in the report of the journey of Wen Amon, the Egyptian. The event takes place in the Canaanite port of Byblos about the eleventh century BC, and thus in chronological and geographical proximity to Israel. At a much later date these ecstatic appearances spread over the whole Mediterranean basin, as in the case of Cassandra in the *Agamemnon* and the case of the Sybil at Cumae in Book VI of the *Aeneid*. Speaking with tongues in the church at Corinth also probably goes back to phenomena of ecstasy.

We can conclude with certainty from the Old Testament that there were forms of ecstasy in early Israel also; I Sam. 10.5ff. describes how Saul, after he had been anointed by Samuel, fell in with a band of prophets who were in ecstasy, and how he was infected by them. Similarly I Sam. 19.15ff. shows us how Saul, in pursuit of David, was attacked by ecstasy in the prophet's house at Ramah, just as his servants whom he had sent before him had been. The phenomenon is described more closely on this occasion : those who are attacked by the ecstasy throw their clothes from their bodies and lie naked on the ground in a trance. Moreover a whole series of other passages speaks of ecstatic conditions, and of men possessed by ecstasy.

At the beginning of this century ecstasy played a special rôle in explanations of prophecy. There was an attempt to explain prophecy as a whole on the basis of ecstasy. It was thought that in this way what the prophets said could be explained psychologically. As a result of excessive spiritual tension at moments of crisis certain men, who were prone to psychic influences, were possessed by ecstasy, in which words formed of their own accord so to speak. They understood and transmitted these words as God's word mediated to them in ecstasy. There was a great number of works written on this 'theory of ecstasy' and it was thought that the riddle of prophecy had been solved. The explanation is not as such to be rejected; why should not God make his words known to men by means of ecstasy? That there was such ecstatic prophecy in the early period and that it was recognized as serving God cannot be disputed. The attempt to explain prophecy as a whole from this root of ecstasy, however, was not a success. The attempt failed for the simple reason that it is not possible, in the case of the written prophets, to locate the source of their words in ecstasy, even when a great deal of imagination is used. A much more characteristic element of prophecy is the strong secrecy observed in regard to *how* the prophets received their words from God. Prophets like Amos, Isaiah and Jeremiah are not men of ecstasy. Nevertheless ecstasy too has its place and importance in the birth of prophecy.

A third root of prophecy is *the man of God*, a man endowed by

God with special powers, who worked miracles, healed, and in many ways stood nearer to God than other men. We know even less of him than of the seer. It is clear that many a man of God was also a seer. In I Kings 13 we are told how such a man of God came from Judah to Bethel, in order to proclaim God's judgement on Jeroboam; he is a seer and miracle worker. The figure of the man of God emerges a little more clearly in the Elijah-Elisha stories, which are sometimes strikingly reminiscent of the portrait of Jesus in the Gospels. Probably there were quite a few such men of God, who worked unobtrusively and only occasionally came into the limelight. Now and again there are traces in the written prophets which remind us of the man of God, as when Isaiah declares to King Hezekiah that he would be healed and also how he will be healed, or in the relation of Jeremiah to his companion, Baruch. But even here we find only a few traces. Prophecy has many different roots and it cannot be explained from these traces.

The simplest and most certain explanation of prophecy is derived from the prophets' own language. It is a stylized language, based on given prescribed forms. The language of the prophets has its own given clear arrangement, which is never, however, schematized. There are fixed formulae, which all have a particular function, in this language. One of these *formulae* is 'thus has Jahwe spoken' (Ko *amar jhwh*; usually translated 'thus says the Lord'). The origin and meaning of this formula has only been discovered very recently (by Ludwig Köhler). It is the messenger's formula with which the messenger introduced the message given to him when he stood before the person to whom he had to deliver it. For a proper understanding of the meaning and significance of this formula we must try to imagine a time when—still before the invention of writing— a message could *only* be communicated by means of a messenger who had to memorize it as he stood before the sender of the message, keep it in his mind throughout his journey, and when he entered the presence of the recipient deliver it orally to him. This was in direct speech, introduced by the messenger: '*Thus has X spoken* ....' At that time everything depended on the faithful and reliable transmission of the messenger. The first step in mechanizing the messengers' report was the invention of writing, which made it possible to give a message permanence by mechanical means; one could now 'have it in black and white'. Consequently the importance of the messenger declined a great deal; he was now no longer the bearer of the message in the real sense but only a 'postman'. For the recipient of a written message everything now depended on the signature under the letter; if the signature were genuine, he could depend on the contents of the letter. The signature of the letter took the place once occupied by the messenger's formula, 'Thus has X spoken'.

By introducing their words with 'Thus has Jahwe spoken' the prophets show they are *messengers* in the old, original sense of the word. Between God and man there is no mechanical link but only a personal link, made possible by the fact that God created man in his own image. The messenger between God and man cannot produce anything in writing; he is dependent on the fact that those to whom he is sent believe that his message really comes from God. This is another indication of how very opposite the prophet is to 'instrumental man'. He is a messenger such as existed when the technique of writing had not yet been invented, a messenger who heard and spoke, and upon whose hearing and speaking, receiving and delivering, everything depended without there being the slightest possibility of objective verification.

A word must be said at this point about a misunderstanding of the word of Scripture which is deeply rooted in the history of the Church. This misunderstanding concerns the doctrine of the 'verbal inspiration' or 'infallibility' of the Scriptures. What is meant by this is generally understood. This doctrine of the infallibility of the Scriptures constitutes the first attempt to mechanize or depersonalize the relationship of man to the Bible, and consequently to God. If the Bible's human origin, human transmission and human fallibility and frailty are excluded, and it is thought that it arose out of the mechanical inspiration of the word and letters, this will be the death of a truth abundantly clear in prophecy : that the words of God were not given to the prophet in writing, were not dictated to him, but were spoken, spoken without any guarantee. It is characteristic of the words of the prophets that they are not 'guaranteed genuine' but depend on the hearers' attitude of trust. This is true of the word of Scripture as a whole. It has no guarantee of genuineness such as would be conferred on it by a mechanical process of inspiration, but it is dependent on the trust of the hearers. Because this attitude of trust would no longer be necessary if this doctrine of inspiration were true it has caused great harm in the Church. It has robbed the Bible not only of its character as the word of man but also of its character as the word of God; for God does not mediate his word mechanically—as prophecy shows—but personally, in a way befitting man's humanity.

It is very indicative that the doctine of verbal inspiration in the seventeenth century hesitated over the question whether in the Hebrew text of the Old Testament simply the consonants or the vowel signs also were inspired. When it became known that the original texts were written without vowel signs and that these were only added to the unvocalized text hundreds of years later through the learned work of the synagogue, this was a severe blow for the theory of verbal inspiration. No, the words of the Bible have not been transmitted to us mechanically, but through men. We can never get beyond the formula of the messenger, 'This is the word of God'. There is no dictation or signature of God for us. If we do not trust his messengers, we cannot understand his message.

The prophets' understanding of themselves as messengers who have to transmit God's words to their people is a claim which we cannot evade by any explanation of prophecy. In the last resort therefore it will depend on whether we accept the words they speak as coming from God. There is another important correspondence between the Old Testament and the New Testament here. To a large extent, the New Testament also is mediated to us by messengers. The Apostles (*apostoloi*) are messengers. They are messengers in another way, messengers of Jesus of Nazareth as the word of God become man. But the important thing in both cases is the same: there is no guarantee that the words of the messengers really come from God, even in the latter case. One must trust that they have been commissioned by God and really are messengers.

The matter has yet another side to it. The messengers are *men*, the apostles as much as the prophets. As men they are fallible. We cannot escape the fact that there were true and false prophets in the history of prophecy, and that occasionally in the New Testament apostle opposed apostle. Not every word of every messenger is as such guaranteed true, we cannot have God's word except in the fallible and frail word of man. The affirmation and recognition of this in the Church has constantly proved very difficult. Time and time again the Church has tried to evade this fact and has sought guarantees. The history of prophecy can show that God is honoured and taken seriously by the very fact that his word accomplishes his purposes through messengers who are not infallible.

4 · The Prophetic Books

O u r knowledge of prophetic activity has come to us in two ways. In part it has come through the prophet's own words, which were written down and collected—whether by himself or others—after his activity began. Such collections are described in the prophets about whom we have information. The second way is the brief account of a prophet's activity in the context of a historical report. Such narratives sometimes contain a citation or a paraphrase of a prophet's word; sometimes, however, we are only told that a prophet was active at a certain time and in a certain place. Reports of this sort occur in all the historical books. These two streams of tradition may cross, overlap or agree. In addition to the words of the prophets one part of the prophetic books also contains accounts of his activity and destiny, including the picture of the historical situation to which the prophets addressed themselves: hence the same account may occur both in a historical and a prophetic book.

The brief accounts of a prophet's activity concern for the most part the period before written prophecy. If the collected words of all the prophets named in this period had come down to us, the range of the prophetic books would have been greatly extended. Only a fragment of Israel's prophecy has been transmitted to us.

One obvious and important reason for this is that the words of the prophets were rarely collected and handed down in the early period. At that time the importance of the words of the prophets was related solely to the hour when they were uttered and to quite a small area. The punishment they announced soon took place. This is true of Nathan's word to David, and Elijah's word to Ahab. It was soon seen whether what was announced took place or not. If it did interest died. It was only necessary afterwards to record the fact that a prophet had been active there on that occasion. The content of the historical report—plus the occasional addition of a particularly memorable word such as the two words just mentioned—was then transmitted to the coming generation. It is, of course, regrettable for our knowledge of the early history of Israel that we know so little about the early prophets; but these brief, matter of fact reports of a prophet's activity can give one side of the nature of prophecy with a special clarity: for a brief moment the prophet steps into the spotlight of history. Where he comes from and what happens to him later is not told; it is not the full curve of his life which stretches from birth to death, but the one point which intersects the line of the history of the people of God that is important; it is the moment of his call which points the way at a time of danger that is important. Or described from another angle: the way in which God came of old at Sinai and the Sea of Reeds to help his people—suddenly erupting like a volcano, intervening in the hour of need—lives on in the prophets.

We come next to the prophetic books themselves. False notions about them are widespread. They were not written in the way we write today. Their structure can be compared with that of the cathedrals of the Middle Ages, built over generations as we can see from the different building materials, styles and art-forms. Each of the prophetic books has a period of growth behind it, before it was given the form in which it has come down to us. Many of the prophetic books, specially the Book of Isaiah, took centuries to become what they now are. Even more important, however, is the fact that up to the exile the prophetic books did not exist as books, that is as written words, but as 'oral tradition'. At the beginning of the prophetic book stands the prophetic *utterance*, the individual prophetic word. This constitutes another important correspondence between the Old and New Testaments: the word of the prophet, the message of Jesus and the message of the apostles were all originally spoken, living words not yet fixed in writing. This is the basic reason why in the two thousand years of the Church's history the life of the Church has depended not only on the written but on the spoken word and the living message. The written word can never replace the spoken word. Accordingly we must moderate our claims from the start if we have no knowledge of actual prophecy but only of its written outcome.

From the spoken prophetic word to the prophetic book the way is long and not always straight. Most of the prophetic books, far from representing only collections of prophetic words, contain much else besides.

The prophetic books stand out as the real centre of the Old Testament, in that in them—or at any rate many of them—all three of the main parts of the Old Testament come together. In addition to the prophetic word we have history (corresponding with the history books) and conversation with God, or prayer (corresponding with the Psalms). To give an example: the Book of Isaiah arose gradually out of many separate collections. Isa. 1-12 consists of such a collection of parts. The conclusion of the collection is formed by a psalm in chapter 12. Consequently as we read the Book of Isaiah in our Bibles today we read without question the words of chapter 12 as if this were one of the words of Isaiah. It was, however, never intended as such. It should be understood from the analogy of a modern sermon, for example, closing with the verse of a hymn. There is a great number of such psalms and parts of psalms in the prophetic books; they can show us in a wonderful way how the words of the prophets entered into the life of the community and were joined with the hymns and prayers of the community. Likewise there is a detailed historical report to be found in Isa. 36-9, coinciding in parts with II Kings 18-9. The prophetic books, then, are very complex structures. The Books of Isaiah, Jeremiah and Ezekiel, above all, are large collections, containing an abundance of diverse elements, which in time, form and content are far removed from each other.

5 · The Prophet Speaks

T H E prophetic utterance is thus a messenger's utterance. It is in this light that its different forms must be understood. A messenger provokes two questions on his journey. To whom does he come? What does he bring? All the prophetic utterances contained in the Old Testament congregate round these two questions. The question 'To whom does he come?' receives a threefold answer: the prophetic utterance is addressed to the people of God (Judah or Israel or both), to someone in authority among the people or a group of people in authority (king, royal family, priests, prophets, judges, officers, commanders), or to other nations. This is a clear indication that prophecy has to do with history. A prophet's word is never addressed to anyone taken at random; a prophet's word is never concerned simply with meditation on God or abstract theology. The fact that a large number of prophetic words are addressed to other nations which have different beliefs and different religions is another clear indication that the prophets recognize the God of Israel as the Lord of the world's history. If prophecy has to do with history, it has to do with the whole of what happens in the world.

The second question 'What does the messenger bring?' can only be given a twofold answer: good news or bad news. In order to understand properly what this means the reader should recall a situation in his own life when he himself experienced this alternative of good news or bad news in the form of a message. Everyone knows this tension in opening a telegram or a letter, or in opening the door to someone who is bringing news. Everyone knows how in such moments we catch our breath and all our thoughts and feelings are tensed with breathless expectation: what does the message bring? At a time when men reckoned with God as the one from whom all salvation and disaster came, a messenger of God could count on this breathless tension among the people to whom he was sent. What it must have meant, then, that the prophets had to be messengers of judgement and bad news for hundreds of years! If we cast our eye over prophecy as a whole, words of judgement and bad news preponderate from the time when the monarchy began to the time when it ended, and subsequently to the exile. None of the prophets at this period proclaimed only judgement, but the message of disaster preponderated in them all. Change comes at the moment of collapse: the prophet Ezekiel, who had really been a messenger of judgement up to this hour, now becomes a prophet of salvation, and Deutero-Isaiah, the prophet of the exile, is purely and simply a prophet of salvation. Salvation-prophecy preponderates in the period of the exile also.

The message to foreign nations is almost wholly one of bad news; but not absolutely. Here and there in the pre-exilic period, during the exile and afterwards also, as well as at the end, the recognition that God still has a plan for the nations and that his last word to the nations is not judgement but salvation, breaks through with radiant clarity.

Individual utterances also display a great number of forms and styles. Whether the message brings good news or bad news, the announcement can be expressed in so many ways that no two prophetic words are ever completely alike. This is all the more surprising in view of the fact that a basic form of prophetic utterance can be recognized amidst this prolific diversity—the word of the messenger announcing judgement. The plainest example of this form is to be found in the word which Elijah spoke to King Ahab when he committed the crime against Naboth. This word had the structure:

Accusation (consisting here simply of an establishment of the facts).
Messenger's formula ('Therefore thus says the Lord ...').
Announcement of God's punishment.

The prophetic word contains two parts, the announcement of God's punishment or judgement and the accusation giving the reason for the punishment. The two parts are joined by the messenger's *formula*. In the written prophets this remained the basic form of prophetic speech by which the two parts were usually linked together once more. The following structure appears in a great number of prophetic words:

$$\text{Reason} \left\{ \begin{array}{l} \text{Accusation} \\ \\ \text{Development of accusation} \end{array} \right.$$

Messenger's Formula

$$\text{Announcement of Judgement} \left\{ \begin{array}{l} \text{God's intervention} \\ \\ \text{The result of God's intervention} \end{array} \right.$$

Both parts can also be reversed; sometimes the announcement of judgement stands alone, sometimes the accusation, or both parts can be amplified at will; there are numerous possible variations. But if one examines prophecy as a whole, then the basic form of a messenger's utterance consists in his having to announce God's judgement, from Amos to Ezekiel and even in the case of Zechariah and Malachi. If, in spite of this, the prophetic announcement never assumes exactly the same form but displays such a lively diversity, this depends chiefly on the fact that the prophets transformed and made use of other forms of speech and song which were in use among the people for their message. It will be sufficient if I give two examples: Amos begins a lament for the virgin Israel (5.1-2); Isaiah sings a popular song about his friend's vineyard (5.1-7) which suddenly changes into a hard word of judgement. The prophet can speak in the form of the priestly *Torah* (Isa. 1.10-7) or assume the style of wisdom-speech (Isa. 28.23-9). The prophets are real messengers; they use the everyday language of their people, not theological jargon. They strive to be understood; they are not hedged around with abstract ideas, but they speak simply and concretely in a way everyone can understand. Their own particular times come to life in their work. As we listen to their word we come near to the people to whom the prophets were sent, we see them laughing and weeping, at their work and at their festivals, on the streets of their cities and outside in their fields. We see the children playing, the young maidens dancing and the men in battle; we learn how hard is the task of God's messengers and how they themselves suffer from the disaster which they are sent to announce.

6 · Amos Prophet to Society

I N the first period of prophecy, about the middle of the eighth century, two prophets appear with an especially passionate social accusation : in the northern kingdom Amos, in the southern kingdom Micah.

We must pause for a moment over the word 'social'. The term has completely changed its meaning in modern speech in an incredibly short time. After the First World War, as a result of the battle cry of a small group, it became alternatively a confession of faith and a term of abuse. Meanwhile it has been used to describe a large number of institutions (social welfare, social rehousing) and it has lost its value as a battle cry because everyone is 'social' today. It is part of the programme of all parties; today *everyone* is social. The word has been completely tamed, it has lost its horns and teeth, it no longer has any opponents. This rapid change of meaning throws a strong light on the chaotic agitation surrounding the 'social question' in an age of revolution. From a dispassionate inquiry into the result of social revolutions in the West since the French Revolution, two things must probably be said : they were all necessary, but in no case has the 'social question' been solved. This probably means that there is nowhere in the world where agitation produced by the social question can be ruled out. We must press our questions further; and in doing so we should not ignore the prophets. Their social message was often ignored by the churches of the nineteenth century; for which they are still paying the penalty today.

No one who is prepared to listen to the Bible as a whole can ignore the fact that the prophets—especially Amos and Micah—

were passionately interested in social questions. When there was a court action in Israel at the time of Amos at which a poor man was condemned because his rich opponent had succeeded in influencing the judgement in his own favour, then the prophet knew that he was called to cry out.

> *Because they sell the righteous for silver, and the needy for a pair of shoes—they that trample the head of the poor into the dust of the earth, and turn aside the way of the afflicted* (2.6-7).
>
> *...see the great tumults within her, and the oppressions in her midst. They do not know how to do right, those who store up violence and robbery in their strongholds* (3.9-10).
>
> *Hear this word you cows of Bashan, who are in the mountain of Samaria, who oppress the poor, who crush the needy, who say to their husbands, 'Bring, that we may drink!'* (4.1-3).
>
> *O you who turn justice to wormwood and cast down righteousness to the earth! They hate him who reproves in the gate, and they abhor him who speaks the truth* (5.7-10).
>
> *You who afflict the righteous, who take a bribe, and turn aside the needy in the gate* (5.12).
>
> *Hear this, you who trample upon the needy, and bring the poor of the land to an end, saying, 'When will the new moon be over that we may sell grain? And the sabbath that we may offer wheat for sale, that we may make the ephah small and the shekel great, and deal deceitfully with false balances, that we may buy the poor for silver and the needy for a pair of sandals, and sell the refuse of the wheat?'* (8.4-6).

In this social accusation which Amos brings against his people the evils at issue in the life of the nation are the same as those which have led to the great social revolutions. It is, of course, healthy and normal for a community to contain both rich and poor. This is not what is meant. Amos is not at all concerned with a principle, even the principle of equality. His accusation is not directed against richness or the rich as such, but it begins where obvious evils and destructive influences have forced their way into the relationship of rich and poor. He instances three such evils in particular: the perversion of justice through the bribery and influence of the rich, the dispossession of the poor under the cover of justice (distraint), and the 'oppression' of the poor by forcing an entry and taking possession, which can take many forms but has one permanent feature—disrespect for the poor. The prophets recognized that the social question is, at bottom, a question of mutual self-respect.

All three accusations assume that something is taken away which belongs indisputably to the person who has been robbed of it, even where the confiscation is 'lawful'. This is dispossession in its original sense. Karl Marx's understanding of the revolution as the dispossession of the dispossessors by the dispossessed agrees with the prophets in one point: the deep gulf between rich and poor in Israel arose in fact through a dispossession characterized by the three evils described above. The social accusation of the prophets parts company from Marx in that it does not regard this situation as a matter of principle but holds it as basically possible for rich and poor to live together in a healthy relationship. It parts company from Marx even more decisively, however, in that it grounds the existence of a classless society—which, like Marx, it regards as the healthy and normal position of society—directly, frankly and firmly in the activity of God. God gave Israel the land in which they now live. This is not a pious phrase but a historical fact, expressed in the right of every Israelite to receive a share in this gift of his God. Every Israelite has a right to his share in the land. The confession of faith 'Jahwe is our God' reaches right into social and economic realities. This is clearly and unequivocally expressed in Deuteronomy especially in the giving of the law. The Israelites and above all the prophets were far too realistic to make this into a right of equality. They knew too well that one man would make something quite different from another man out of the share which came to him. They knew that there would always be rich and poor. But they remained absolutely firm in their belief that the coexistence of rich and poor should never lead to class warfare. This is not Utopian illusion but historical fact. It can be proved quite definitely that Israel did not yet possess important social stratifications when it settled in Canaan. A comparison of Hammurabi's Code (*c.* 1700 BC in Assyria) and the Book of the Covenant, which display many similarities, can demonstrate this. Whereas the Code of Hammurabi reveals social distinctions in the application of its laws, in Israel all laws apply equally to all Israelites. The first important social differences in Israel come from the time of the kings, especially Solomon, although with the division of the kingdom this development was probably halted again. Under Jeroboam, too, Israel experienced a new period of prosperity; as a result social tensions emerged and, as so often in a period of sudden prosperity, serious social evils appeared. It is in this situation that Amos brings his accusation. Amos may have exaggerated. He was certainly one-sided; he did not see what the concentration of wealth in a few hands would produce in terms of cultural values. This can be conceded without any difficulty. But the cry which he raised at the time retains its far reaching significance for the whole human history.

The social accusation of Israel's prophets is the only place in history which preserves the moment when the separation of a nation's community into social strata or classes began. In fact the prophetic office consists in using the future, namely the coming judgement of God which they have to proclaim, to bring the very beginning of the social cleavage clearly into the light of history. We may say that has never happened anywhere else in the history of the world. Everywhere else movements of social renewal only begin at a much later stage of social stratification.

The accusation of Amos against his people at the moment of this first dispossession of the weak makes the point that this first dispossession has not been brought about by a particularly severe period of distress, in which the stronger dispossessed the weaker because of their need. On the contrary, it has happened simply because a small nation has not been able to digest a new and quickly won wealth. Amos sees this event as something which happens between this people and its God. This first dispossession is wanton sin, it is an act of direct aggression against God and provokes his judgement. For Amos there are no social events which can be separated from this relationship of God to his people. The social question *as such* stems from a departure from God, marked by the separation of real and formal justice. By addressing themselves to these symptons of sickness and by intervening with their call, the prophets, as God's messengers, are saying in effect that this separation of formal and real justice, which was given an appearance of justice by the social cleavage, cannot be healed by anything else but the intervention of God's word. Whether the nation will continue or be wiped out depends now on whether they hear this word or not.

Social preaching is not to be found only in Amos. Micah makes a protest of equal sharpness and passion in the southern kingdom; the prophetic accusation is to be found with equal lack of compromise in Isaiah and Jeremiah, and also in post-exilic prophetic texts. It is an important and indisputable part of the word of God in the Bible. It is the same line which is taken up in the New Testament when Jesus knows that he is sent above all to the poor, the handicapped and the despised.

The Church has ignored the social preaching of the prophets too often and too long. It is not an easy position to adopt. Today the time has come to recall it with all seriousness. We can no longer shut our eyes to the fact that the social revolutions of the nineteenth and twentieth centuries had to come because the social preaching of the prophets in the Church had ceased to be vital. Meanwhile a new position has arisen. Today this section of the Bible presents a question which goes even deeper. Do we still honestly believe that God, who sent his messengers at the time when the first serious cracks threatened to disorganize the community life of God's people, can still heal the disorganization, cleavage and estrangement of a community? This would have to apply both to the smallest community (e.g. a group at work) and to the largest form of community. The Church in our world does not exist to nurse its own fellowship, but to heal the rifts and cracks and weaknesses of the communities into which it is sent. The Church still stands as a testimony to the fact that the first dispossesion which led to the thunder of Amos was not God's will for the common life of man.

In the history of the West the Church has increasingly become a guardian of tradition and a conservative power. This applies to

almost every area of life. This is, doubtless, an important task of
the Church. But if it becomes the *only* task, if the Church is *only*
conservative, it can no longer appeal to the Bible. It is not pure
invention to suppose that, even to the present day, anti-ecclesiasti-
cal propaganda could turn to account the view that the Church
exists to support and justify an existing patriarchal or capitalistic
order of society. The purely conservative character has been too
obvious. The social preaching of the prophets contained an important revolutionary element. The prophets dared to stand up
against the existing order and against those in authority for the
oppressed, the handicapped and those deprived of their rights, for
the downtrodden and insulted, regardless of their own position.
They did this in the name of God and did not ask about the consequences. This is what we should listen to today.

Who was Amos? The Book of Amos contains a single report:
the meeting of Amos with the high priest Amaziah (7.10-17).
A brief episode of pregnant clarity which sheds a bright light not
only on the man Amos but on an important feature of prophecy
as a whole. Amaziah, priest of the royal shrine of Bethel (the bull-
image which Jeroboam I had had erected still stood there!) had
denounced Amos to the king. In doing this Amaziah had only done
his duty. As high priest he had the responsibility of providing for
peace and order in the country, and the preaching of Amos must
have seemed dangerous to him. He had been commissioned by the
king to prohibit the prophet Amos from speaking publicly in any
temple in Israel and to banish him from the country. Now the two
men stand opposite to each other, a priest and a prophet. Two men
who both speak and act on the orders of God, the God of Israel,
and who both wish to serve their country. We must picture the
conversation taking place in public. It must have happened in
front of witnesses. The men of Israel saw before them two representatives of God, standing against each other. The one spoke by
right of his office and on the orders of the divinely anointed king.
The other spoke in the name of God without any badge of authority,
without any official position and without any authority behind
him. And he declared God's judgement to the divinely anointed

king, to the ecclesiastically appointed priest: destruction, disgrace.
What a heavy demand this scene must have made on the witnesses!

As the reason for forbidding Amos to preach and for expelling
him Amaziah quoted a saying of Amos: *For thus Amos has said,
'Jeroboam shall die by the sword, and Israel must go into exile away
from his land'*. It is very significant that the priest mentions Amos'
announcement of judgement but is silent about the reasons given
by Amos (i.e. the accusation). So it is, right up to the present day!
Whenever a totalitarian state in the twentieth century makes public
the reasons for its measures against the Church, then it takes
exactly the same course that the royal priest Amaziah took at that
time. It is publicly announced that the Church threatens the state,
but there is silence about the fact that the Church has put its finger
on a weak spot. This is where the weakness of authority shows itself.
It is true the prophet's mouth is stopped and he has to leave the
country. But it is not long before it becomes clear that God is not on
the side of the loyal priest, but on the side of the powerless prophet.

Amaziah acts according to instructions. But when he says, in
expelling Amos, *Flee away to the land of Judah, and eat bread there
and prophesy there!* it is intended as a friendly gesture. He assumes
that Amos earns his living by his prophetic preaching; he suggests
to him that he could surely earn his bread by prophesying in the
land of Judah. Amaziah could only speak in this way if this was
the normal practice at that time. We have already heard of the
schools or guilds of prophets at the shrines and at court; these did
exist, and Amaziah thought Amos belonged to one. In reply Amos
says, *I am no prophet, nor a prophet's son; but I am a herdsman, and
a dresser of sycamore trees, and the Lord took me from following the
flock, and the Lord said to me, 'Go, prophesy to my people Israel'*.

'The Lord took me from following the flock': this describes Amos
and it is the most important thing in prophecy. These sentences still
challenge us and ask us whether we really believe what they say.
We are at the one decisive point at which God's activity touches
our earth: God chooses himself a man and does his work through
him. What is here expected of those who believe in God is something vexatious, repellent and quite unheard of. Why could not

God do what he had in mind here through Amaziah? Surely there was a Church? Were there not enough priests, enough professional prophets, in Amos's day? Why did God not act through the institutions which were at his service? Why did he choose himself a farmer, a shepherd? Nor was Amos the only one. It continued. Time and time again a man came from outside, a man who was not prepared for the service of the Church, a man who could show nothing, absolutely nothing, to prove the assertion—with which Amos came before Amaziah—that he was called by God. But the importance of prophecy lies in its being able to point to the freedom and majesty of God's call, God's activity and God's ways with men, a freedom which cannot be contained by any institutions. Ever since God called Abraham it has always been true that a new call, a new impulse, a fresh faith has produced, after a while, a structure to which people grew accustomed and in which they felt secure. In this they settled themselves as they thought proper and convenient; in fact, they had an institution. And then it soon came about that God's voice was no longer really heard. Information about God became such common knowledge that a new word and a new instruction were no longer wanted; they grew secure and became cold. This happened soon after the activity of the Apostles, soon after the great missionary enterprises, soon after Francis of Assissi's call to repentance, and soon after the Reformation. If this direct, personal call of God to a man's life, to which Amos here appeals, were to cease, then the Church too would cease to be.

There is something else here which is important for us. Amos is a simple man. He is not a cultured person. He speaks a simple language which all can understand. He did not need any theological terms for his prophetic message. This, too, is generally characteristic of prophecy: it needs no special, stylized, theological language, but it speaks the everyday language of the people to whom it is addressed. The language of the priest and the language of the Church have a strong tendency to inflexible religious jargon. It can be established even in the Old Testament: the 'priestly writing' in the Pentateuch employs a stylized, in fact almost liturgical, language studded with many inflexible theological terms. This priestly, ecclesiastical, liturgical language has a strong tendency to stiffness. It cannot follow the change which every living language undergoes in the course of time, and thus it gains its ancient sound and its timeless character which makes it so suitable for a liturgy. Prophecy shows unanimously that the preaching of the Church must be in the everyday language of the people to whom it is addressed. In our Protestant Church today there is still, unfortunately, a great deal of uncertainty prevalent.[1]

What Amos appealed to ('the Lord took me from following the flock') in opposing Amaziah is emphasized by him in another word. He recounts a number of experiences which stand in a necessary connection with one another:

Do two walk together unless they have made an appointment?
Does a lion roar in the forest when he has no prey?
Does a bird fall in a snare on the earth, when there is no trap for it?

What he really wants to say comes at the end of this series (Amos 3.3-8):

The lion has roared—who will not fear?
The Lord God has spoken—who can but prophesy?

Amos is here explaining or demonstrating why he is God's messenger. It corresponds to the account of the call in other prophetic books. He does not speak of himself. He hides himself completely behind the fact on which he takes his stand. He wants to say only

[1] Luther, who could sometimes call himself 'the prophet of the Germans", definitely broke with the religious language of the Roman Church, in order to speak to the people in their own language – in preaching and liturgy, be it noted. He really wanted to preach in the language spoken by the men to whom he had been sent. This was the language into which he translated the Bible. It is a well-nigh tragic development that within the Lutheran Church the language of Luther should itself have become like a sacred language, not only in its liturgy (and its preaching also to some extent), but also in its version of the Bible. This is the exact opposite of what Luther intended with his translation of the Bible, his preaching in the mother tongue and his German liturgy. The language of the prophets could lead us to see more clearly at this point.

one thing in this word: *I must.* It is a series of rhetorical questions
which answer themselves. To be a messenger is as inevitable and
necessary for the man who hears God speaking to him, says Amos,
as it is for one thing to be produced by another in each of these
cases. A man can no more avoid prophesying when God has spoken
than he can avoid being afraid when he hears a lion's roar. As the
lion's roar has its inevitable corollary, so has the word of Jahwe in
the obedience of the hearer.

That God speaks is simply assumed here. It is quite as real for
Amos as the roaring of the lion. Our distinctions between physical
and metaphysical, between real and transcendant, between historical and meta-historical, simply break down before this word of
Amos. Here there is *only one* reality. This reality includes the word
of God as well as the roaring of the lion.

Amos then asserts that it is equally necessary for a man to listen
to this word of God and obey it. Once again, Amos says only one
thing: in the whole of this word: *I must.* This word of Amos
should never be read without pausing for a moment in quiet reverence. Words like this make us feel that this life with all its riddles
and obscurities is worth-while. That men have spoken like this
brings us nearer to the reality of God than all the thoughts that
men have had about God. There is a deep kinship between this
word of Amos and the death of the martyrs. Behind both stands
this *I must.* And in the centre of both stands the *I must* of
the Saviour. That is why people go calmly and willingly to their
death, today as two thousand years ago. That is why the Church
exists; men have found in this their only comfort in life and death.
This absolute certainty is the only fixed point from which faith
can lift the world off its hinges; as those who have no faith know.
That is why men have praised God from the depths, because there
is this fixed point, this absolute, which enables a man to say *I must.*

While the words in chapter 3 are extremely reserved as to what
is involved in being confronted by God and in being spoken to and
called by him, another passage seems to bring us closer to what
happened between God and the prophet. In Amos 7.1-9; 8.1-3;
9.1-6, five visions of Amos which are clearly connected are described.

In the first two visions (7.1-3 and 7.4-6) Amos sees a plague
of locusts and a drought, the two scourges most dreaded by the
farmers in Palestine, for they could destroy a whole year's crops.
Both visions make Amos turn to God in prayer for his people. O
Lord God, cease! Forgive! How can Jacob stand? He is so small.
On both occasions God prevents the plague's occurrence in response to the prophet's supplication. These first two visions show
us an important part of the unknown early history of prophecy.
We see how a line can be drawn from Moses to the prophets. As
Moses came before God in prayer for the people, similarly it was
clearly the prophet's task also, from the early times right up to the
last; for the same experience occurs in Jeremiah also. The prophet
Jeremiah is forbidden by God—also in a drought (Jer. 14)—to pray
for the people in their distress because they are weighed down with
sin. This obviously happened much more frequently than we know
about. It is perhaps at this point that the mission of the 'cultic'
prophets and that of the judgement-prophets coincides. It is very
important for the picture of prophecy as a whole that we note here
that the judgement-prophets including a prophet like Amos, who
otherwise meets us as an uncompromising messenger of judgement,
also had the task of acting as mediators in prayer between the
people and God. In times of distress they were the ones who brought
the people's supplications before God and by virtue of the power
thus given them implored God that disaster might be averted, children receive their bread and young people lead happy lives. But
their supplication had a limit. The third to the fifth of Amos's
visions deal with this. Amos sees 'a man standing on a wall with a
plumb line in his hand' and God explains the vision to him, 'Behold,
I am setting a plumb line in the midst of my people Israel !' This is
meant to describe God's guiding intervention in the history of his
people. The fourth picture shows Amos the consequence of God's
intervention. Amos sees a basket with fruit and the vision is explained to him 'My people Israel are ripe for destruction !' The
Hebrew word for late summer can stand at the same time for the
fruit belonging to this time of year; and it sounds similar to the
word for 'destruction' (or end). In the last vision Amos sees Jahwe

standing beside (or upon) the altar 'and he smote the capitals till the thresholds shook'. The judgement announced in the two previous visions will inevitably take place. The blow which will hit the people begins in the centre of the nation's life, at the altar. What an outrageous picture! God destroys the altar on which sacrifices are offered to him, the sign of his presence, the place where he is worshipped! But Amos must declare even this terrible calamity, he is told here. The coming judgement involves the whole life of the nation including its worship, the serious defects of which Amos has to declare. Spreading outwards from this centre the judgement of God envelops the whole nation. No one will be able to escape it:

> Though they dig into Sheol
> From there shall my hand take them;
> Though they climb up to heaven,
> From there I will bring them down (9.2).

The five visions contain the message which Amos is commissioned to bring, the message of inexorable judgement. They make it clear that it is not the prophet, Amos, who desires the judgement. He would willingly help his people to preserve peace and prosperity by acting as a mediator in prayer, as the first two visions demonstrate. And twice God is moved by entreaties; he, too, desires the salvation of his people. But then a time comes when judgement can no longer be averted. One man sees this: the messenger of God. And he must now become the messenger of judgement. The stern, unyielding, destructive activity of God is expressed first of all in a word. Thus, the message of Amos is without mercy. Yet that God announces his judgement in advance is itself an act of mercy. He gives his people one more last chance, the offer of which is brought by the messenger of judgement. This paradoxical offer of mercy in the message of judgement survived the judgement: the messenger of judgement belongs to the history of salvation. Here too we trace the activity of God, who when the time was fulfilled gave to the world salvation in the form of the Cross.

One final word about the visions themselves. They do not reveal any trace of mystical experiences, of ecstasy or trance or hallucination. Amos saw these things when he was fully conscious and his mind clear; he was wide awake and sober. Anything else would be out of keeping with the shepherd from Tekoa, his clear sober speech and very realistic message. Only the fifth vision in which Amos sees God lift his arm to strike the altar is a vision in our sense. Within the five visions as a whole, however, the fifth signifies only the inescapability and inevitability of the previous visions. The third and fourth visions have already said what will happen. To this must be added the fact that each of the visions was only intelligible through the word which comes to Amos. What Amos sees is only a confirmation or realization of what he hears. The reality of what is heard becomes more real by what is seen; the messenger is also the eye-witness. He not only hears what is to take place, he also sees it. When God makes a man the messenger of his word, then inevitably he sees more than others. It is characteristic of early prophecy that it is extremely reserved in giving information about what the prophets saw. This care and sobriety authenticates their message for us and bridges the centuries which divide us from them. We shall see that after the exile things changed. It is highly significant that visions only become rampant when the power of prophecy begins to fade. We must therefore see the visions of Amos only as an extremely faint hint of the world of visions opened to the prophet, a world not confined by the narrow horizons of time and space which limit our sight. What Amos had the power to see was not the decisive thing for him; he could leave it on one side. The only important thing is the word which he had to bring as a messenger, the word which faces his people with a final decision on the edge of the precipice. They did not listen to the word; but the word was not in vain.

7 · Isaiah Prophet of the Holy

'H O L Y' is a word which is as little understood as what it refers to. What this means is perhaps best explained by the negative. We can say of a man 'he regards nothing as holy any more'. We mean much more by this than simply 'he no longer believes in God'. We mean that a man who regards nothing as holy any more no longer acknowledges any limits. He does whatever he likes. He shrinks from nothing, he makes his way in brutal fashion, and it does not matter to him what he destroys in the process. It does not occur to him that he is trampling under foot what is holy for others. This makes it clear that 'holy' is not only a religious term. It does have to do with God, but it also has to do with the world and with people. We all know that when those who hold nothing 'holy' gain complete power this means chaos and destruction for everyone, including, ultimately, those for whom nothing is holy. We all feel that the existence of the world depends on people holding something as holy. This feeling has always been kept alive, even where faith in God has disappeared. Today, however, this knowledge has been brought to the fore-front of human consciousness once more by weapons of mass destruction. Whether these weapons are used or not will depend not so much on political treaties or resolutions as on whether people still hold anything holy.

The holy has an extremely fascinating history in the development of humanity. All the religions of mankind at all times know something of the holy, even the religions which recognize no personal God. And wherever 'enlightenment' has displaced religion something else must inevitably take the place of the holy, even if it seems quite different and is given quite a different name. We live at a time when the holy has become attached in a special manner to the political field. The extremes of the totalitarian state in explaining its government as holy and claiming for it the veneration due to the holy is only the final consequence of that nationalism produced by the Enlightenment, when ties with God were loosened.

There is a great deal which a man can esteem holy, and as long as he knows that what he regards as holy points to God in some sense, this has value and meaning. It becomes dangerous only when what a person regards as holy, whether it is an idea, a power, or a memory itself becomes God. People for whom something is holy can live peaceably together even if they differ in their views of what is holy. They can trust one another because they have this in common—

the *fact* that they regard something as holy. But one can no longer trust a person who no longer regards anything as holy. There is, however, still the possibility that a person or a group of people says a great deal about the holy, the word is used very frequently and a great number of rites are performed, all intended to give expression to veneration for the holy, but everything has become empty form, empty words, a matter of rigid habit. This is generally the case where too many holy places, holy ceremonies and holy objects accumulate round the holy God. It is religion's threat to the holy. It was to meet this threat that Isaiah was sent. If anyone were to ask in what chapter the distinctiveness of the Old Testament is to be found, then without hesitation we point to Isa. 6, the account of Isaiah's call. All three parts of the Old Testament come together here. It is a historical report ('in the year that King Uzziah died . . . '); it is a prophet's call to his service as a messenger, and it contains the two basic elements of the psalm—praise and lament. We should then have to tell the questioner, it is true, that we are unable to explain this chapter. Explanation stops here. What Isaiah describes here, and what happened to him, can only be properly understood by a person for whom God is not a hypothesis but reality. But then there is no longer much that needs to be explained. The story of Isaiah's call has three parts. Every encounter with the living God has these three aspects which are described here in the three parts of the account of the call. It is immaterial whether it is Amos, Isaiah, Jeremiah, Peter or Paul, Luther or anyone else : when a person knows of God's reality in his own life, then he understands what happened when Isaiah was called to be God's messenger. Encounter with God has these three aspects :

1. *God meets Isaiah as the Holy One* (6.1-4).
2. *Isaiah discovers he is unclean before God and is cleansed* (6.5-7).
3. *Isaiah is sent* (6.8-11).

1. *God meets Isaiah as the Holy One.* Isaiah sees God enthroned in the temple. What Isaiah sees is something very contemporary and representative of his time. Michaiah ben Imlah has a similar

account of a vision of God enthroned (I Kings 22). It is a picture of lordship and majesty which has been dominant for thousands of years: the king seated on his throne, giving orders to his servants who surround his throne. This picture is the absolute embodiment of the concept of lordship. The picture is completed by the addition of the holy place, the temple, the place where man comes before God. Instead of the servants and ministers who surround the king's throne there are seraphim on this occasion, winged heavenly beings (the walls of the temple and the Holy of Holies were decorated with pictures of such beings) who adore God and serve him; it is adoration and worship on a higher plane.

In all this Isaiah did not see anything in his vision that any Israelite who entered the temple at Jerusalem in the year King Uzziah died could not have seen. Isaiah saw nothing exceptional. He saw nothing but what his whole nation already believed. One could go even further and say that what is described in the first four verses of Isa. 6 could have happened within the framework of many religions. It is the classic expression of encounter with the holy. The distinctiveness of this picture lies in the unsurpassed simplicity and directness of the description. There will be few who will be able to deny that Isaiah here is bearing testimony to an actual event. The song of the seraphim is the archetype of the adoration of God. On this higher plane adoration may be on one note. The abundance and variety of human words cease. All the various ways of adoring God come back to adoring God as God, adoring the Holy in his Holiness. The one unchanging eternal adoration answers to the oneness of God and his eternity.

At the end of the picture stands the sentence 'and the house was full of smoke'. For a moment Isaiah has seen—now all is hidden again. The vision does not stay. It is not to be clung to. The vision is not the important thing.

2. *Having seen the holiness of God, Isaiah recognizes who he is.* Man is such that he cannot bear to look upon God. And Isaiah cries out, 'Woe is me! I am lost ... !' In the presence of God's holiness he recognizes that he is a man of unclean lips. This central section of Isaiah's vision is of decisive importance for what the Bible says

about sin. Sin can only be taken seriously as sin when a person has seen God. Everything else is mere talk. One cannot persuade a person that he is a sinner. Nor can one prove theologically or otherwise that all men are sinners. We have become accustomed, unfortunately, to speak far too generally and theoretically about sin. The result is that this word 'sin' has lost its edge and its power. The story of Isaiah's call can convey to a man of our own age what sin is. But if a man has never for one moment been frightened in the presence of God, tremendously afraid that he is a sinner before God and unclean before him, then he will never see this. It is as possible for this knowledge to overtake a man in the mid-twentieth century as in the year when King Uzziah died. We learn to treat this word sin more warily and reverently in the light of this chapter.

When Isaiah is suddenly possessed by a sense of his uncleanness before God, this is not anything exceptional. What is exceptional does not begin until this point. The world of Isaiah and the people of Isaiah were not without a remedy against sin. One could be cleansed from sin by a liturgical or cultic ceremony. There was an abundance of such purification, or expiation, ceremonies. But Isaiah knew that the uncleanness which he had discovered in himself in the presence of God could not be removed by any cultic remedy. He reports that it was removed by God himself through one of his servants acting on God's word. One of the seraphim takes a burning coal from the altar with the tongs and touches Isaiah's mouth with it. Together with this action he pronounces the word of forgiveness. This passage is particularly important for the understanding of prophecy. The movement of liturgical expiation ceremonies is one which proceeds upwards from below. By means of the sacrifice offered to him God is influenced by the priest to forgive the sin. This movement is reversed on this occasion; the sacrificial implements (the tongs, the burning coal) in the hand of God's servant are employed in the opposite direction, from above downwards! In opposition to every cult which in its self-confidence thinks it can provide for God's forgiveness, Isaiah here gives the glory to God. He makes it clear that God alone can forgive sins, God alone can make a man clean in his sight. God's forgiveness can never be imprisoned in a cultic institution. What Isaiah describes must and always will be so: a man may experience the forgiveness of God directly without any cultic medium, and through this forgiveness be freed from the misery of his sin. There is always the danger in the case of an institution for forgiving sins that the institution may take the place of God. To prevent this happening God went the opposite way about it: what Isaiah experienced for himself has now become possible for all men, in that God has freely given from above the work of atonement for all and the directly spoken word of forgiveness by sending his Son.

3. This is not the end, however, of what takes place between Isaiah and God. *Isaiah is sent*, for this is not an event 'between God and the soul', but between God and his people and therefore between God and the world. The holiness of God is not there just for God, and the purification of man is not just for the bliss of man, but in order that, as a result of this encounter, something might go forth into the world. There is no genuine encounter with God without this third aspect, without this sending to others. God asks, 'Whom shall I send?' and Isaiah answers, 'Here I am! Send me!' The deep, insurmountable opposition between all mystical piety and biblical faith is to be found at this point. In the Bible what takes place between God and man is not concluded by what happens to the man involved. It does not take place for the building up, advancement, enjoyment or pious meditation of the individual whom God encountered, but in order that something may go forth from him to others. The touch of the burning coal left Isaiah a quite ordinary man. But something changed for him. He now knew—not through himself, but through what had happened to him—that he was empowered to be God's messenger. Now, when he is ordered by God, 'Go and say ... !' he will go and he will speak. And no power in the world or weakness of his will prevent him.

One further point: this call could have had another conclusion. It would have been conceivable that the expiation would have fitted Isaiah for something quite different, namely to join in the songs of the seraphim and to set by the side of their heavenly liturgy an earthly liturgy which could correspond here on earth, in the earthly temple and with human voices, to the heavenly liturgy. This did not happen. Isaiah did not encounter God that he might purify and renew or reform the liturgy of the temple in Jerusalem as a priest but that he might be God's messenger. It should not be overlooked that here in the middle of the Old Testament praise of God's holiness finds its earthly counterpart not in the liturgy but in the service of the messenger, in the preaching of God's word. In the New Testament the story of the transfiguration points in the same direction.

And now a final word on the tripartite division of the story of Isaiah's call. The story is the Church's Old Testament lesson for Trinity Sunday. This probably came about because the threefold 'holy' was interpreted as referring to the trinitarian God. We may raise the question whether the three parts of the encounter with God in Isa. 6 do not correspond to what is meant by the tripartite division of the Apostles' Creed. We do not need to draw that out further; the correspondence of the three parts of Isa. 6 to the three sections of the Creed will quickly be apparent to everyone. This would imply, of course, that we think of the essential threeness of God as a threeness which arises as a matter of necessity out of the encounter of God with the world or with a person. When God encounters our world in Jesus Christ, this encounter must have the same three aspects which the encounter of God with Isaiah had: God in his majesty; God stooping down to men; God sending forth the purified one. A further question is whether every act of worship ought not to be concerned with this threefold event which determines the call of Isaiah.

Isaiah encounters God as the Holy One. He often describes God as 'the Holy One of Israel', a particularly characteristic expression of his for God. He is the messenger of the Holy One. In Isa. 1.10-17 a word spoken by the prophet against the worship of his people has been preserved. It is a truly staggering word. After the introduction which summons men to listen to God's word, God asks:

> What to me is the multitude of your sacrifices? says the Lord;
> I have had enough of burnt offerings of rams and the fat of
> fed beasts.

There follows a word which overturns the religious festivals, and then God's word is directed even against prayer :

> *When you spread forth your hands I will hide my eyes from*
> *you;*
> *Even though you make many prayers I will not listen;*
> *Your hands are full of blood!*

And the word rings out in a call of God, in which he summons the people to do what he really wants from them :

> *Cease to do evil, learn to do good;*
> *Seek justice, correct oppression;*
> *Defend the fatherless, plead for the widow.*

The three most important ceremonies which determine the whole religious life of Israel are here overthrown by God : sacrifice, prayer and festival. The words of Isaiah paint us a picture which has the elements of a great drama.

Standing in the forecourt of the temple at Jerusalem are men with their hands stretched upwards in prayer. And over against them a man calls out, a man who speaks at the command of the God to whom their prayers are addressed. *God doesn't hear you! God won't listen to you! Your hands are full of blood!*

One can understand that the prophets cause offence ! This word of Isaiah, it is true, does not want to destroy or abolish worship as a matter of principle. But it does want to say that this worship, as held in Jerusalem at present, cannot be accepted or recognized by God. For it does not take God seriously. The same hands which are now raised in prayer to God have just taken a poor man's last possession, or voted in court for those in authority against the underprivileged. In the life of those to whom Isaiah's word goes forth both the egoistic hardness of daily life and the pious practices of religion go together. They dare to enter God's presence without the rest of their life being affected in any way. Isaiah sees God's holiness is very deeply damaged by this. God cannot really be holy for these people ! But this means that all their religious ceremonies are worthless and meaningless; it would be better to abandon them altogether. If the people in Jerusalem are not really willing to make basic alterations in the way they live together with their fellow men, then God despises and overthrows their worship. If God were holy for them, then encounter with God would lead to a change in their whole existence, beginning with the sphere of social intercourse. If they remain obdurate, however, then judgement must come and the judgement will be upon Israel's worship also. Amos had said the very same thing in northern Israel; this was the meaning of his last vision; and there are also in Amos a number of passages in which he brings the same charge against worship in northern Israel as Isaiah brings against worship in Judah and Jerusalem. We shall hear the same charges in Jeremiah later.

What the prophets attack is not worship as such but the dichotomy of genuine worship and purely superficial and formal turning to God, the deadly consuming lie of a worship that is a pious Sunday practice and does not penetrate into the hard realities of every day. In doing this they pointed to a danger which threatens every act of worship which is held regularly. Their warning of the deadly danger of worship which runs a purely regular course has seldom been listened to in the Church. It is worth reflecting how in Germany, after the Second World War, the question was asked with great zeal and intensity: 'What is the correct way for worship to be conducted?' But it was not asked with the same intensity: 'How can our acts of worship be so ordered that what takes place in them reaches into homes and workshops, on to the streets and into the large areas of public life?' If in an act of worship minister and congregation see that the forgiveness there received changes a hardness in everyday life, that the wisdom heard in the sermon brings about a conversion, and that the peace imparted through words can silence a worrying anxiety, then that worship is worth more in God's eyes than a large number of services which liturgically are unobjectionable and edifying, but which remain enclosed within the walls of the church.

The holiness of God includes his majesty or highness. Isaiah saw the Lord sitting on a high and lofty throne. In his preaching Isaiah takes seriously this concept of God's highness or eminence. His attitude is similar to the one he took with regard to worship.

There Isaiah said : one can hold a great number of beautiful, solemn services and yet not really serve God with it all, that is, not really recognize him as Lord, Lord of the whole of life. Here he says : one can talk a great deal about God's highness, about his eminence and majesty, without really respecting God in his highness. Only a man who is prepared to see the consequences of God's eminence can do this. Isaiah announces the day of judgement when God will judge everything that is high and exalted :

> For the Lord of hosts has a day against all that is proud
> and lofty,
> Against all that is lifted up and high (2.12-17).

What is high and lifted up is now specified, from the cedars of Lebanon to the high towers and fortified walls, and then the word concludes :

> And the haughtiness of men shall be humbled
> and the pride of men shall be brought low
> and the Lord alone will be exalted in that day.

The whole word terminates in this 'alone'. God's highness and eminence is not the highest point of what is high and exalted among men in this world; it is highness of another sort. Everything high and exalted on this earth advances towards the day when it will be destroyed. It does not have the character of the eternal. Whether it is a building, an empire, or a philosophical system everything great, high and exalted awakens surprise, wonder and perhaps awe; but this is the very point where man is in especial danger of overstepping the limit by conferring on a created object or something made by man a highness which belongs only to God. Only the man who sees the limitations of all human and created greatness can recognize God's eminence.

This word must be seen against the background of Judah's history during Isaiah's lifetime. The small land of Judah had the gigantic Assyrian empire as its neighbour. It witnessed the fall of the city of Damascus, the capture of Samaria, the exile of the northern kingdom. It witnessed the continual growth in size and strength of a great political power, an empire to which the small countries surrendered and to which those with any foresight capitulated without any resistance. What was the God of Israel, in fact? Was it not simply foolishness still to want to affirm that the God of the small nation of Israel was the Lord of history and that the king of Assyria had to submit to his will? It was in the light of this question that what was meant by the highness and majesty of God had to be explained. And it was in the light of this question that the prophet Isaiah dared to preach the God who makes Assyria the instrument of his anger, his rod to punish his disobedient people, but who has power to compel overpowering, proud Assyria to withdraw from beleaguered Jerusalem at the moment of its greatest danger (701). In fact, said Isaiah, God declares he will soon judge this colossal power of Assyria because it has turned somersault in its greatness and its intoxication with power.

Let us pause for a moment. There stands Isaiah, in the land of his fathers which has become very small and very poor. He sees the great Assyrian empire arise and grow, and it can only be a matter of time, by human calculations, before it incorporates Judah also. This did in fact take place, and Judah became an Assyrian province. But the Assyrian power block could not impress Isaiah. Scorning political realities he stuck to the word which he had to deliver as God's messenger. God has announced a day of judgement on everything high and exalted. This day will come; therefore Isaiah can contemplate the growth of the towering might of Assyria calmly and unmoved. He sees the mounting power of Assyria as outbidding itself and already lying broken on the ground one day. It can still accomplish or destroy a great deal, but this does not affect the day which will come:

and the pride of men shall be brought low ...

Isaiah takes God's highness seriously in that he does not allow himself to be fascinated any longer by the highness of human power, be it never so powerful.

This was when our concept of faith was coined. Isaiah coined it. The word had existed for a long time before this, but the real significance of faith has its origin here. In Isa. 7 and 8 we are told how Isaiah was sent with a message to the king at a moment of far-reaching historical importance. Syria and northern Israel have made an alliance against Assyria. King Ahaz of Judah refuses to join the alliance. The confederates want to compel him and they march against Jerusalem. The enemy is no longer far away, the king is in the process of testing the city's water supply in case of a siege. Isaiah goes to meet them. He declares to him that the plan of the confederates will miscarry; they will not capture Jerusalem. Isaiah concludes his word with the call: 'if you will not believe you shall not be established!' This scene with its final word makes it classically clear what the word 'to believe' means in the Bible. The call was necessary. The king does not believe what Isaiah declares. Isaiah asks him to ask for some sign or other to confirm his word. The king rejects the sign; he does not want to tempt God. The scene ends with the rescue of the city from the approaching enemy and with Isaiah warning the king of a coming judgement, *because he has not believed.* King Ahaz does not rely on the word of Isaiah; he calls the Assyrians to his aid, and this is the beginning of the end.

It was a moment of great tragedy. The king acted with full knowledge of his responsibility. Political events had taken on such an independent existence of their own for him that he believed a decision had to be made on the basis of the political situation alone. Isaiah, however, demanded unconditional faith from him. At this juncture it becomes clear for the first time that God and his people will no longer remain a unity; the community of those who have faith will take the place of the nation as a political entity. And the community of the faithful will wait for another king.

The call to faith occurs again in a similar context in another much later word of Isaiah (Isa. 28.14-22). It is directed against the politicians in Jerusalem who think they have insured themselves against every catastrophe by a clever political alliance. Isaiah tells them that their whole political alliance is being swept away; it cannot stave off the coming catastrophe. The safety of God's people in the face of this can only come about in quite another way: *Behold, I am laying in Zion for a foundation a stone, a tested stone, a precious corner stone, of a sure foundation: 'He who believes*

will not be in haste'. The city which now stands on Zion, the
temple which now crowns Zion, all that now exists, which the
politicians think they can secure by their alliances, will be hurled
into the coming catastrophe. But through the collapse God begins
something new, he establishes a new order in which only those
who have faith stand the test. Isaiah points even more clearly than
in Isa. 7 beyond the unity of the nation as a political and religious
entity to another community, a new people of God, whose only
continuity is in faith.

The word of judgement about mockers and the corner stone is
concluded by a parable (Isa. 28.23-9). Isaiah does not say this as a
messenger of God, it is his own word in a conversation in which
he answers an implicit objection. The objection is understandable;
it is one brought against many prophets. They were told: 'You
messengers of judgement talk so much of a coming catastrophe but
everything goes on quite well as before; we live and enjoy ourselves.
You only disturb and frighten the anxious with your threats!'
Isaiah quotes these opponents on one occasion: *They say: 'Let
him make haste, let him speed his work that we may see it; let the
purpose of the Holy One of Israel draw near, and let it come that
we may know it!'* (5.19).

Isaiah answers this objection with a parable. Like so many para-
bles in both Old and New Testament, it has two parts. He points to
the work of the farmer. The farmer does not always do the same
work; he ploughs in season, but there is also a season for sowing.
The farmer's work shows something else as well. He does not treat
all fruit the same at harvest time; rather, each fruit is harvested
according to what it is. The farmer has learnt two things from God;
it is God's way to do everything in due season and fittingly. At
the back of everything stands the wonderful counsel of God, with
whose praise the parable ends. God's plan is all embracing; it is
represented in the parable by the total activity of the farmer
sowing and harvesting, ploughing and threshing. In the reality
to which the parable refers God's plan embraces history as a whole,
in which judgement and salvation have their season. The prophet
is well aware that as God's messenger he has only *one* thing to say,

namely, what the people need to hear at a particular moment. He
knows that God's plan for his people among the nations contains
much more than he can say. It corresponds entirely to God's all-
embracing counsel if judgement is held in abeyance. God does everything in due season. It is enough that he knows the hour of judgement. Isaiah is aware that his parable of God's activity can only
hint at an activity which embraces all history, and that he, the
messenger, cannot explain everything. He can do no more than call
the mockers and doubters to reverence: 'He is wonderful in counsel,
excellent in wisdom!' Here we hear Isaiah, the prophet of the holy,
again. He is commissioned to preach about God's activity.

He himself cannot recognize God's plans, he himself can never
say more than he is newly commanded to say for each new moment;
his knowledge is only a pointer to the majestic power of the Lord of
history, whose horizons are far too powerful for human understanding.

There are other passages also where we discover how very
reverently Isaiah contemplated the often unintelligible activity of
God in history. On one occasion he announces the coming judgement (Isa. 18.4-6) and a word of God explains the delay:

> I will quietly look from my dwelling like clear heat in sunshine,
> like a cloud of dew in the heat of harvest.

These words of God, these long periods in which none of the things
foretold in God's word happened, have their counterpart on the
human level in silent trustful waiting for God, come what may.

> For thus says the Lord God, the Holy One of Israel,
> 'In returning and rest you shall be saved;
> in quietness and trust shall be your strength'.
> But you would not (30.15).

8 · Jeremiah Prophet of Torment

I N the first period prophets were active both in the northern kingdom of Israel and the southern kingdom of Judah. What the
prophets of the northern kingdom, Amos and Hosea, had declared

came to pass: Samaria was conquered, the majority of the people deported and the land became an Assyrian province with foreign settlers. Jeremiah was active in Judah about a hundred years later. As the messenger of judgement he had to announce the downfall now of the southern kingdom also, the destruction of Jerusalem and the end of the rule of David's house. Everything took place just as Jeremiah had said it would a decade before. Nation and king heard the voice of warning and the offer of salvation, right up to the hour of collapse. But the voice was not heeded, the catastrophe took its course. The task of the prophet who had to accompany this final stretch of Israel's history up to that time was almost superhumanly difficult. For over forty years he had to tread a path which he knew—knew from the beginning—would lead to ruin. He was not heeded, he was shunned and despised, he was finally arrested as a traitor, but he could not leave these people who were running to their own destruction. He had to be with them to the end.

His life and work cover a time of ferment. At the time of his birth (*c.* 650) Assyria was at the height of its power. From the time of his call (627) Assyria's power began to decline and in the year 612 the great Assyrian empire was overthrown. Nineveh fell, and the triumphal march of the Babylonian empire began. It succeeded to the Assyrian empire and after a short time became even greater and more powerful than its predecessor.

At first the small land of Judah breathed again when the pressure of Assyria was removed; it could be free once more from the yoke of foreign overlords, and King Josiah could extend the country's boundaries once more and win back a large part of the area belonging formerly to northern Israel. He carried through a reform (622) which restored public worship and the ordering of society to its former purity and strength, and Judah experienced another fine period of prosperity. The defeat at Megiddo (609) was the prelude to a precipitate end. Josiah opposed the Pharaoh Necho who wanted to hasten to the help of declining Assyria. He was defeated and fell. After his death the irretrievable impulse to catastrophe began; Judah was tossed to and fro between Egypt and the rising power of Babylon. It was worn out in this struggle and in 586 came the end of Jerusalem, the end of Judah and the end of the Davidic monarchy.

The distinctiveness of Jeremiah's prophecy is to be seen against this background. Jeremiah is the prophet in whom, for the first time in the history of God with his people, torment receives a positive meaning. This can be seen in the structure and style of the Book of Jeremiah. The book has two main parts—the words of Jeremiah (Jer. 1-24 and 30-3 words to Israel; Jer. 25 and 46-51 words to the nations) and an account of his life (Jer. 26-9 and 34-45). The account covers only the last period of his activity, and for the most part describes the prophet's sufferings. This reveals a certain similarity with the gospels, which likewise in the first part contain chiefly words of Jesus and in the second part a connected story of his passion. There are in addition a number of laments of Jeremiah (between Jer. 10 and 20) which only occur in this prophet and give expression to the difficulty of the task in the moving words of one in torment. Equally in the laments which Jeremiah wrote personally and in the story of his passion, which his companion Baruch wrote down, one feels that this is the beginning of something quite new. One is bound to feel it if one looks back to Amos, who in his passionate, uncompromising sharpness, in his untamed, exuberant language, represents the youthful stage of prophecy; and if one looks back to Isaiah, in whom prophecy came to maturity in the masculine clarity and calm of the messenger of the holy. With Jeremiah prophecy pushes forward into new territory. One cannot under any circumstances say that Jeremiah marks a stage of prophecy's old age. Rather, this prophet sets himself a superhumanly heavy task, persevering and waiting, even when the pressure of suffering is heaviest, for God to begin something new and different, some transformation.

It is as if in the figure of this prophet and his sufferings the destruction of the people of God cast its shadows forward and was already realized in advance, as it hurried forward pointing to a New Event. The more difficult it became for the man Jeremiah who loved life and longed for happiness and companionship and groaned under the burden which was laid upon him, the clearer it became that there was a meaning in the suffering of this individual which must benefit others, in fact the nation as a whole. The line from Abraham through Moses, Elijah, the prophets and the suffering servant of Deutero-Isaiah to Jesus Christ is to be seen most clearly here in Jeremiah. At the same time this line makes it clear what is the meaning of the work of salvation accomplished by the suffering of Christ in the New Testament. The fact that at the end of God's work for our world and for us men salvation comes through the suffering of the Son of God, who was a man, can only be appreciated properly when one contemplates the journey which led to this destination. All other possibilities of mediation or transmission of salvation led up to this last possibility, and prepared the way for it. Moses was mediator of both word and deed together; the judges and kings were mediators of the deed, the prophets mediators of the word. The history of prophecy, however, leads directly to the necessity of suffering for the coming of salvation to men. That is why the figure of Jeremiah stands at the end of the line of God's messengers before the exile; the message which he had to bring leads to suffering.

Realization of this can prevent any false understanding of suffering as the exclusive way of God's salvation for men. One sees first of all that Christ not only suffered, but the word which brings joy and the deed which brings salvation are an integral part of his work. In him all the three ways of salvation found in the mediators of the Old Testament converge. Suffering as a way of redemption for men does not do away with the other ways. Suffering for others, suffering for the world, presupposes that our existence can give joy and happiness for which it is worth suffering. Christ did not suffer for us in order that everyone else might now suffer also, but that under the protection of his suffering joy and peace might blossom.

This becomes clear when one reads the prophet Jeremiah. He helps one to understand the New Testament better. It is possible to see the extensive background of the sufferings of Jesus Christ for us with greater clarity. Jeremiah was called to be a prophet when he was quite a young man. He describes his call in the first chapter. It is distinguished from that of Isaiah by characteristic features. Jeremiah draws back from the task. *Ah, Lord God! Behold, I do*

not know how to speak, for I am only a youth! Here in the first
words of Jeremiah, we meet the human feelings of this prophet;
they are not completely absorbed in his office as in the case of Amos,
but constantly come into conflict with his heavy task. God sets
before him in his agitation the age-old promise of the helping
presence. *Do not be afraid, for I am with you!* Jeremiah feels something touch his lips and hears, *Behold, I have put my words in your
mouth.* The call of Isaiah was dominated by the tension between
the holy God and the sinful people. In Jeremiah's call the tension
is located in the messenger's task; in the demand made on a youth
who draws back from the messenger's mission. *See, I have set you
this day over nations and over kingdoms . . .*

The messenger is shown his task in two pictures (vv. 11-6). He
sees an almond branch and the vision is explained to him: *I am
watching over my word* (the Hebrew word for 'watch over' sounds
like that for 'almond branch'). He sees a pot boiling over from the
north and the vision is explained to him, *Out of the north evil
shall break forth upon all the inhabitants of the land.* These two
pictures embrace the basic constituents of the prophetic word of
judgement, which announces God's intervention and the results of
his intervention. Jeremiah will now have to say this for a whole
lifetime. The two pictures have shown him only a piece of the
reality which surrounds him, but the event which the pictures
portray is a piece of reality with the inevitability, the inexorability,
characteristic of life. Jeremiah, standing by this reality which he
has seen has to remain quite alone, a solitary figure, ignored or
hated or despised by others. He knows that God watches over his
word, that is, the word which has announced the coming judgement. But he had to wait a lifetime between the announcement
and the fulfilment, while life went on around him as before and
attempts were made to suppress and silence the tedious messenger
of judgement. It is understandable that Jeremiah almost broke
down sometimes under this burden. It is understandable that he
brings the accusation, *Thy hand was upon me, I sat alone.*

The laments of Jeremiah (in Jer. 11, 15, 17, 18, 20) belong to
the most powerful and the most terrible sections of our Bible. They

are concerned with the most human of human needs: loneliness, rejection, solitude.

We can only hint here at what this means. We are emerging from the romantic experience of loneliness as classically expressed in Hermann Hesse's poem *In the Mist*: 'To wander alone in the mist. To live is to be alone. No man knows another; each man is alone ...'. We are entering into a different, more serious, more deadly experience of loneliness: the loneliness of functional man. There are a number of functions in political, and economic industrial life which can isolate a man in a way never possible before. In many places there is a compulsion to silence or concealment or deceit which isolates those who participate in these functions in a way whose consequences we have not yet been able to measure. Today a person can be lonely because, like a machine, he is 'switched off'. We can only throw out suggestions here. They can show one thing: the romantic experience of loneliness meant that loneliness was an event involving two people or the lonely one and the rest of mankind. Today we are beginning to feel and learn again that real, lethal loneliness is three dimensional. This loneliness has to do not only with one's fellow men, but with a third authority or a third power. This is gradually becoming clear again in the harshness of our machine-ordered existence—simply because the machine or the organization cannot be companions.

Today therefore we are again in a position to understand the laments of Jeremiah better. The loneliness which Jeremiah laments is three-dimensional. There is first of all, isolation from men. Jeremiah is commanded by God to remain alone—without wife, without children, without a group of friends among whom he can be at ease (Jer. 16.1-13). But it doesn't stop there. His eyes are suddenly opened; the people of Anathoth among whom his daily life is spent, his neighbours with whom he is bound by everyday business, have planned to attack him. He has done nothing to them, he goes to meet them unarmed. Jeremiah complains of his suffering to God, he asks how God could allow it and receives an incomprehensibly hard answer: it will be much worse yet. You should not even trust your next of kin! At this point the third dimension of his loneliness is revealed: the lonely person wants to pour out his heart to God and is—apparently—roughly rejected (Jer. 11.18-12.6) Jeremiah longs for the company of happy people. He would so like to be happy with the happy. He rises up against this dreadful solitude (15.10-20):

> *I sat alone because thy hand was upon me*
> *for thou hadst filled me with indignation.*

And his lament turns to accusation:

> *Wilt thou be to me like a deceitful brook, like waters that fail?*

We shrink from this word, but we shall not lightly condemn it. Today we have again been brought to realize in many respects how far men can be driven. We are realizing again that the loneliness of man among men is not yet the final loneliness. By listening to this outcry of the man who has become lonely under God's hand, we shall also listen more earnestly to the cry of Jesus on the Cross. It is good for us to know that in this deeper loneliness men have held fast to God against God. It is deadly serious, in fact, here. Jeremiah has to fight not only against a feeling of loneliness. It is his mission, his *raison d'être*, which casts him into deeper loneliness:

> *The word of the Lord has become for me a reproach*
> *and derision all day long* (Jer. 20.8).

The same word of which Jeremiah can also say,

> *Thy words were found, and I ate them,*
> *and thy words became to me a joy* (Jer. 15.16).

There were moments in Jeremiah's life when this conflict became unbearable and he tried to get rid of the burden and cease to be a prophet. But then it was like a burning fire within him, he could not escape from God, he was bound to continue standing for him before men (Jer. 20.7-11).

The story of Jeremiah's passion begins with the temple-speech (here for once both the speech itself, Jer. 7, and the story of the speech, Jer. 26, have been preserved). He brings a biting accusation of false worship against those who want to go to worship in the temple; the same accusation which Amos (e.g., Amos 5) and Isaiah

(Isa. 1.10-17) also brought. *Will you steal, murder, commit adultery, swear falsely ... and then come and stand before me in this house ... and say, 'We are delivered!'—only to go on doing all these abominations? Has this house which is called by my name become a den of robbers in your eyes?*

The infuriated citizens of Jerusalem, especially the priests, rise up against Jeremiah and they would probably have killed him, if the officials had not intervened demanding a proper trial. This trial makes clear what had been promised the weak and tormented Jeremiah when he was called: *I will make you a wall of brass.* The majesty and dignity of his mission echo in the word he now directs at the angry crowd. There is not a word to extricate or defend himself, but only a warning to those he had been sent to and who now in their rage want nothing more than to get rid of him. Jeremiah is delivered at this moment by the officials remembering a word of the prophet Micah, who had also spoken a word of judgement on the temple at Jerusalem a hundred years before and who had been allowed to do so without being punished.

The false security of the people in Jerusalem, whom Jeremiah attacked sharply in his speech in the temple, stands in blunt contrast to the torment of the lonely prophet. He was constantly involved with this stupid, growing security. In his temple speech he attacked this complacency among the people and the priests. More serious still was the fact that he found it also among the prophets who preached, like himself, in the name of God. After the first siege of Jerusalem, when a part of the population and the valuable vessels of the temple had been carried away to Babylon, hopeful reliance on Egypt awakened a blind and dangerous optimism in Jerusalem. One of the salvation-prophets, Hananiah, advanced the following statement in Jerusalem, ostensibly as a word of God, 'Within two years I will bring back the vessels of God's house!' Hananiah met Jeremiah, and Jeremiah was wearing a yoke, an acted symbol of their blind optimism. This gave Hananiah his opportunity. He tore the yoke from Jeremiah's neck, broke it in pieces and as he did so said, 'Even so, I shall break the yoke of Nebuchadnezzar within two years!' We can imagine how this was taken by the people of Jerusalem. And now follows a deeply moving scene; at this moment of deepest humiliation Jeremiah has nothing to say. All that is said is, 'And the prophet Jeremiah went his way'. Only later, after an interval, is Jeremiah ordered to go to meet Hananiah once again. In a single sentence he tells Hananiah that his action condemns him and his word is empty: 'You have broken a wooden yoke and made an iron one'. Jeremiah denies Hananiah's prophetic authority. For his misuse of God's word he must die. The report closes, 'The prophet Hananiah died in the same year in the seventh month'.

The highest responsible authority in Judah, the king, closes his ears to the warning of the prophet as do the people, the priests, and the salvation-prophets. At a festival when there are a large number of people in the temple, Jeremiah has the word of God, which has been laid upon him, read out in the temple court by Baruch, his companion and scribe. He himself has been forbidden to enter the temple. Among those listening is a court official. When Jeremiah's words are read out his reaction is just like that of the high priest Amaziah to the words of Amos: he thinks they are dangerous to the state. He brings the matter before the princes, therefore, and they report it to the king. The king is sitting in his winter house, with a brazier of burning coal in front of him. A servant of the king reads from the scroll of the book, word for word. The officials, princes and servants stand round in a circle. After each section the king cuts off what has been read and throws it into the fire till the whole scroll is destroyed. How deeply this act of wantonness impressed the reporter of the incident is shown by the words: *Yet neither the king, nor any of his servants who heard all these words, was afraid, nor did they rend their garments* (36.24).

This is the first time the written word of God influences history. The story just told happened to a piece of our Bible. It should be noticed that the public reading had anything but a religious character. The words make their own way in this situation. They find no response, but they represent the last dramatic warning to the king and a leading statesman. The act of cutting up and burning this warning signifies the final judgement on the king's house and the state of Judah. The destroyed words, however, survive the burning. God's words cannot be destroyed even though the book in which they are written is destroyed. This has often been demonstrated in the following thousands of years. Many attempts have been made to silence it. But this book cannot be silenced by any power of man.

Jeremiah lived through the reigns of five kings. King Jehoiakim, who burnt the book of Jeremiah, led the first deportation to Babylon in 597, and among those deported was his son Jehoiakin, who reigned only a few months. The last king, Zedekiah, was appointed by Nebuchadnezzar. He vacillated this way and that between surrender and rebellion, and Jerusalem was torn by party strife. These last ten years up to the fall of Jerusalem in 586 are like a drunken dance up to the edge of the precipice.

Once again the conflict between king and prophet came to a head in a very extreme way. The constant calm of the prophet who had *one* thing to say and who said it in spite of all the ups and downs of the situation, in spite of threats and prison and the danger of death, in spite of being accused of treachery, contrasted uncomfortably with the zig-zag line of the politics of these last ten years. The king was weak and uncertain. He left Jeremiah in prison, but made a friendly request for a guiding word of God. He was told nothing but what Jeremiah had constantly said, yet was unable to decide. Unafraid, Jeremiah risked his own life in order to rescue the last life in the city. He was thrown into a cistern, in which he would have perished if an Ethiopian had not rescued him. But he stayed in Jerusalem to the end. And after Jerusalem had fallen and the Babylonian commander set him free either to stay in the country or to go with them to Babylon and spend the rest of his life there in peace and safety, Jeremiah decided of his own free will to stay with the poor, battered remnant; with those who had fought against him, suspected him and despised him throughout his life. They were his people, God had sent him to these people. Even with this wretched remnant he had to continue being what he had been, a messenger of God whose words were not accepted. He was taken to Egypt with those who fled and had finally to witness how they served foreign gods.

But Jeremiah knew now that this was not the end. He had shared his people's destiny to the bitter end. But when he was imprisoned during the siege, he received a new commission. A kinsman offered to sell him a field outside the city. At God's injunction Jeremiah bought this field and the deal was completed in every detail in his prison cell. There were witnesses present who heard the word of God which was set forth in the symbolic action of the purchase of the land: *Houses and fields and vineyards shall again be bought in this land* (32.15). It was, indeed, an extremely modest and discreet word of good news; it simply affirmed that destruction, ruin and collapse are not the end. There is something else after them. This sober modesty gave the word an even stronger effect than the most radiant pictures of the coming state of prosperity. To understand it one must know the situation in which it was spoken.

Jeremiah says only this about what will come to pass one day in the future—it will be quite new and quite different. God will make a new covenant with his people. The new covenant will no longer be based on the written law: *I will put my law within them and I will write it upon their hearts. I will be their God and they shall be my people* (Jer. 31.3). It cannot be said that the time after the exile corresponded to this announcement of the new covenant. Jeremiah points beyond this to a new period in the history of God and his people. This word can only be explained as referring to the time of fulfilment.

9 : The Prophet of Consolation

PROPHECY in the narrower sense of the term accompanied Israel's monarchy from its beginning to its end. It began when Samuel opposed King Saul and Nathan opposed David. It ended with the last words with which Jeremiah prophesied the fall of Jerusalem to King Zedekiah. But prophecy had a history during the exile and after the exile. The prophet of the exile whom we call

Deutero-Isaiah—the name used by custom to describe the unknown prophet whose words were joined to the book of the prophet Isaiah and are preserved in Isa. 40-55—stands in quite a close relationship to the old classical prophecy. (Whether chaps. 56-66 belong wholly or partly to him, whether they are the prophecy of a third person, the so called 'Trito-Isaiah', or whether they represent additions to Deutero-Isaiah, is not clear.)

The work of scholars on the Bible has rendered the Church an excellent and valuable service here. As early as 1775 scholars saw in this part of the Book of Isaiah the words of a man speaking during the exile, about two hundred years later than Isaiah himself. Gradually it was seen with increasing clarity that this unknown prophet spoke a completely different language, had a different style, used different forms of speech and above all had a different message to bring to a different period of time. As a result we can be quite sure today that here, in addition to the prophets known to us, a new prophet has been discovered, another voice has been added to the chorus of prophecy.

Deutero-Isaiah is a messenger of consolation. This is announced as his mission in the prologue of his book (Isa. 40.1-11). God calls for a messenger of consolation for the people in exile, *Comfort, comfort my people*! He has forgiven his people after a time of suffering; this is now to be announced and with it the clear way into a new future, redemption from captivity. There is only a passing and obscure reference to the prophet's call. An unnamed man has heard the call. But he asks, *What shall I cry?* and bases his question on the transitoriness of all living things. We can only feel that behind these words stands the deep scepticism of a man who can no longer believe that new life can waken from the mutilated and scattered remnant of the people. He receives an answer which confirms this transitoriness, *The grass withers, the flower fades.* But a different order of reality is set over against this order: *but the word of our God will stand for ever.* This is a reference to the word of God which has gone forth through the prophets to Israel. The prophets' message of judgement has come to pass. It has proved true. But the prophets also said that all was not ended with the judgement and that something could still be expected from God. It is enough to point to the words of Jeremiah. That is why now in the middle of the exile a message of consolation can go out, and why the messenger of consolation has something to build on: the promises of God abide through the collapse, yes even through the nation's death.

The Book of Deutero-Isaiah begins and ends with the declaration that God's word abides. At the end of Isa. 55 it is confirmed once more in the simile of the rain which makes the fruit sprout from the earth: *so shall my word be that goes forth from my mouth; it shall not return to me empty but it shall accomplish that which I purpose, and prosper in the thing for which I sent it.* These sentences at the beginning and end of Deutero-Isaiah are like a seal to the history of prophecy. The words of the messengers have gone forth to Israel for hundreds of years—apparently without success. They have not, however, fallen into oblivion. The words sent by God do not come to an end; one messenger succeeds another right up to the last one to whom this word brought joy and pain. Only now at the end of the line of messengers does the meaning of the line show itself: the death of the nation in exile can be connected with the—not empty—words of the long line of prophets. The word proclaimed by them now provides the foundation on which the messenger of consolation—himself a despondent man—can stand.

The best example of the comfortable words of Deutero-Isaiah follows immediately on the prologue (Isa. 40.12-31). One sees here how different from the previous prophets are his words. The whole passage is a series of questions: *Who has measured the waters in the hollow of his hand? To whom will you liken God? Have you not known? Have you not heard? Who created these things? Why do you say, O Jacob. . .?* One feels immediately that they are words of a conversation which the prophet had with those who shared his fate in exile. He takes up their complaints which had also been his own complaints. *My way is hid from the Lord, and my right is disregarded by my God.* Those who lament in this way and blame God are pointed to the majesty of the Creator with words of won-

derful poetry and are then promised that God cares for them:
*The Lord, the everlasting God, the Creator of the ends of the earth
. . . gives power to the faint.*

If one reads this strong poetry through without interruption and
listens to it carefully, one is surprised to discover that this is the
language of the Psalms. The complaint of the exiles taken up by
Deutero-Isaiah (Isa. 40.27) could stand, word for word, in a psalm
of corporate lament; and the praise of God in his majesty, the praise
of God as Creator and Lord of history, could stand in a psalm of
praise in precisely the same way. This is characteristic of the prophet of the exile: the two streams of prophecy and psalmody flow
together in him. One can trace it clearly through all the words of
Deutero-Isaiah. One of the important features of the history of
God's people becomes clear at this point: prophecy in the narrower
sense came to an end with the destruction of Jerusalem. The rebirth
of prophecy in the exile points in a new direction: the Psalms, as
response to the acts of God, response in the community's prayer and
song, now receive their lasting importance for the long time of
waiting, in which actual prophecy is silent until something quite
different, the time of fulfilment, arrives.

The word at the end of chapter 43 (vv.22-8) also grew out of a
debate, but here the debate became a judicial contest between God
and the people. God faces a charge which is brought against him:
'How could you, God, so completely reject us! Have we not served
you faithfully since you brought us into the promised land? Have
we not brought you sacrifices for hundreds of years from our possessions, our cattle and our crops? Has it all proved in vain?' The
answer to this accusatory question of the people in exile is a
moving, radically negative judgement on the nation's sacrificial
worship through the whole history of the settlement; it is a complete, conclusive confirmation of the words which the prophets
have spoken from time to time about the sacrificial worship of their
people. This is the answer: The sacrifices which you have brought
all this time were not brought to *me* at all. For this sacrificial worship has not changed you, it has not altered your life. You have not
really done me any service by it. Rather, in the course of its history

you have heaped up a mountain of sins, which have not been expiated by the sacrifices. *You have burdened me with your sins, you have wearied me with your iniquities.* If the history between you and me is to continue then there is nothing there to which you can appeal against me. There is only the mountain of sins there. It can only continue therefore in this way: *I, I am he who blots out your transgressions for my own sake, and I will not remember your sins.* But it is hard work even for God to remove the mountain of sins.

The songs of the servant of God which have been attached to the prophecy of Deutero-Isaiah follow at this point. They are the passages 42.1-4, 49.1-6, 50.4-9, 52.13-53.12. These songs raise many questions and have received a great number of explanations which can no longer be taken in at a glance. The following remarks can only represent one attempted explanation among many others. We should be clear from the first, however, that the never-ending question as to who is meant by the suffering servant of God probably corresponds to a deliberate obscurity in the words of the text, which does not on the whole allow a precise and certain solution to the question.

The songs can only be understood correctly against the background of Israel's whole history. God always worked on this people through individuals. Right at the beginning there is *one* mediator, Moses, who was the nation's leader and God's spokesman simultaneously; Moses was called God's servant. In the land of Canaan the line of mediators divided. Side by side with the mediators of the deed (the judges and kings) were the mediators of the word. In the servant of God in Deutero-Isaiah the two lines come together again. The mediator of God's work to his people is now *one* man again, and this individual is called, like Moses, God's servant. The fact that this new mediator of salvation is a servant forms a definite link with the royal line: the time of the political kings is finally past, and the servant has taken the place of the king. This receives expression in the song of Isa. 42.1-4 particularly, where the words clearly link up with the old designation of the king at his anointing (cf. Ps. 2). The work of the servant is here contrasted deliber-

ately with the exercise of power by the king : his office is to bring
forth truth. The conversation between Jesus and Pilate is a close
parallel to this in the New Testament.

The office of bringing forth the truth is in fact the office of the
messenger of God, the prophet. The servant stands at the end of the
line of prophets as the second song Isa. 49.1-6 says. The servant is
called at birth just like Jeremiah (chap. 1), and he works by means
of his word (vv.1-2). Just as many prophets struggled at first against
their call, so too the servant. As he looks back on what has happened :

> But I said, 'I have laboured in vain,
> I have spent my strength for nothing and vanity'.

This is evidently a retrospective view of prophecy as a whole, of
the long line of prophets, all of whose activity to all outward
appearance was in vain. But instead of easing the heavy and
apparently useless work of the servant, God answers this complaint: It is too light a thing that you should be my servant to
raise up the tribes of Jacob and to restore the preserved of Israel;
I will give you as a light to the nations. What was already hinted
at in the first servant song is asserted quite clearly and emphatically in this second song : the servant of God receives a mission
which extends beyond Israel to the nations.

We must look back here for a moment. The Old Testament begins with the creation of the world, and at the end of the primaeval
history (Gen. 10) stands a list of the nations. This makes it clear
from the first that the God of the Bible is the God of the whole
world, all men are his creation and his activity extends to all
creatures. The special history of God with the one whom he calls
and who becomes the one nation chosen by him begins later; and
with this nation God goes his special way. But in the first words of
this history, right at the beginning of Gen. 12, the promise to
Abraham ends with the words, '. . . and in you shall all the families of the earth be blessed'. The servant songs follow on immediately after this promise. Right from the first God had the whole
world in view in his special activity with this nation : it is in this

nation that God journeyed with the nations of the world who all share in this journey, from the wandering ancestor and the growing tribe to a full-grown community in all stages of its history up to the collapse of the state and the uprooting of the nation.

It is certainly no accident, therefore, but a clear sign of the deep historical purport of the Bible that, while the nation's catastrophe is still reverberating, and at the very place where by human standards the nation's journey is at an end, the original, world-wide scope of God's acts reappears: the new era of salvation-history has to do with the whole world again, the servant who is commissioned to do the new work of God is to be the light of the nations and the plan which stands behind this becomes clear at the end of the song: *that my salvation may reach to the ends of the earth.*

Who the servant is, cannot be perceived from the first two songs. Clearly, there are two conditions of his work: he is the new mediator of God's salvation, and in him the two lines of kings and prophets come together again; he is once more the *one* mediator. He is commanded to carry on the apparently useless work of the prophets in establishing and restoring Israel. Furthermore, however, he is to bring God's salvation to the nations.

The third and fourth songs give, in addition, a harmonious and clear definition of the work of this servant: vicarious suffering. In the third song (Isa. 50.4-9) the servant's special task of bringing consolation is linked with blows and ignominy; the servant accepts suffering and disgrace and patiently takes it upon himself. In the fourth song (Isa. 53) this line of thought is developed further in two respects: the blows lead to the death of the servant. The servant has taken suffering and death on himself vicariously. This death, however, is not the end; this death bears fruit and a community, overcome by the suffering and death of the servant, confesses, 'We know now that all this happened for our sakes'.

In the four servant songs the work of the servant is thus set out clearly, in a way everyone can understand, but the person of the servant remains in the dark. It is clear that he belongs to the people of God; it is clear too, that he continues the prophetic line in some way, or rather brings it to an end. But it is not at all certain whether an individual is meant by the servant or whether he is meant to embody a community. It is equally uncertain whether the servant's suffering is thought to be past, present or future. This much is certain: in the post-exilic community up to the coming of Christ the servant songs are not referred to a definite individual of the period of the exile or shortly after. If Deutero-Isaiah had been thinking of a definite historical figure or of himself, at least there was no definite tradition connecting the work of the servant with this person. Consequently it is more probable that by the servant the 'last prophet' is meant; he becomes the new mediator through vicarious suffering. This last prophet was not a historical figure for Deutero-Isaiah, who sees in him the whole prophetic line including himself. He also includes himself in the servant songs, but they are not, exclusively or strictly speaking, autobiographical. The fulfilment of these songs in Jesus of Nazareth, who had not yet come at the time of Deutero-Isaiah but was born five hundred years later 'when the time was fulfilled', has the most significance if Deutero-Isaiah meant the servant in the way explained above. The servant songs can then be seen according to their true meaning, without reading into them a meaning they did not originally have. They are the most clear, direct and profound pointer in the Old Testament to Jesus Christ.

10 · The Importance of Prophecy for the History of Mankind

T H E prophets can only be understood as coming from a period of human existence and thought in which God or gods still belonged to the presuppositions of thought rather than to the objects of thought. It was probably the most decisive change in the whole history of mankind when God, the gods or the divine, became the objects of human reflection and when man could take an independent, objective standpoint in his attitude to the divine, and could decide whether he would accept God or reject him. Emancipation from God began with reflection about him. The boundary separating thinking about God—as a man in prison thinks about his wife and children, or as Psalm 23 thinks about God—and thinking which sets God in the series of objective facts, in the series of objects contemplated by the human intellect, was crossed. This is a long, many-sided process, which can be recognized in many places of the world. Everywhere it is connected with what we call, in its historical manifestation, the 'Enlightenment'. Often this process has taken centuries. Everywhere it ends with human thought or the spirit of men being set above everything that can be said of God or the gods or the divine. The term 'religion' is also a product of this process.

The people of Israel were not exempt from this process, but in Israel it took a different course from the usual one. In Israel's case there was an uneasy decline enacted with unique drama, the most striking part of which is the first steps of this process of separation from God. In this small nation, of no world historical importance, the first and earliest signs of emancipation from God were noted and resisted by a few men. They saw the first cracks appear and stepped into the breach.

Herein lies the importance of prophecy for the present. What the prophets thought about God may be interesting but it need not be of vital importance for us today. As religious personalities the prophets of God were unique, but the same objections apply. It is understandable if someone today says with regard to the prophets: our problems are different. Nevertheless they are vital for us, for they concern us when they treat of what is our basic problem: Can we live without God? As far as the individual goes, for hundreds of years this question has been answered in the affirmative by millions of people. As far as community life goes, the question has not yet been answered. The time since the Enlightenment is still too short for us to be able to say what will become of a community which, *as a community*, denies God. The forsaking of God by individuals cannot answer our question as to what happens where a nation or state has decided for atheism. Because we cannot by-pass this question today it is important for us to know what happened at the beginning of that line, at the end of which we stand today.

The drama of this process in Israel is rooted in the peculiar course of its early history, at the beginning of which stood a confession of faith in the God who delivered Israel in its hour of greatest need. This confession lasted through the time in the wilderness up to the first period of the occupation of Canaan. It created its own special political form of expression in the tribal confederacy which was held together by this common confession, and in the charismatic leadership. With the rise of the monarchy the authority of the confession was called in question. The monarchy, which appealed to a divine foundation, succeeded entirely by its own efforts in bringing the religious life of Israel into a permanent, ordered form, in which the important decisions of a political and a religious nature were left more and more to the leaders, that is the kings and the priests. A state-religion grew up, in which the individual stood over against a rigid institution which had both a political and a religious side. Now, for example, if something which was against the will of God were carried out in the country by the king's will, it was extremely difficult for the individual Israelite to oppose this will. Politics received an emphasis of its own. Political necessities arose which appeared unavoidable even if it was not certain whether they coincided with the will of God. Not only the field of politics however, but also the social sphere and the field of religion gradually became a law unto themselves. When, for example, Solomon's wives had altars to their native gods erected in Jerusalem, this was probably a political necessity.

This development could have taken place smoothly. Political, social and economic necessities would have been able to break through gradually and gain the upper hand—as has happened in fact almost everywhere. The will of God would not simply have been abandoned, but it would have been increasingly limited to the private sphere. The state-religion would have become a solemn confirmation and embellishment of political events and would have left room alongside for private religious devotion. Then Israelite religion would have become one of the Oriental religions along with many others.

The prophets set themselves against this development. Why they did so cannot be fully explained. They were not understood in their own time, although they were not totally ignored. Their counterparts, the kings, were not opposed to the prophets simply because they were godless or thoughtless, but because they were responsible to God for looking after religious worship, as God's anointed. The conflict between prophet and king was a tragic conflict. Nor should the prophets be idealized in contrast to the people. For the people the emphasis of religious life was on permanency, on the permanent, recurrent, firmly established institutions. The attacks of the prophets on worship and the politics of the kings were hard to understand. The fact that the prophets often attacked the priests, and that prophet and priest often stood in opposition, must have been confusing. It was hardly conceivable that the prophets should have gained the following of the nation as a whole. Thus prophecy was condemned to failure from the very beginning. It was this which made it a living symbol. The life of the nation, which had gradually detached itself from God in the political, social and economic fields, was on the decline. Prophecy was an exception to this trend. This is the reason why Israel's history was not brought to an end by the Babylonian exile. The history of prophecy points beyond itself to the Man who, as fulfiller of this history, trod the same path of failure right to the end and in doing so made possible a new beginning. This history of unsuccessful resistance to the separation from God, which is brought about by the most prominent areas of life becoming independent, still lies like a huge boulder across the path of mankind in its journeying away from God; it is impossible to remove it. But here is the one great sign in the course of the world's history that the increasing tendency nowadays to separation from God and to independence is not the only possibility. This process was once halted in one place ! This is a fact of world history, beginning in prophecy and ending in Christ and his Church. The existence and activity of the Church is the continuance of this sign to the present day.

VII · AFTER THE EXILE

1 · Disenchantment

T H E day came for the Jews who had been exiled to Babylon to return home. After the capture of Jerusalem the Babylonian empire only held together for another fifty years. In the year 539 Babylon fell into the hand of Cyrus, king of the Persians, whom Deutero-Isaiah had greeted with enthusiasm. In 538 Cyrus allowed the Jews to return home and gave them permission to rebuild the temple in Jerusalem (the king's decree is preserved in Ezra 6.3-5). What Deutero-Isaiah had declared to the exiles had come to pass: they were free again!

But now something happened which had little in common with the hope that had been cherished for fifty years, or with the glowing colours in which Deutero-Isaiah had pictured the return home: disenchantment and disillusion, which quickly cooled every glow of hope and expectation.

We can get some idea of this today. We still read in the German newspapers from time to time of men who, years after the end of the war, are only just returning home. Such a return is seldom happy. The time was too long. The exile of the Jews lasted fifty years; and in the case of those deported in 598, sixty years. Of those who were thirty years old when Jerusalem was destroyed there could only have been a few old people among those returning; of those deported in 598 there could have been hardly anyone to return. The children of the exiles, however, had grown up in another land, they knew the homeland of their parents only by hearsay, they had had to settle in Babylon whether they liked it or not. All this must be borne in mind in comparing the expectation of return with what really happened.

There is, moreover, another side to the story: the land to which they were coming home was not empty. The houses, insofar as they had not been destroyed, had been appropriated by others, the fields and vineyards had been taken over by others. There were, of course, many Jews who had remained in Palestine, many had returned from hiding after the end of the wars and here and there immigrants from other countries had also settled. All of these were probably not very enthusiastic about the return of the exiles. No one had reckoned with returning exiles; life had continued. Finally, in addition to all this, there was the fact that those returning were not coming back to a free country of their own, but to a province of the Persian empire. It was under Persian rule and under foreign laws. One came across foreign officials and soldiers; taxes had to be paid to the governor; and those with power, importance and authority were enemies. There was a repetition of something which must have been experienced right at the beginning of Israel's history: deliverance was promised by God and, moreover, it really happened, but those delivered found themselves in the wilderness. After the jubilation at being delivered had died down, there was no rest, no fulfilment; instead, hard, difficult years of testing. This happened after the deliverance at the Sea of Reeds, and again after the arrival in the Promised Land, and now once again after the Babylonian exile, though now, under the burden of God's judgement which had struck the nation as a whole, it was incomparably harder and more difficult. The dreams of greatness and glory, of a restoration of David's former empire, of destruction for all the enemies of God's people, who would themselves rise up in dazzling glory and power, very soon faded away in the face of this reality. Instead they had laboriously to adapt themselves to restricted circumstances, worn out by petty provocations and trivial rivalries and the wearisome struggle for daily bread, while houses and community life and relations with those in authority were built up only very gradually. That it ever came to this at all was a miracle. Only the bridge of God's activity, which spanned the abyss, made it possible.

The new beginning was only possible under the sign of repentance. The Deuteronomic work of history, which came into existence during the exile, grew out of the confession of guilt as we have already seen. A group of exiles had seen that everything had happened as the prophets had declared it would, and in doing so had discovered the possibility of a new beginning, which acknowledged God's judgements as right; they waited therefore with empty hands for God's future plans for his people. This work of history, covering the period from the crossing of the Jordan to the fall of Jerusalem, was composed from the standpoint of returning exiles who had been humbled by God's judgement, but it was also conceived as a work which should call the children, the coming generation, to accept their history as the history of a downfall and to repent and wait for Gods activity which could *never* come to an end.

We feel something of the strength which did not quail before the heaviest blow—the beginning from which, humanly speaking, nothing but trouble, distress and difficulty was to be expected. In fact it was only a section of the exiles who had the courage to return. There were only groups of people who returned and by no means large groups. About a hundred years after Cyrus's edict, a fresh, decisive attack by those who had stayed in Babylon was needed to help the pitiful beginnings of the new Jerusalem and to give the new community a fresh composition. It was no longer a question of the whole nation returning; the Babylonian exile marked the beginning of the Diaspora, the dispersion of the people of Israel, and this is still the position today in spite of every attempt to form a new state. Judah, Jerusalem and the new temple were the centre, of course, but this was no longer now the whole, it was no longer a closed entity. The absence of the old boundaries showed itself in another quite different way. From the Babylonian exile onwards foreign influences surged into the life of the nation and exerted a decisive influence. This resulted, almost necessarily, in deep cleavages within the body of the nation. From now on throughout the Persian, Greek and Roman periods there was a tendency amongst some to come to terms with the fact that Judah was nothing more than a province of a great empire and adapt themselves to the new situation, language, manners and mode of life. This had consequences for faith and worship; this group was 'liberal' and disposed to all kinds of compromise. Others, of an opposite tendency, were completely determined by the past in their thoughts and expectations; they were hermetically sealed against everything new and foreign, and lived to carry on the past and preserve it for the future.

There was a further deep-seated contrast which could not be resolved. The province of Judah had lost all independence in the realm of politics, but it retained its religious independence. Hence it was almost inevitable that the strength and spirit of the nation was now wholly concentrated on this possibility of free development which remained, and worship governed the corporate life of the nation to an extraordinarily high degree. Here the nation had a rallying point linking it to its past and at the same time providing a source of new life which pointed to the future. The great reform of Ezra, a hundred years after the first return, gave the Jews a form as a worshipping community. It left its mark on the coming centuries, and lasted through many generations as the community's foundation. But it could not fail to be noticed that the worship in the temple at Jerusalem, which dominated the whole life of the nation, became callous and formal in many respects and began to propagate very human tendencies and pretensions. It took on a strong institutional character; active participation in worship was increasingly limited to the clergy, while the community became merely the public audience of religious shows; thus, the central act of worship, the sacrifice, took on more and more strongly the character of an *opus operatum*, a holy event operating mechanically. Connected with this was the steep rise in the quantity of sacrifices made; the number of sacrificial animals grew and grew, and likewise the number of the clergy. The priests formed themselves into a hierarchy, divided into a higher and lower clergy, with the high priest at the head. There were times when the office of the high priest was very secular and struggles broke out round this office. It is understandable, therefore, that a silent opposition to the superficial practice of religion arose and accounts from both the early and late post-exilic period have come down to us of a number of witnesses who are full of deep distrust of worship which has become a profession and who openly advance the conviction that God does not want the sacrifice of animals. As a result there were whole sections of the nation who, while not fighting against sacrificial worship, ceased to expect salvation for the nation from it.

A third contrast showed itself in the attitude to other nations. This contrast is probably the sharpest. There were two expectations for the future, roughly side by side: the expectation that the time of salvation would bring richness, greatness and prosperity for Israel, judgement and utter destruction for the heathen. (Here for the first time in the post-exilic period the word *goim*, nations, is given the connotation which we hear in the word 'heathen'.) Side by side with it is the very different expectation that God's ultimate aim for the other nations also is salvation, peace and the worship of their Creator and Redeemer, who journeyed with Israel in order that all nations might know him and recognize him as the Lord of heaven and earth and find rest and deliverance with him under the sign of his salvation.

These contrasts, which the above remarks have only sketched, extend throughout the whole post-exilic period of the Old Testament. We must simply admit that a single, clearly recognizable thread running through the history of God's people, such as was described previously in the history of prophecy, can no longer be found after God's judgement on Israel, and the announcement of a new, quite different way of God by the prophets of the exile. We must admit that after the exile, in the later writings, a path can be recognized which leads finally to John the Baptist and Jesus of Nazareth, and side by side with it another path which leads to those who rejected Jesus of Nazareth and drove him out. We can only just trace both paths, but these paths point in different directions. This indicates what the New Testament confirms. In the words of Jesus Christ about the Old Testament, a full affirmation of the Old Testament (e.g. in the Sermon on the Mount, Matt. 5. 17-19) can be found side by side with a very clear critique of it (e.g. in the contrasting words, Matt. 5.: 'You have heard that it was said of old. . . but I say to you. . .').

For the understanding of the late parts of the Old Testament it is important to recognize these two lines from the start; many a difficulty will be elucidated if this is done.

2 · Postscript to Prophecy

I N a late psalm we once hear the lament, 'There is no longer any prophet' (Ps. 74.9). The word simply establishes that it is so and presupposes in doing so that prophecy belongs to a limited period, in a way in which the priestly office for instance does not. We saw that prophecy accompanied the monarchy from the first to the last king; it is allied with the period of the state of Israel and Judah. If prophets are mentioned prior to this the word is being used in an extended sense; these appearances belong to the preparation or pre-history of prophecy. If the history of prophecy seems to continue for quite a long time after the exile and prophetic books are handed down from this period, then this is simply like an echo of what prophecy once was. This late prophecy has certain characteristics in common with pre-exilic prophecy, but the activity of this late prophecy as a whole is something substantially different. Something similar often happens in the political field. If a definite form of government such as monarchical rule has embedded itself deeply in a country's history, then even when another form of government has been adopted the monarchy may still exist for centuries, although it has surrendered the functions which it once exercised. Or if a dictatorship takes the place of democracy, 'the party' can continue, although it now has a completely different function than it had in the democracy. The continuance of the old form is always a sign of the influence it exercised in its own time. Similarly with post-exilic prophecy in Israel : its importance lies less in itself than in its keeping alive what prophecy once was.

Three prophets of the restoration, Haggai, Zechariah and Malachi, belong to the first ten years after the return. The words of Haggai and Zechariah are dated precisely; those of Haggai to the second year of Darius, 520 BC, those of Zechariah to the years

520-518 BC. From Chronicles we learn that the building of the temple, which Cyrus had already authorized and aided in 538, had not been carried out, and that it needed a new royal decree to set the work in motion again; it was not ready till the year 515.

The few words of the prophet *Haggai* that have come down to us are almost exclusively concerned with the rebuilding of the temple. The returned exiles had so much to do with themselves, their own houses and the reconstruction of a new existence, that it had been widely suggested, 'The time has not yet come to rebuild the House of the Lord' (1.2). As a result of Haggai's challenge 'they came and worked on the house of the Lord of hosts, their God' (1.14). It is characteristic that he no longer bases his challenge to build the temple simply on God's command, as the earlier prophets would have done. Rather, he gives a very rational reason: he points the people in Jerusalem to their laborious and poverty-stricken beginnings, to the set-backs through drought and bad harvests. 'You have looked for much, and, lo, it came to little'. This, he says, comes of letting God's house lie in ruins till now. If you will tackle the building, then you will see how God blesses you! This is the gist of Haggai's message. The tremendous distance that separates him from the earlier prophets is obvious. His words lie more in the direction of the pre-exilic salvation and cult-prophets. One could say that it is simply an appeal to rebuild the temple clothed in the form of a prophetic word.

Thus a continuance of pre-exilic prophecy cannot be looked for in Haggai; and his promise of a new and greater glory for Judah and the new temple has dangers in its directness. Yet there is so much in this small book that reminds us of the first years after the Second World War. Then, the same arguments were used to concentrate rebuilding efforts on the economic sphere, on the building of houses and the 'revving up' of trade—with such one sidedness that the consequences were as clear as noonday in the following years. It is perhaps a significant sign that in those hard years of rebuilding Jerusalem the one record considered worth handing down, out of all that was achieved at that time in order that the nation might live in its own country again, was that of the one voice which called for the rebuilding of the church in spite of the difficulties of the time.

The prophecy of *Zechariah* corresponds with that of Haggai in the most important feature: he, too, is a salvation-prophet and a cult-prophet. There is one important new feature, however: the visions in which he sees the future concealed in pictures. In Zechariah, as in Haggai, the future salvation depends on the building of the temple (Zech. 8.9-12). This brings out even more strikingly the figures of the two men who were in power at that time, the governor, Zerubbabel, and the high priest, Joshua. Zechariah announces, 'The hands of Zerubbabel have laid the foundation of this house; his hands shall also complete it (Zech. 4.8-10). As the completion of the temple will usher in the time of salvation, so Zerubbabel will be the king in the time of salvation, the Anointed, a scion of David's house. Zechariah is commanded to crown him now and to appoint him as the one who will be king in the time of salvation. Joshua shall stand by his side as high priest. In a vision Zechariah sees two olive trees, on the right- and left-hand of the lampstand: the two anointed, the king and priest of the time of salvation (Zech. 4.11-4). The high expectations which Zechariah placed in the person of Zerubbabel, the governor under Persian high authority, were not fulfilled. In the later words of Zechariah dealing with salvation the name of Zerubbabel is missing and we do not learn anything further about him from the historical account in Chronicles. The non-fulfilment of this message can be recognized in the Book of Zechariah itself. In Zech. 6.11, according to the received text, it appears as if the crown was placed on the head of Joshua, the priest. This is very improbable. It is therefore assumed that the name of Zerubbabel stood here originally and the name of Joshua was substituted later. Verse 13a, at any rate, fits not the office of the priest but that of the king. With the end of the royal house of David we find the first reference to political Messianic expectation in Zechariah: the expectation of a king from the house of David who would restore to Israel its former greatness and glory. From now on it constantly appears; it lives on among the people until the day of John the

Baptist and Jesus, where it once more plays a decisive rôle as the background of Jesus's activity. Jesus of Nazareth sides clearly and unconditionally (see the temptation-story) with the line of the suffering servant of God, beheld by Deutero-Isaiah, against the hope of a political Messiah. In this connection we must observe that the promise of a time of salvation which Zerubbabel was to usher in as 'the anointed' did not materialize.

The visions of Zechariah, the seven night visions, mark the transition from prophecy to apocalyptic, the first traces of which are to be bound in Ezekiel, the prophet of the exile. It is obvious as soon as one compares the call of Ezekiel with the calls of Isaiah or Jeremiah. Isaiah, too, has a vision, an apparition; but it is described with the greatest reserve and awe; it is only for a moment that Isaiah sees the Lord enthroned, surrounded by seraphim; the emphasis is entirely on the word which is spoken to him. In Ezekiel the call-vision has a highly baroque character. What he sees is a many-sided, complicated picture, which needs a long, intricate explanation, and the picture leads to a sequence of changing pictures. This is apocalyptic announcing itself; the Book of Daniel and later the Revelation of John are its essential expression in the Old Testament and the New.

The night visions of Zechariah all amount to a revelation of God's saving activity which is coming. In the first, for example, Zechariah sees a man on a red-brown horse, with many horses following. They are messengers who are patrolling the earth; they report that everything is still quiet. The lament of God's people who have to suffer so long is raised; the answer is the announcement that God will again return to Jerusalem in mercy, but full of blazing anger for his enemies. 'The Lord will again comfort Zion and again choose Jerusalem.'

The subsequent night visions need no enumeration; the vision of the lamp-stand and the two olive trees (Zech. 4) has already been referred to. It will be obvious that, in this catalogue of different fantastic visions which extend from the first to the sixth chapter of the Book of Zechariah, prophecy has been replaced by something substantially different, the vision of the apocalyptist. The change is particularly striking in one respect: if today we are confused and dismayed by this sequence of visions, in which horses and riders, horns and smiths, a man with a measuring line, lamp-stand and olive trees, a flying scroll, a woman in an ephah, four chariots between two mountains of brass with red, black, white and dappled-grey horses appear, this is true also of the man who first saw these visions. He himself cannot explain these visions, he is helpless when faced with them. They have to be explained to him from the other side first. It is significant that they are not explained by God, but a mediating angel comes between God and the prophet and explains the vision to him (Zech. 1.9-10). God and the divine world are here sharply separated from the world of men. The seer has visions from the world beyond, it is true, but they exceed his powers of comprehension. On the other hand God is so majestic and remote that a mediator is necessary to convey God's wishes to the prophet by means of these visions. This interpreter-angel bridged the inordinate gap between God and man in the late period of prophecy during the transition to apocalyptic. The angel occurs in exactly the same way in the Book of Daniel and the Revelation of John. The command to prophesy also (Zech. 1.14-5) no longer proceeds directly from God to the prophet, but *via* the angel. Even the people's lament, 'how long?' (Zech. 1.12-3) is no longer expressed by the people but by the mediating angel!

This indirect relation between the prophet and God, mediated by intermediary beings in the late period, corresponded to worship at that time: the community's part in worship became increasingly passive and what had to be said and done was done exclusively by priests. Again we find the same remoteness the same transcendence of God: God is such a majestically long way away that an ordinary layman can no longer dare to appear directly before his face, or to act and speak in God's presence as it is in his heart to do; he is much happier for everything to be taken over by specialists, by those who have been entrusted, as servants of the shrine, with its holiness. The laymen 'attends' worship; it is ordered by the clergy. We find the same basic features in both the apocalyptic and the cult of the late period: God is far removed from man, he is exalted and distant; mediation provides the only way to him, and from him.

Parallels come to mind without prompting. How quickly something similar happened within the Christian Church! And how striking that at the time of the greatest separation of clergy and laity in the Middle Ages visions again become very important in the Church; not, it is true, apocalyptic visions, but mystic visions.

Likewise the special development of ecclesiastical learning, scholasticism, in the late Middle Ages alongside clerically ordered worship and mysticism had its parallels in the late Jewish community after the exile. And just as apocalyptic developed from prophecy, so too did this other trend, scribal wisdom. The small book of *Malachi* points the way.

It originated about fifty years after Haggai and Zechariah, about 470. Malachi is the last prophet whose prophecy we possess; his prophecy is small but complete. Afterwards, it is true, there were many individual prophetic words and men who were called prophets still appeared: but a complete prophetic figure and book did not occur again. We do not know, to be sure, that the prophet of these three chapters was called Malachi; it may be that the name was derived subsequently from Mal. 3.1 (my messenger = *malaki*), and that at first the small book was transmitted anonymously.

Malachi is absolutely in line with Haggai and Zechariah, in that his words refer to worship and liturgical events to a great extent; likewise he is a thorough cult-prophet. One of his complaints (Mal. 1) is that people offer God imperfect sacrifices. Quite a new development, however, here makes its appearance. In Malachi, at the end of prophecy, the *reply* of those whom the prophet accuses makes its way into the prophetic word. It is a defence which verges on blasphemy. (Mal. 1.7; 2.2, 14,17; 3.7, 13-15.) Loud voices are raised saying 'It is vain to serve God. What is the good of our keeping his charge....?' In each of the sayings of Malachi what he has to say in the name of God is in opposition to such voices; these sayings report a dialogue and we stand on the boundary between the prophetic word which goes forth in the name of God and the learned disputation (scribal wisdom) of the synagogue. Even if the prophecy of Malachi is almost entirely limited to the cult, and even if one feels the narrowness of circumstances after the exile very acutely, these four chapters of the small Book of Malachi are a stirring piece of evidence of the initial stages of the conflict between belief and unbelief, which now brings division into the people of God, between those who remain true to God and the many others who pursue their own interests without worrying themselves any more about what God commands. From now on faithful and unfaithful, loyal and disloyal, live next to each other in the cities of Judah and the streets of Jerusalem, until the day comes (Mal. 3.1 ff.; 4.1 ff.) when God sits in judgement so that it will leave them neither root nor branch. *But for you who fear my name the sun of righteousness shall rise* (Mal. 4.2).

3 · The Law

T H E people's impulse to build the temple after its destruction resulted in its being rebuilt, it is true, but the great hopes which the prophets Haggai and Zechariah—and not only they, of course—had associated with the restoration of the temple were not fulfilled. What men had looked forward to was a restoration of the life of the old political structure under a new king with a high priest by his side, and this longing continued through the centuries in the political Messianic expectation. When, however, it was no longer possible to think of a realization of this dream, something else inevitably took its place—the nation must preserve its independence and identity.

The new order was brought by the scribe, Ezra, an official of the Persian court who was of Jewish origin and who came to Jerusalem with a new group of returned exiles about 450. A detailed description of his work and Nehemiah's is given by the books named after them. Certain matters, especially the chronological sequence of events in the work of the two men, are not clear from the account, but Ezra, soon after his arrival in Jerusalem, had a document which was declared to be binding read out. In the Book of Ezra this was called 'the law of the God of heaven'. Scholars agree on the whole in assuming that this is a reference to the so called 'Priestly writing' (or the priests' *codex*) which was the framework of the Pentateuch (the five Books of Moses). Whether the Book of Ezra is *only* the Priestly writing or whether it is the whole Pentateuch which is now included within the framework of the Priestly writing may remain undecided. At any rate—whether before or after or through Ezra —the older traditions of Israel's early history, from the creation to the settlement in Canaan, have been worked into the Priestly writing, and from this arose the Pentateuch, the book which was then simply called 'the Law'; this is a description found in the New Testament also.

This marks the beginning of the period of Israel's history which is determined, for the most part, by the Law—a period which begins soon after the exile and lasts up to the coming of Christ and, in the Jewish Synagogue, far beyond. In order to understand the Old Testament it is very important that we should see the references to the Law, as we find them in the Old Testament and as they are continued in the New, in chronological perspective. For this a glance at the history of Old Testament scholarship is necessary. Already soon after the Reformation, doubt had arisen as to whether Moses was the author of the five books named after him. It was discovered that this great picture was not homogeneous, but that it originated in different periods. The question of the sources of the Pentateuch became one of the chief questions of Old Testament scholarship. In the long and complicated history of source criticism, linked with the name of Wellhausen among others, the most important discovery was that the Priestly source or Priestly strata of tradition, which had already been recognized for a long time as a special stratum by its stylized language, was the *latest* source, which first originated in the exile or after the exile, in the sixth and fifth centuries. This discovery quite radically changed the whole picture of Israel's history. The large sections of the Pentateuch which contain the Law, from Ex. 25 through the whole of Leviticus to Num. 10 (with a few interruptions), belong to the Priestly writing. They insert the Law in the account of Israel's beginnings in such a way that the sum total of these laws is delivered to the people, immediately after the escape from Egypt, by Moses on Mount Sinai. (This gives them authority.) On the assumption that this was to be accepted as a historical account the period of the prophets had previously been placed after the period of the Priestly laws. The early period of Israel was seen as determined by these laws and prophecy was understood as a countermovement following the period of the Law. This view proved untenable for many reasons. When it was realized that the Priestly writing only originated towards the end of the exile, and that the full sweep of the Law contained in it first gained sway in the post-exilic period, the account of the whole Law being mediated by Moses on Sinai was interpreted differently. The Priestly writing—or the circle in which it was composed—did not want to make any historical assertions. They wanted to set the whole complex of the Law, which evolved only gradually, under the authority of Moses and thus under the authority of God's original saving work in liberating the nation from bondage. If, as a result of our present view, we say, 'Then it is not true that all the laws from Ex. 25 to Num. 10 were revealed by God to Moses on Mount Sinai and that he wrote them down; it is a falsification', we are applying concepts and standards to those old documents which simply do not fit. This association with Moses and Sinai was never meant as a historical assertion; rather, it gives expression to the authority of Moses for the giving of the Law as a whole to the nation. This applied equally to the Deuteronomic law, which was declared to be the law of the nation in the reform of Josiah (621); as we have seen, it, too, was drawn up and described as a law mediated to the people by Moses. To understand this properly we must be quite clear that our modern idea of history and historical development is quite recent. The authors of these laws wanted to express the historical connection of the laws which originated later with the nation's early history and with the fundamentals of that history. They did this by saying that they were mediated to the people by Moses.

To ask a simple reader of the Bible to accept this is asking a great deal. We may therefore add one more consideration. Everywhere in the world a community of men needs at first only a few basic rules or commands or laws in order to regulate its common life. Then, the more it grows and the more diversely this community is gradually organized, the more rules become necessary. The illustration which lies nearest to hand is the development of traffic regulations in the last thirty years. It was exactly the same in Israel. In the beginning the Ten Commandments, the Decalogue, were sufficient for the nation's early period. When they settled in Canaan new regulations were needed for a new way of life. The Book of the Covenant (Ex.20-3) belongs to the first period of the settlement. In the period which followed, the Law gradually grew; an entirely new compilation has been preserved for us from the end of the period of the kings, the Deuteronomic law (Deut.12-26). Every new collection of laws is more comprehensive in important respects than the previous one. By far the most comprehensive is the Priestly law. That is why it can be accepted that it is also the latest. Naturally one should not use growth and size to measure age simply in a mechanical fashion. There are also smaller collections inserted into the main tradition; for example, the so-called 'Holiness Law' in Lev. 19-26 (now joined to the Priestly law, but once an independent collection). One can say, nevertheless, that the growth of laws in the course of history is a widespread phenomenon, produced by the nature of the case.

Above all, however, the Priestly law can only really be understood in the post-exilic period. Israel had ceased to be a political state. It could only preserve its own life as a religious community. Hence the ordinances of the religious life were given an importance which affected the whole life of the community. The existence of the community now depended in fact on holding fast to the Law. The Deuteronomic work of history, which rests on the law of Josiah's reform, is pervaded by the one strong, dominant motif: 'If you obey God, this means life. If you turn away from God to other powers, this means death.' The post-exilic community accepted this Either-Or, and thus accepted the guilt of their fathers and built their new life on obedience to God's Law.

4 · The Psalms

A N important difference between the Old and New Testaments lies in the fact that the Old Testament, in addition to reporting God's mighty acts and handing on the words which proceeded from God, has preserved the response to the acts and words of God in a third part and has made it part of the Bible. The kernel of this third part, which is called 'The Writings' and to which a number of very different writings were gradually attached, is the Psalter. The Book of Job and Lamentations belong with the Psalter; in the books of this group response to God's deeds consists of songs of lament and praise of many different varieties. The second main group, containing Proverbs and the Book of Ecclesiastes (one strain of the Book of Job also belongs here) describes quite a different response to the mighty acts of God, that of Wisdom. The work of the Chronicler —the first and second Book of Chronicles, Ezra and Nehemiah— and the Book of Esther from the historical books belonged to this third part of the Bible originally. They are not really to be compared with the other historical books which extend up to the Babylonian exile. Among the prophetic books the Book of Daniel belonged originally to this third part; it is not really a prophecy but an apocalypse.

To understand the Old Testament in its living entirety it is important to see the difference between the three parts clearly. They should not be seen simply as three items of a sum, which can be added together to obtain the whole. The first part reports the mighty acts of God in a definite time and place. The second part completes this history in the call of the prophets, who hurl God's word into this history where it is necessary. The third part presupposes the first two and is like an answer of all sorts and shapes by the people of God to what has been done and said in the first two parts. The simple fact that the Bible contains both words coming from God and the response of men to God demonstrates something which was important for the people of God: God's

word is always, of necessity, part of a dialogue; it demands a response and is not really God's word until it receives an answer and
awakens a response.

Thus the answer to God's activity and God's words is not confined to particular parts of the Bible; rather it runs throughout the
Bible in both Old and New Testaments.

In the Old Testament, therefore, there are psalms, prayers and
songs not only in the Book of Psalms but in all books. We may
recall just two places where the response in the historical and
prophetic books is expressed in a hymn of praise to God : in Ex. 15,
the hymn of praise sung in response to God's miracle by those
delivered at the Sea of Reeds; and Isa. 12, the conclusion, composed
of psalms, to the first collection of the words of the prophet Isaiah.
One could, however, go through all the books of the Old
Testament, as of the New, and find that in none of them is praise
of God completely missing, from the Book of Genesis to the Revelation of John. In this connection special attention may be drawn
to the work of the Chronicler, which is studded with psalms inserted in the historical narrative at places where the response of
the people should be expressed in a hymn of praise or prayer of
repentance on the occasion of an important event or section of
history. The psalms are a whole book of response to God's deeds
and God's words. They are a response; they must be understood in
this light; they are part of the exchange between God and man. A
psalm is never something which only proceeds from man. It is
always preceded by something that proceeded from God. Consequently the psalms cannot be fully comprehended by any of our
modern terms. They are prayers and hymns at the same time, but
they do not correspond exactly either to our hymns or to our
prayers. They are addressed to God, and yet this talking to God can
change abruptly into talking *about* God; an address to God can
change in an address to the community. They are hymns with a
definite connected form but again something quite different from
our hymns which are sung according to set tunes in equal verses;
it is a different singing from that to which we are accustomed,
more akin to our speaking than our singing. They elude our

terminology in a further respect also, in that they are poetry and prayer in one, prayed poetry. The psalms are the words of men whose whole being—in prosperity and in adversity—is in such a personal relation with God that poetry is included almost automatically when they talk to God. In the thousands of years of human history since then this connection between poetry and prayer has never been completely forgotten. In the poetry of all nations there are heights when poetry has again become prayer or at any rate something like prayer.

The fact that in the last few decades the psalms have had a renewed lease of life in many places, and have begun to speak clearly and forcibly again for many people, can in every case be accounted for in a way which we can understand. The psalms reveal a directness in speaking to God which we have progressively lost. Their prevailing climate is not that of moderate, pious sameness, but a contrast of hot and cold; the lament which vibrates with pain exchanges with jubiliant praise, and behind the quiet words of trust one still hears the raging of the powers with which this trust is confronted. What transpires between God and man is elemental and involves all the possibilities of men, not only the pious but also the rebellious, the fighting and the despairing. One further point speaks to our time with special force. What takes place here between God and man embraces man's whole existence in the world and God's activity throughout the world, throughout history and throughout the cosmos. The Psalter's invitation to all creation to praise God (especially Ps. 148)—the mountains, the fields, the stars and the beasts—presents us with an interpretation of nature which excludes the view that our world or any component part of it is a substance whose ultimate meaning lies in being used or governed by men. Everything created, yes everything, has its ultimate meaning in its creatureliness, that is in its relationship to God; nothing can alter this, not even the most highly developed capacity of man for utilizing what this world is composed of. The true extent and meaning of this ability, however, together with all man's technical potentialities, is to be found in the realization by technical work that it is sustained in all its developments by the joyful gratitude of the creation and the humility of the creature which bows before its creator.

Whenever we watch an aeroplane rising from the ground of the airport, or whenever we take our seat in one and the motors are revving up and slowing down again before the start, the words of the psalms may come to our lips quite spontaneously. How power, fully the praise of the eternal God could rise from the churches today if we were to take up technical activity with all its terrifying, as well as its beneficial, life-enriching and life-preserving possibilities into the prayer of the Church ! Just as in Psalm 8 the praise of the Creator rejoices in the ability of man to tame animals and have sway over them and use them in the service of man, so today the abundance of possible ways of controlling the earth's powers and making them serve the purposes of men could enrich the praise of the Creator and the Lord of history and make it more relevant. The colossal dangers which this same technical development has brought with it need today—and it is certainly high time—the care and prayer of a Church which will open itself fully in its worship to the changed, machine-governed existence of our time, in order to oppose to these dangers a message and a prayer in which those who live in the age of the machine cannot help feeling understood and accepted for once, so that they might also be enabled to hear the voice of warning and the call to repentance wherever it is necessary.

Today, when a man in an office-building with many hundreds of rooms works on one of a thousand documents, and a worker has to make one of a thousand handles, without ever having the personal satisfaction of creating anything entire, then for him to hear in one of the psalms, say Psalm 139, that someone thousands of years before him spoke to God as the one who purposely brought his existence into the scheme of the great creation and gave eternal significance to this trifling existence by giving him to understand : 'Wherever you are, whatever you are doing, wherever you hide yourself, you are in my presence, for I hold everything in my hands, and your criteria of near and far, small and great, whole and part are overturned in my presence'. This can give something no one else can in any other way, something which the man needs like nourishment and joy. This mighty, clear certainty of a direct approach to God, for every man as for every smallest member of creation, permeates the whole Psalter and makes it speak in quite a new way to the people of our time.

One must also recognize in all soberness that what has just been said about the nearness of the Psalter to modern times is by no means true of every psalm or every word of the Psalter. We cannot automatically join in the prayer of many psalms today in the Christian Church. There is much that remains completely unintelligible to us, and a great deal only makes sense to us when we have explained the psalms chiefly by means of their world and environment. But to do this is possible only to a limited extent; there is much in the Psalter that will always remain obscure to us. It is not difficult to understand why. The psalms were alive for hundreds of years in the prayers and hymns of the community before they were written down. In the course of this long time much was changed, much was left out and much was added. Above all, these psalms developed a stylized language with picturesque expressions, which for men at that time embodied quite concrete pictures which we are no longer familiar with. In the individual psalms of lament a great deal is said about the enemies of the suppliant. But everything which is said of them is so schematic and general that even today it is not really clear who is meant by these enemies of the individual who is praying.

This general and strongly picturesque manner of speaking was necessary for this reason also: in the laments the various ills which could overtake an individual were described in words of lamentation which had been coined hundreds of years previously and which were meant to give expression to the suffering of very many, very different people. When, for example, enemies are spoken of as if they were wild animals and their activity is described as the setting of a trap or attack of a robber, this referred to a very definite act by the enemies. Our only clue to it now is what we can guess from the picture.

This talk of enemies presents a particular difficulty to our understanding the psalms and sharing in their prayer. In very many of these psalms prayers *against* the enemies occur. The psalms in which they are predominant have been called 'vengeance psalms'. This description is false and misleading. One can revenge oneself or take vengeance, but one cannot *pray* for revenge! There is, it is true,—and for the ancient world to a much greater extent than today—such a thing as verbal vengeance; but that is certainly not prayer but imprecation or curse. The distinctiveness of the curse lies in the fact that it is aimed *directly*, without any detour via God, at the one it is meant to hit. A curse is a word of power which the swearer releases without recourse to God. There are enough examples in the Old Testament to show that this imprecation must have played an important role at an early period and that its effectiveness was generally believed in. Above all it was the weapon of the powerless against the over-powerful enemy.

Seen against this background the prayers against enemies in the psalms appear in a different light. All these psalms renounce the curse, as is recognized in the sentence, 'Vengeance is mine; I will repay, says the Lord'. Consequently the prayers and wishes against enemies (e.g. in Ps. 109), which often appear so terrible to us today, represented for the time when they originated something very different from what we see in them.

But this has still not really explained them. The reason for this prayer against enemies, this wish that God would punish the enemies as severely as possible, lies deeper. They are rooted in the fact that, for those who prayed the psalms, God's activity is limited to this life. God's dealings with men are simply ended by death. This is where the really important newness and difference of the message of the New Testament, compared with the Old Testament, lies: through the death and resurrection of Christ, this barrier to God's activity is broken through. But because this barrier still exists for the Old Testament, because all God's dealings with men are played out between birth and death, God's 'yes' to a human life can, in the eyes of the suppliant of the Old Testament, only be spoken *before* the end of that life. If the distress in which a man cries to God is brought about by other men, the suppliant can see God's 'yes' only in God's intervention in his favour, and that for him inevitably means intervention against his enemies. This presupposes that his enemies are also God's enemies. How these enemies despise God and mock him is often described in the psalms. If God really sides with the pious against the godless, then this decision must take place on earth; and in the thought of these men it can only be a two-sided decision—for the one and against the other.

If this explanation is correct, then the Church of Christ *no longer* needs to join in these prayers in the psalms against enemies. For the Church, the death and resurrection of Christ have made a fundamental difference at this point. It receives its clearest and most direct expression in Christ's prayer for his enemies from the Cross. By this event prayer directed *against* men has been eliminated from the Church's prayer. Attempts have been made to preserve these prayers which are directed against enemies in the psalms for the prayer of the Church, by saying that for enemies we should substitute either the devil or sin or our own sinful ego. This can be done; but it is a deliberate change which requires a conscious effort every time it is done. It seems rather more clear and honest to admit unequivocally that these prayers in the psalms against people have been done away for us by the work of Christ. If then it is the practice of a church to repeat the psalms in unison or antiphonally, as at Matins or Evensong, the whole of the Bible completely justifies the omission of psalms or parts of psalms in which such prayers against enemies occupy a particularly large amount of room, as in Ps. 109 or Ps. 69.23-9. It should be mentioned also at this point that Psalm 137 which, because of its terrible ending, is a serious stumbling block for many who love the Psalter, is not a psalm in the literal sense but a folk song from the exile which was appended to the Book of Psalms.

In addition to this there is still a great deal in the Psalter that remains difficult and obscure for us; this is not to be wondered at in view of the great distance which separates us. It is all the more surprising and amazing that despite its distance it speaks to us directly and without any explanation today and can be repeated by us.

The whole Psalter is characterized by two basic notes: praise and lament. They correspond to the two basic ways of God's activity: judgement and mercy. Lament answers judgement, praise mercy. These two basic notes are absolutely fundamental like the great polarities in creation, day and night, quiet and storm, ebb and flow, life and death. This contrast of lament and praise finds its perfect counterpart in the sort of sentence which frequently recurs in a group of psalms, *Lord, thou hast brought my soul back from the kingdom of the dead and called me back to life.* Fear of death and the joys of life are voiced in lament and praise.

Both lament and praise are developed with boundless diversity in the psalms, and yet there are certain broad clear outlines discernible in all of them, which make the diversity a compact whole. They are not individualistic poems, but have all arisen out of the great dialogue between God and his people, in which every poet and every suppliant of the psalms takes part. Every individual is something special, but every individual is much more a part of the whole, that is, of the total response to God's activity. That is why certain large groups or types of psalms grew out of the nature of this answer, and within these groups an abundance of smaller types and groups. They are like a tree with two large branches and many small branches, a living organism in which even the smallest unit shares in the essential structure of the whole.

A word must be said about Psalm 73. Its high-water mark is an expression of trust:

> *Nevertheless I am continually with thee;*
> *thou dost hold my right hand.*
> *Thou dost guide me with thy counsel,*
> *and afterward thou wilt receive me to glory.*

The translation of the last sentence is uncertain. These and the following words sound to us if it were being stated, or at least hinted, that God continued his dealings with his faithful beyond death. We are probably reading into the words something which was not intended. The emphasis at any rate is on the unconditional trust of the suppliant, who in spite of the threat of death maintains his trust in God and his activity calmly and unshaken, although he cannot understand. He holds fast to his faith even in the presence of death. The suppliant is not concerned to make a statement about the position after death, but he is most concerned to affirm God's activity, in spite of everything, till he dies. In this psalm we can feel something of a confidence which is prepared to go beyond even the furthest limit of human or divine possibilities, (as understood at that time) a confidence which trusted God in the impossible and unthinkable, and is thus on the way to believing in the possibility of breaking through death's frontier. The most serious obstacle to this belief was the fact that the godless prospered. The beginning of the psalm describes how the Psalmist is almost shipwrecked on this point. How is it possible in God's world that the wicked thrive and the faithful have to suffer greatly? This is precisely the question asked by the author of Job; Psalm 73 and the Book of Job are quite close together at this point. Both writers give one the feeling that this was the question which provoked the greatest conflict of soul at that time, this was where they struggled and suffered to understand God's dark dealings, and this was where the pressure to abandon the old and espouse the new was strongest. It was felt acutely that those who took God and his activity deadly seriously were the ones who encountered the hardest conflict which called for a solution.

Lamentations and the Book of Job belong with the Psalter. The former are laments of the people after the capture of Jerusalem in 587. The Book of Job is an individual's lament which has been formed into a powerful drama; it undergoes a wonderful transformation at the end. This book is excitingly near to our time and may speak particularly to those who are struggling with doubt and despair.

5 · The Literature of Wisdom

FINALLY reference at least must be made to the wisdom
literature, represented in the Old Testament by the Book of Proverbs, the Book of Ecclesiastes, parts of the Book of Job, and
continued in the Apocrypha in the Book of Jesus Sirach. In these
books we meet the forerunners of science. Everywhere in the world
science is preceded by a practical wisdom, the distinctive form of
which is short sayings or, as we say, maxims. This wisdom is an
expression of everyday practical common sense and has nothing to
do with God or God's word originally. Hence even the proverbs in
the biblical Book of Proverbs contain for the most part a thoroughly
secular common sense. They became a part of the Bible because it
was recognized that this secular common sense had its roots—
often quite hidden—in reverence for God and that no human
wisdom can exist without this root. This proverbial wisdom stands
right on the edge of the Bible, but it has an important task to do
there. At a time in which that part of wisdom called science is
strongly separated from other areas of life and has developed great
ramifications within itself, attention to the beginnings and first
developments of wisdom can help us to see more clearly again the
common attributes of all science and the deep connection of scientific questioning and research with reverence for God and recognition
of man's God-given limitations.

There is one further aspect of the Wisdom writings of the Old
Testament which is important for us today particularly. In its
wisdom literature the Bible is open to other cultures. Words of
wisdom from other nations have been admitted into the Book of
Proverbs; the Israelites learned from the wisdom of Egypt, Arabia
and elsewhere and incorporated a great deal from them. Here in
the Bible itself, then, the international character of wisdom is
recognized: in this field even the people of God have to listen to
others and learn from them. This characteristic of wisdom—not to
be tied to any national, territorial, religious or philosophical

boundaries—has been taken over by science. When the international character of science is threatened today by the divisions of the world we can assert, in the name of the Bible, that it is God's will for wisdom and science to remain common to men.

We look back today on centuries in which an ever deeper rift between religious faith and science has arisen; during this time in many places faith in God has been attacked in the name of science. The first signs of a reaction are now beginning to appear. Even this attempt of wisdom to draw men away from God has its first traces in the Bible. In the few wisdom books we possess a line of development nevertheless stands out : at first it is very simple common sense; later it attaches itself to discussion about God, similar to the way Aristotle and the Bible were joined together in scholasticism; ultimately wisdom flows into a resigned scepticism (the Book of Ecclesiastes), for which there is no longer anything certain. It is true the Ecclesiastes' faith in God has not been shattered, but God has been removed to a distant transcendental beyond for him, almost like the God of the Deists. If scepticism, resignation and traces of nihilism are alluded to in the Bible itself, even if only peripherally, this is some comfort when we stand in a world in which many have turned away from God and in which there is often a battle against faith. These sceptical, atheistic and nihilistic explorations of man are anticipated in the Bible.

6 · The Open Book

T H E Old Testament points to the future. The promises which span the history of the Old Covenant are always, within the history reported in this book, fulfilled in a purely partial or spasmodic manner, if at all. Above all in the period after the exile, which brought much more disappointment than fulfilment, the power of God's people became increasingly the power of waiting. The fulfilment which came in Jesus of Nazareth, his preaching and his works, his passion, death and resurrection, was, however, not such that it guaranteed automatic understanding and acceptance. It was like the sign which Moses erected in the wilderness among those bitten by the serpents; one had to look and believe, only then was one made whole. This Jesus of Nazareth did not simply bring redemption for all, but he brought an offer which could be accepted or rejected. It is still the same today.

It cannot be proved—any more than the claim of Jesus of Nazareth that God would bring salvation to the world through him can be proved—that, in the thousand years of the Old Testament, God, the Creator of the world and Lord of all history, journeyed specially with this *one* nation, and in doing so had in mind the whole of the world and its history. And therefore it cannot be proved, and never will be, that the thousand years were moving to the one day on which Jesus of Nazareth died on the Cross. Every new generation through the centuries and millenia is challenged afresh at this point, and brought again to face the secret of God's dealings with our world in matters both great and small. The book which speaks of this, the Bible of Old and New Testaments, defies a final reading or exhaustive explanation. We live in different times and speak a different language, but it is still open for us to find new wonders in the Bible. There we meet him in whose sight a thousand years are but as yesterday when it is past.

INDEXES

INDEX OF SUBJECTS

INDEX OF BIBLICAL REFERENCES